ALL COLOUR COLLECTION

365
CAKES
AND
PUDDINGS

ALL COLOUR COLLECTION

365

CAKES
AND
PUDDINGS

EBURY PRESS LONDON

First published by Ebury Press
an imprint of The Random Century Group
Random Century House
20 Vauxhall Bridge Road
London SWIV 2SA

A catalogue record for this book is available from the British Library

ISBN 0–09–175–349–X

Photography by Jan Baldwin, Martin Brigdale,
Laurie Evans, Ken Field, Melvin Grey, John Heseltine, Tim Hill,
James Jackson, David Johnson, Paul Kemp, Don Last, James Murphy,
Peter Myers, Alan Newnham, Charlie Stebbings, Grant Symon,
Rosemary Weller, Andrew Whittuck, Paul Williams

Typeset by Clive Dorman
Printed and bound in Italy by New Interlitho S.p.a., Milan

COOK'S NOTES

- Both metric and imperial measures are given in the recipes in this book. Follow one set of measures only as they are not interchangeable.
- All spoon measures are level unless otherwise stated.
- All ovens should be preheated to the specified temperature.
- Microwave cooking instructions are given for some of the recipes in this book. When using these, please note that HIGH refers to 100% full power output of a 600-700 watt cooker; MEDIUM refers to 60% of full power; LOW refers to 35% of full power.

  If your microwave power output is lower than 600 watts, it may be necessary to allow longer than recommended. In any event you should always check food before the end of the cooking time, to ensure that it does not overcook.

CONTENTS

SMALL CAKES & BISCUITS

A tempting collection of recipes for teatime treats and lunchboxes, featuring traditional small cakes, children's favourites, moist chewy traybakes and crunchy cookies. Quick and easy griddle pancakes, irresistible muffins and melt-in-the-mouth shortbread are also included.

MADELEINES

MAKES 10

100 g (4 oz) butter or block margarine	30 ml (2 level tbsp) red jam, sieved and melted
100 g (4 oz) caster sugar	50 g (2 oz) desiccated coconut
2 eggs, beaten	5 glacé cherries, halved
100 g (4 oz) self-raising flour	angelica leaves

1 Grease 10 dariole moulds. Cream the fat and sugar until pale and fluffy. Add the eggs, a little at a time, beating well after each addition before adding more.
2 Fold in the flour, using a metal spoon, then three-quarters fill the moulds.
3 Bake in the oven at 180°C (350°F) mark 4 for about 20 minutes, or until firm and browned. Turn them out of the moulds and leave to cool on a wire rack.
4 Trim off the bottoms, so that the cakes stand firmly and are of even height. When they are nearly cold, brush with melted jam, then holding them on a skewer, roll in coconut.
5 Top each madeleine with a glacé cherry half and two angelica leaves.

MAIDS OF HONOUR

MAKES 12

600 ml (1 pint) milk	1 egg, beaten
15 ml (1 tbsp) rennet	15 g (½ oz) butter or margarine, melted
212 g (7½ oz) packet frozen puff pastry, thawed	50 g (2 oz) caster sugar

1 Gently heat the milk in a saucepan until just warm to the finger. Remove from the heat and stir in the rennet. Leave for 1½-2 hours until set.
2 When set, put the junket into a muslin bag and leave to drain overnight. Next day, chill the curd for several hours or until very firm.
3 Grease twelve 6 cm (2½ inch) patty tins. On a lightly floured surface, roll out the pastry very thinly and using a 7.5 cm (3 inch) plain cutter, cut out 12 rounds. Line the patty tins with the pastry rounds and prick well.
4 Stir the egg, butter and sugar into the drained curd. Divide the mixture between the pastry cases and bake in the oven at 200°C (400°F) mark 6 for 30 minutes, until well risen and just firm to the touch. Serve warm.

QUEEN CAKES

MAKES 16

100 g (4 oz) butter	100 g (4 oz) self-raising flour
100 g (4 oz) caster sugar	50 g (2 oz) sultanas
2 eggs, beaten	

1 Spread out 16 paper cases on baking sheets, or put them into patty tins.
2 Cream the butter and sugar together until pale and fluffy. Gradually beat in the eggs, a little at a time, beating well after each addition. Fold in the flour, then the fruit.
3 Fill the paper cases half full. Bake at 190°C (375°F) mark 5 for 15-20 minutes, until golden brown. Transfer to a wire rack to cool.

VARIATIONS

Replace the sultanas with one of the following: 50 g (2 oz) chopped dates; 50 g (2 oz) chopped glacé cherries; 50 g (2 oz) chocolate chips.

MINI CHERRY BUNS

MAKES ABOUT 36

50 g (2 oz) soft margarine	1 ripe banana, peeled and mashed
50 g (2 oz) caster sugar	125 g (4 oz) icing sugar, sifted
1 egg, beaten	about 15 ml (1 tbsp) orange juice
50 g (2 oz) self-raising flour	red glacé cherries or red spherical sweets
1.25 ml (¼ level tsp) baking powder	

1 Put the margarine, sugar, egg, flour and baking powder in a food processor and process until smooth and well mixed. Add the banana and process for 1 minute.
2 Put a teaspoonful of the mixture into about 36 small petits fours cases. Arrange the filled cases on a baking sheet and bake in the oven at 190°C (375°F) mark 5 for about 12-15 minutes or until golden brown. Cool on a wire rack.
3 When the buns are cold, make the glacé icing by mixing the icing sugar with the orange juice until smooth and just thick enough to coat the back of a spoon. Top each bun with a small blob of icing and stick half a cherry or a sweet onto each. Leave to set.

CINNAMON CHERRY BARS

MAKES 24

125 g (4 oz) ground almonds	5 ml (1 level tsp) ground cinnamon
1 egg	finely grated rind of 1 lemon
225 g (8 oz) plain flour	125 g (4 oz) black cherry jam
225 g (8 oz) caster sugar	icing sugar, for dredging
175 g (6 oz) butter or margarine	

1 Lightly grease a 28 x 18 cm (11 x 7 inch) shallow tin.
2 Put the first seven ingredients into a large bowl and beat well.
3 Knead lightly. Cover and refrigerate for at least 30 minutes. Press half of the dough evenly into the prepared tin. Spread the jam over the surface.
4 On a lightly floured work surface, lightly knead the remaining dough. With well-floured hands, roll into pencil-thin strips. Arrange over the jam to form a close lattice pattern. Refrigerate for 30 minutes.
5 Bake at 180°C (350°F) mark 4 for 40 minutes or until golden brown and firm to the touch. Leave to cool then dredge with icing sugar. Cut into 24 bars and ease out of the tin.

COOK'S TIP

If you haven't got the right size tin use two small sandwich tins instead and cut the baked mixture into wedges.

LAMINGTONS

MAKES 12

	FOR THE TOPPING
40 g (1½ oz) butter or margarine	450 g (1 lb) icing sugar
65 g (2½ oz) plain flour	75 g (3 oz) cocoa powder
15 ml (1 level tbsp) cornflour	15 g (½ oz) butter
3 eggs, size 2	100 ml (4 fl oz) milk
75 g (3 oz) caster sugar	75 g (3 oz) desiccated coconut

1 Grease a 28 x 18 cm (11 x 7 inch) cake tin. Line with greased greaseproof paper.
2 To make the cakes, melt the butter and let it stand for a few minutes for the salt and any sediment to settle. Sift the flour and cornflour.
3 Put the eggs and sugar into a deep bowl, place over a pan of simmering water and whisk until light and creamy – the mixture should leave a trail on the surface for a few seconds when the whisk is lifted. Remove from the heat and whisk for 5-10 minutes until cool.
4 Re-sift the flours and fold half into the egg mixture with a metal spoon.
5 Pour the cooled but still flowing butter round the edge of the mixture, taking care not to let the sediment run in.
6 Fold the butter very lightly into the mixture, alternating with the rest of the flour.
7 Turn the mixture into the prepared tin. Bake in the oven at 190°C (375°F) mark 5 for 20-25 minutes until firm to the touch. Turn out on to a wire rack and leave to cool.
8 Meanwhile, make the icing. Sift the icing sugar and cocoa into a heatproof bowl placed over a pan of simmering water. Add the butter and the milk and stir over a gentle heat to a coating consistency.
9 Cut the cake into twelve even-sized pieces. Place on a wire cooling rack and stand the rack on a baking sheet. Spoon the icing over each cake to cover completely. Sprinkle the tops with coconut. Leave until set.

ORANGE AND CARAWAY CASTLES

MAKES 10

75 g (3 oz) butter or margarine	2 eggs, beaten
50 g (2 oz) caster sugar	125 g (4 oz) self-raising flour
120 ml (8 level tbsp) fine shred marmalade	pinch of salt
finely grated rind of 1 orange	2.5-5 ml (½-1 level tsp) caraway seeds
	125 g (4 oz) toasted flaked almonds, roughly chopped

1 Grease 10 small dariole moulds and stand them on a baking sheet.
2 Cream together the butter and sugar until pale and fluffy. Beat in 30 ml (2 level tbsp) marmalade and the orange rind. Gradually beat in the eggs, then fold in the flour, salt and caraway seeds.
3 Divide the mixture between the prepared dariole moulds and bake at 170°C (325°F) mark 3 for 25 minutes or until well risen and firm to the touch. Turn out and cool on a wire rack.
4 Trim the bases of the cakes so that they stand level. Heat the remaining marmalade gently in a saucepan until melted. Spread the nuts out on a large plate. Spear each cake on a skewer, brush the tops and sides with marmalade, then roll in the nuts to coat.

COOK'S TIP

We used dariole moulds with a capacity of 75 ml (3 fl oz). If yours are slightly larger you can still use them but you will make fewer cakes.

UPSIDE DOWN CURRANT BUNS

MAKES 15

30 ml (2 tbsp) currants	2 eggs, beaten
30 ml (2 tbsp) nibbed almonds	2.5 ml (½ tsp) vanilla flavouring
150 g (5 oz) butter or margarine	finely grated rind of 1 lemon
150 g (5 oz) caster sugar	100 g (4 oz) plain flour

1 Grease 15 fluted bun tins and divide the currants and almonds between the bases.
2 Cream together the butter and sugar until light and fluffy. Gradually beat in the eggs, vanilla flavouring and grated lemon rind. Sift over the flour and fold in.
3 Divide the mixture evenly between the tins and level with a knife.
4 Bake at 190°C (375°F) mark 5 for 25-30 minutes or until firm to the touch and golden brown. Ease out of the tins immediately and cool on a wire rack.

COOK'S TIP

Try other combinations of dried fruit and chopped nuts such as pistachios and apricots, or pecans and raisins.

ECCLES CAKES

MAKES 8-10

TRADITIONAL CAKE-IN-THE-PAN

MAKES 4

212 g (7½ oz) packet frozen puff pastry, thawed	25 g (1 oz) finely chopped mixed peel
25 g (1 oz) butter or block margarine, softened	50 g (2 oz) currants
25 g (1 oz) soft dark brown sugar	caster sugar, to sprinkle

1 Roll out the pastry on a lightly floured surface and cut into eight to ten 9 cm (3½ inch) rounds.
2 Mix the butter, sugar, mixed peel and currants in a bowl.
3 Place 5 ml (1 tsp) of the fruit and butter mixture in the centre of each pastry round. Draw up the edges of each pastry round to enclose the filling, then re-shape.
4 Turn each round over and roll lightly until the currants just show through. Prick the top of each with a fork. Leave to 'rest' for about 10 minutes in a cool place.
5 Transfer the rounds to a dampened baking sheet. Bake in the oven at 230°C (450°F) mark 8 for about 15 minutes until golden. Transfer to a wire rack to cool. Sprinkle with sugar while warm.

225 g (8 oz) wholemeal self-raising flour	50 g (2 oz) lard, cut into pieces
pinch of salt	50 g (2 oz) caster sugar
pinch of freshly grated nutmeg	100 g (4 oz) seedless raisins

1 Sift the flour, salt and nutmeg together into a bowl. Rub in the lard, then add the caster sugar and seedless raisins.
2 Mix in 150 ml (¼ pint) cold water to make a soft dough and divide into four equal pieces.
3 Form each quarter of dough into a ball and roll out on a lightly floured surface into a round about 12 cm (5 inches) in diameter.
4 Lightly grease a griddle or frying pan and place over a low heat. Cook the rounds for about 10 minutes on each side. Serve at once.

GRIDDLE PANCAKES

MAKES 15-18

100 g (4 oz) self-raising flour	1 egg, beaten
30 ml (2 tbsp) caster sugar	150 ml (¼ pint) milk

1 Mix the flour and sugar in a bowl. Make a well in the centre and stir in the egg, with enough of the milk to make a batter the consistency of thick cream; the mixing should be done as quickly and lightly as possible.
2 Drop the mixture in spoonfuls on to a greased hot griddle or heavy-based frying pan. For round pancakes, drop it from the point of the spoon; for oval ones, drop from the side.
3 Keep the griddle at a steady heat and when bubbles rise to the surface of the pancakes and burst, after 2-3 minutes, turn the pancakes over with a palette knife. Continue cooking for a further 2-3 minutes.

COOK'S TIP

Today's cookers make cooking on a griddle much less of a hit and miss business than when the griddle or bakestone was perched over the coals of the fire. These pancakes or drop scones should be eaten as soon as they are cooked. They are quick and easy to make but don't reheat well.

TRADITIONAL MUFFINS

MAKES ABOUT 14

5 ml (1 level tsp) caster sugar	5 ml (1 level tsp) salt
300 ml (½ pint) warm milk	5 ml (1 level tsp) plain flour, for dusting
10 ml (2 level tsp) dried yeast	5 ml (1 level tsp) fine semolina
450 g (1 lb) strong plain flour	

1 Dissolve the sugar in the milk, sprinkle the yeast over the surface and leave in a warm place for about 20 minutes or until frothy.
2 Sift the flour and salt together. Form a well in the centre. Pour the yeast liquid into the well, draw in the flour and mix to a smooth dough.
3 Knead the dough on a lightly floured surface for about 10 minutes until smooth and elastic. Place in a clean bowl, cover with a tea towel and leave in a warm place until doubled in size.
4 Roll out the dough on a lightly floured surface, using a lightly floured rolling pin, to about 5-10 mm (¼-½ inch) thick. Leave to rest, covered, for 5 minutes, then cut into rounds with a 7.5 cm (3 inch) plain cutter.
5 Place the muffins on a well-floured baking sheet. Mix together the flour and semolina and use to dust the tops. Cover with a tea towel and leave in a warm place until doubled in size.
6 Heat a griddle or heavy-based frying pan and grease lightly. Cook the muffins on the griddle or frying pan for about 7 minutes each side. Cool on a wire rack.

COOK'S TIP

The correct way to toast muffins is not to split them and toast the two halves separately, as this makes them tough. Instead, cut them open, then close together again and toast slowly until warm right through, before opening out and buttering generously.

PECAN AND RAISIN MUFFINS

MAKES 12

350 g (12 oz) plain flour	150 ml (¼ pint) milk
15 ml (1 level tbsp) baking powder	60 ml (2 fl oz) corn oil
salt	1.25 ml (¼ tsp) vanilla flavouring
125 g (4 oz) caster sugar	75 g (3 oz) pecan nuts, roughly chopped
2 eggs	75 g (3 oz) raisins

1 Line 12 deep bun or patty tins with paper cake cases, or grease 12 muffin tins.
2 Sift the flour, baking powder and a pinch of salt into a bowl. Mix in the sugar and make a well in the centre.
3 Lightly beat the eggs with the milk, oil and vanilla flavouring and pour into the centre of the dry ingredients. Mix quickly to blend the flour with the liquid. Do not over-mix, the mixture should look slightly lumpy. Lightly stir in the nuts and raisins.
4 Divide the mixture equally between the paper cake cases or muffin tins. Bake in the oven at 190°C (375°F) mark 5 for 25-27 minutes or until well risen, golden brown and cooked through. Leave in the tins to cool for a few minutes. Serve warm or cold.

VARIATION

Blueberry Muffins
Use one third wholemeal flour and two thirds plain white flour. Replace the pecan nuts and raisins with 225 g (8 oz) blueberries. (Illustrated above right.)

DOUBLE CHOCOLATE MUFFINS

MAKES 12

100 g (4 oz) plain chocolate, broken into pieces	pinch of salt
50 g (2 oz) cocoa powder	100 g (4 oz) plain chocolate polka dots
225 g (8 oz) self-raising flour	225 ml (8 fl oz) milk
5 ml (1 level tsp) baking powder	60 ml (4 tbsp) vegetable oil
50 g (2 oz) dark brown soft sugar	5 ml (1 tsp) vaniila flavouring
	1 egg

1 Thoroughly grease 12 deep muffin or bun tins. Place a large paper cake case in each.
2 Put the chocolate into a large bowl and stand over a saucepan of simmering water. Heat gently until the chocolate melts.
3 Remove from the heat and stir in the remaining ingredients. Beat thoroughly together.
4 Spoon the mixture into the paper cases. Bake in the oven at 220°C (425°F) mark 7 for 15 minutes until well risen and firm to the touch. Serve warm.

COOK'S TIP

It's important to use deep bun tins to make muffins. They are quick to make and taste delicious, especially if served fresh from the oven.

EASTER BISCUITS

MAKES ABOUT 30

100 g (4 oz) butter	2.5 ml (½ level tsp) ground cinnamon
75 g (3 oz) caster sugar	50 g (2 oz) currants
1 egg, separated	15 ml (1 tbsp) chopped mixed peel
200 g (7 oz) plain flour	
pinch of salt	15-30 ml (1-2 tbsp) brandy or milk
2.5 ml (½ level tsp) ground mixed spice	caster sugar for sprinkling

1 Cream the butter and sugar together until pale and fluffy, then beat in the egg yolk. Sift in the flour, salt and spices and mix well. Add the fruit and peel and enough brandy or milk to give a fairly soft dough.

2 Knead lightly on a lightly floured surface and roll out until about 5 mm (¼ inch) thick. Cut into 6 cm (2 inch) rounds using a fluted cutter. Place on greased baking sheets and bake at 200°C (400°F) mark 6 for 10 minutes.

3 Remove from the oven, brush with the lightly beaten egg white, sprinkle with a little caster sugar and return to the oven to bake for about 5 minutes longer, until the tops are golden brown. Transfer to a wire rack to cool. Store in an airtight container.

SHREWSBURY BISCUITS

MAKES 20-24

125 g (4 oz) butter or block margarine	225 g (8 oz) plain flour
150 g (5 oz) caster sugar	grated rind of 1 lemon or orange
2 egg yolks	

1 Grease two large baking sheets.

2 Cream the butter and sugar until pale and fluffy. Add the egg yolks and beat well.

3 Stir in the flour and grated lemon rind and mix to a fairly firm dough with a round-bladed knife.

4 Turn out on to a lightly floured surface and knead lightly.

5 Roll out to about 5 mm (¼ inch) thick. Cut into rounds with a 6 cm (2½ inch) fluted cutter and place on the baking sheets.

6 Bake in the oven at 180°C (350°F) mark 4 for about 15 minutes, until firm and a very light brown colour.

VARIATION

Add 50 g (2 oz) chopped dried fruit to the mixture with the flour.

ALMOND CRISPS

MAKES 24

125 g (4 oz) butter or block margarine	few drops of almond flavouring
75 g (3 oz) caster sugar	150 g (5 oz) self-raising flour
1 egg yolk	75 g (3 oz) chopped almonds

1 Grease two or three baking sheets.
2 Cream together the butter and sugar until pale and fluffy. Beat in the egg yolk and almond flavouring and then the flour to give a smooth dough.
3 Form into a neat log shape and cut into twenty-four even slices. Shape each into a barrel, then roll in chopped almonds.
4 Place well apart on the baking sheets and bake in the oven at 190°C (375°F) mark 5 for 15-20 minutes. Cool on a wire rack.

REFRIGERATOR BISCUITS

MAKES ABOUT 32

150 g (5 oz) caster sugar	grated rind of 1 lemon
150 g (5 oz) soft tub margarine	1 egg, beaten
few drops of vanilla flavouring	225 g (8 oz) plain flour

1 Lightly grease two baking sheets.
2 Cream together the sugar and margarine until pale and fluffy. Beat in the vanilla flavouring, lemon rind and egg.
3 Stir in the flour and mix to a firm paste. Knead lightly, wrap and chill in the refrigerator for 30 minutes.
4 Roll the dough to a sausage shape about 5 cm (2 inches) in diameter and 20 cm (8 inches) long. Wrap in greaseproof paper. Refrigerate for at least 30 minutes.
5 When required, cut off 5 mm (¼ inch) slices, place on the baking sheets and bake at 190°C (375°F) mark 5 for 12-15 minutes. Cool the biscuits on a wire rack.

VARIATION

Honey Jumbles

Follow the basic recipe above as far as the end of stage 4. Slice off 5 mm (¼ inch) rounds. Roll into pencil-thin strips 10 cm (4 inches) long. Twist into 'S' shapes and place on lightly greased baking sheets. Chill for 30 minutes. Bake as above. While still warm, glaze with thin honey, sprinkle with demerara sugar and grill for 1-2 minutes until caramelised. Cool.

PECAN COOKIES

MAKES ABOUT 24

125 g (4 oz) plain flour	50 g (2 oz) pecan nuts, finely chopped
50 g (2 oz) cornflour	75 g (3 oz) butter
3.75 ml (¾ level tsp) baking powder	50 g (2 oz) light soft brown sugar
pinch of salt	25 g (1 oz) dark muscovado sugar
10 ml (2 level tsp) ground ginger	40 g (1½ oz) golden syrup
5 ml (1 level tsp) ground mixed spice	30 pecan nut halves, to decorate
5 ml (1 level tsp) ground cinnamon	

1 Lightly grease several baking sheets. Sift the flour, cornflour, baking powder, salt and the spices into a bowl. Stir in the chopped pecans.
2 Beat the butter with the sugars until very soft, light and fluffy. Beat in the golden syrup, then mix in the flour and nut mixture. Knead the dough very lightly on a floured surface until smooth.
3 Divide the dough into walnut-sized pieces. Roll each one into a ball and place on the greased baking sheets, spacing the balls well apart. Flatten each ball of dough with a fork, then press a pecan nut half into the centre of each one.
4 Bake at 180°C (350°F) mark 4 for 15-20 minutes, until just lightly browned around the edges. Allow to cool slightly on the baking sheets, then remove with a palette knife to cooling racks to cool completely.

COOK'S TIP

Pecan nuts belong to the walnut family and are grown in North America where they are known as hickory nuts. They are available in their shells, which are smooth and reddish-brown, or shelled, looking like narrow, elongated walnuts. If pecans are unavailable, walnuts may be used.

CINNAMON BISCUITS

MAKES ABOUT 24

275 g (10 oz) plain flour	225 g (8 oz) butter
90 ml (6 level tbsp) ground almonds	egg yolk, to glaze
10 ml (2 level tsp) ground cinnamon	flaked almonds
125 g (4 oz) caster sugar	icing sugar and drinking chocolate, for dredging

1 Sift the flour into a bowl. Add the almonds, cinnamon and sugar and mix together. Work in the butter with your fingertips. Knead well.
2 Roll out on a surface dusted with icing sugar until about 2.5 cm (½ inch) thick. Cut out heart or flower shapes with small pastry cutters. Brush with egg yolk and sprinkle with a few almonds.
3 Bake in the oven at 170°C (325°F) mark 3 for about 40 minutes, until firm and pale golden brown. Cool on a wire rack. Dredge a few biscuits with sifted icing sugar and a few with drinking chocolate powder.

LEMON AND LIME COOKIES

MAKES ABOUT 24

100 g (4 oz) butter or margarine	175 g (6 oz) plain flour
100 g (4 oz) caster sugar	finely grated rind of 1 small lemon
1 egg yolk	15 ml (1 tbsp) lemon juice
50 g (2 oz) full-fat soft cheese	20 ml (4 tsp) lime marmalade

1 Put the butter and caster sugar in a bowl and beat together until light and fluffy.
2 Beat in the egg yolk, cheese, flour, lemon rind and juice, until a soft mixture is formed.
3 Place small spoonfuls of the mixture on to greased baking sheets, allowing room for spreading.
4 Bake in the oven at 190°C (375°F) mark 5 for about 17 minutes or until light brown. Transfer to a wire rack to cool.
5 Melt the marmalade in a small saucepan and brush over the cookies, to glaze. Leave to set.

COOK'S TIP

These cookies are simplicity itself to make, almost like craggy, flat rock cakes. If you have a food processor, steps 1 and 2 can be made in moments, by working all the ingredients together in one go.

FLORENTINES

MAKES ABOUT 12

90 g (3½ oz) butter or margarine	5 glacé cherries, chopped
100 g (4 oz) caster sugar	25 g (1 oz) chopped mixed peel
100 g (4 oz) flaked almonds, roughly chopped	15 ml (1 tbsp) single cream
25 g (1 oz) sultanas	175 g (6 oz) plain chocolate

1 Line 3 baking sheets with non-stick paper.
2 Melt the butter in a saucepan over a low heat, add the sugar and boil the mixture for 1 minute.
3 Remove pan from the heat and add the remaining ingredients, except chocolate, stirring well to mix.
4 Drop the mixture in small, well-rounded heaps on to the prepared sheets, allowing enough room between each for the mixture to spread.
5 Bake the biscuit rounds in the oven at 180°C (350°F) mark 4 for 10 minutes until golden brown.
6 Remove from the oven and press around the edges of the biscuits with the blade of a knife to neaten the shape. Leave on the baking sheets for 5 minutes until beginning to firm, then lift on to a wire rack to cool for 20 minutes.
7 Break the chocolate into a heatproof bowl and place over simmering water. Stir until the chocolate is melted, then remove from the heat and leave to cool for 10-15 minutes.
8 Just as the chocolate is beginning to set, spread it over the backs of the biscuits. Draw the prongs of a fork across the chocolate to mark wavy lines and leave to set.

COOK'S TIP

If chocolate is overheated, it may curdle or thicken instead of melting smoothly. To guard against this, either melt it in a bowl placed over a pan of hot water, as suggested here, or use a double saucepan. If the chocolate does curdle, add a little blended white vegetable fat in small pieces, stirring into the chocolate until it reaches the desired consistency.

PISTACHIO RINGS

MAKES ABOUT 20

	FOR THE ICING
175 g (6 oz) butter	125 g (4 oz) icing sugar, sifted
50 g (2 oz) caster sugar	30 ml (2 tbsp) fresh lime juice
225 g (8 oz) plain flour, sifted	40 g (1½ oz) shelled pistachio nuts, skinned and chopped
15 ml (1 tbsp) milk	

1 Cream the butter and sugar together until light and creamy. Stir in the flour and milk and mix to form a fairly soft dough.
2 Put the mixture into a piping bag fitted with a 1 cm (½ inch) star nozzle. Pipe the mixture into 5.5 cm (2¼ inch) diameter rings, spaced well apart, on greased baking sheets.
3 Bake at 180°C (350°F) mark 4 for 8-10 minutes until lightly golden and cooked through. Transfer to wire racks to cool slightly.
4 To make the icing, blend the icing sugar with the lime juice to make a thin consistency. Brush over the rings while still warm to glaze and sprinkle at once with chopped nuts. Leave to set before serving.

BRANDY SNAPS

MAKES 10

50 g (2 oz) butter or block margarine	2.5 ml (½ level tsp) ground ginger
50 g (2 oz) caster sugar	5 ml (1 tsp) brandy
30 ml (2 level tbsp) golden syrup	grated rind of ½ a lemon
50 g (2 oz) plain flour, sifted	150 ml (¼ pint) double cream

1 Grease the handles of several wooden spoons and line two or three baking sheets with non-stick baking parchment.
2 Melt the butter with the sugar and syrup in a saucepan over low heat. Remove from the heat. Stir in the flour and ginger, brandy and lemon rind.
3 Put small spoonfuls of the mixture about 10 cm (4 inches) apart on the baking sheets, to allow plenty of room for spreading.
4 Bake one sheet at a time in the oven at 180°C (350°F) mark 4 for 7-10 minutes, until bubbly and golden. Allow to cool for 1-2 minutes, then loosen with a palette knife and roll them round the spoon handles.
5 Leave until set, then twist gently to remove. (If the biscuits cool too much whilst still on the sheet and become too brittle to roll, return the sheet to the oven for a moment to soften them.) Before serving, whisk the cream until thick and fill the brandy snaps.

GINGERBREAD MEN

MAKES 12

350 g (12 oz) plain flour	175 g (6 oz) light soft brown sugar
5 ml (1 level tsp) bicarbonate of soda	60 ml (4 level tbsp) golden syrup
10 ml (2 level tsp) ground ginger	1 egg, beaten
100 g (4 oz) butter or block margarine	currants, to decorate

1 Grease three baking sheets.
2 Sift the flour, bicarbonate of soda and ginger into a bowl. Rub the butter into the flour until the mixture looks like fine crumbs. Stir in the sugar. Beat the syrup into the egg and stir into the bowl.
3 Mix to form a dough and knead until smooth.
4 Divide into two and roll out on a lightly floured surface to about 5 mm (¼ inch) thick. Using a gingerbread man cutter, cut out figures and place them on the baking sheets. Decorate with currants. Bake in the oven at 190°C (375°F) mark 5 for 12-15 minutes, until golden. Cool slightly, then place on a wire rack.

HARLEQUIN BISCUITS

MAKES 30

75 g (3 oz) plain flour	15 ml (1 tbsp) golden syrup
1.25 ml (¼ level tsp) bicarbonate of soda	1 egg, size 6, beaten
2.5 ml (½ level tsp) ground ginger	227 g (8 oz) packet ready-to-roll icing
25 g (1 oz) butter or block margarine	liquid food colourings
40 g (1½ oz) light soft brown sugar	juice of ½ small orange
	edible silver balls, to decorate

1 Grease two large baking sheets. Sift the flour, bicarbonate of soda and ginger into a bowl. Rub the fat into the flour and stir in the sugar. Add the syrup with enough egg to form a soft dough, then turn onto a lightly floured surface and knead until smooth.
2 Using a floured rolling pin, roll out the dough to a 25 cm (10 inch) square. Cut into 2.5 cm (1 inch) wide strips. Separate the strips then, cutting at an angle, cut off pieces to make diamond shapes.
3 Place the biscuits on the prepared baking sheets and bake in the oven at 190°C (375°F) mark 5 for 8-10 minutes until golden brown. Cool slightly then transfer to a wire rack.
4 When the biscuits are completely cold, roll out the icing on a surface dusted with icing sugar. Cut the icing into strips (as when making the biscuits). Paint each strip a different colour using a little food colouring. Wash and dry your brush between each colour. Cut off diamond shapes. Moisten the surface of each biscuit with a little orange juice and top each biscuit with a piece of icing and three edible silver balls. Leave to set.
5 Serve the biscuits on a platter, decoratively arranged in a harlequin pattern.

CHOCOLATE VIENNESE FINGERS

MAKES ABOUT 26

125 g (4 oz) butter or margarine	few drops of vanilla flavouring
25 g (1 oz) icing sugar	50 g (2 oz) plain chocolate or plain chocolate flavour cake covering
125 g (4 oz) plain flour	
1.25 ml (¼ level tsp) baking powder	icing sugar, to decorate (optional)

1 Beat the butter until smooth, then beat in the icing sugar until pale and fluffy.
2 Sift in the flour and baking powder. Beat well, adding the vanilla flavouring.
3 Put into a piping bag fitted with a medium star nozzle. Pipe out finger shapes, about 7.5 cm (3 inch) long, on to two greased baking sheets, spacing them well apart.
4 Bake in the oven at 190°C (375°F) mark 5 for 15-20 minutes. Cool on a wire rack.
5 Break up the chocolate and place in a bowl over a pan of simmering water. Heat gently until the chocolate melts. Dip the ends of each Viennese Finger in the melted chocolate to coat. Leave to set on the wire rack.
6 Dredge with icing sugar to serve if wished.

PETTICOAT TAIL SHORTBREAD

MAKES 8

100 g (4 oz) butter, softened	150 g (5 oz) plain flour
50 g (2 oz) caster sugar, plus extra for dredging	50 g (2 oz) ground rice

1 In a medium bowl, cream the butter and sugar together until pale and fluffy.
2 Gradually stir in the flour and ground rice. Draw the mixture together and press into an 18 cm (7 inch) round sandwich tin.
3 Prick well all over, pinch up the edges with a finger and thumb. Mark into 8 triangles with a sharp knife. Bake at 170°C (325°F) mark 3 for about 40 minutes, until pale straw in colour.
4 Leave in the tin for 5 minutes, cut into 8 triangles, then dredge with caster sugar. Remove from the tin when cold. Store in an airtight container.

COOK'S NOTE

These traditional Scottish shortbread biscuits date back beyond the 12th century. The triangles fit together into a circle and were the same shape as the pieces of fabric used to make a full-gored petticoat in Elizabethan times. The biscuits got their name because in those days the word for a pattern was a 'tally', and so the biscuits became known as 'petticote tallis'.

INVERNESS GINGERNUTS

MAKES ABOUT 36

225 g (8 oz) plain flour	75 g (3 oz) caster sugar
10 ml (2 level tsp) ground ginger	2.5 ml (½ level tsp) bicarbonate of soda
5 ml (1 level tsp) ground mixed spice	175 g (6 oz) treacle
75 g (3 oz) fine oatmeal	50 g (2 oz) butter

1 Put the flour, ginger, spice, oatmeal, sugar and bicarbonate of soda in a bowl and mix together.
2 Heat the treacle and butter in a small pan until melted. Pour on to the dry ingredients and mix to make a smooth dough. Knead well.
3 Roll the dough out until about 5 mm (¼ inch) thick. Prick with a fork and cut out 6.5 cm (2½ inch) rounds with a plain cutter. Place on greased baking sheets and bake at 170°C (325°F) mark 3 for 20-25 minutes, until firm to the touch. Transfer to wire racks to cool.

TONBRIDGE BISCUITS

MAKES ABOUT 24

75 g (3 oz) butter, diced	1 egg, beaten
225 g (8 oz) plain flour	1 egg white, beaten, to glaze
75 g (3 oz) caster sugar	caraway seeds, for sprinkling

1 Rub the butter into the flour until the mixture resembles fine breadcrumbs, then stir in the sugar. Add the egg and mix to a stiff paste.
2 Roll out on a lightly floured surface, until about 5 mm (¼ inch) thick, prick the top with a fork and cut into rounds with a 5 cm (2 inch) plain cutter. Brush with egg white and sprinkle on a few caraway seeds.
3 Put on to greased baking sheets and bake at 180°C (350°F) mark 4 for about 10 minutes or until light brown. Transfer to wire racks to cool. Store in an airtight container.

FRUIT CAKES & TEABREADS

Fruit cakes and teabreads have the advantage that they keep much better than other cakes. Indeed, many actually improve in flavour and are easier to slice after storing closely wrapped, in an airtight tin for 2-3 days.

SAFFRON CAKE

MAKES 8-10 SLICES

2.5 ml (½ tsp) saffron strands	50 g (2 oz) butter, in pieces
7.5 ml (1½ tsp) dried yeast plus a pinch of sugar	50 g (2 oz) lard, in pieces
150 ml (¼ pint) tepid milk	175 g (6 oz) currants
450 g (1 lb) strong plain flour	grated rind of ½ a lemon
5 ml (1 tsp) salt	25 g (1 oz) caster sugar

1 Infuse saffron in 150 ml (¼ pint) boiling water for 2 hours. Grease a 20 cm (8 inch) round cake tin. Sprinkle the yeast and sugar into the milk and leave in a warm place for 15 minutes until frothy.
2 Sift the flour and salt into a bowl. Rub in the butter and lard until the mixture resembles fine breadcrumbs. Stir in the currants, lemon rind and sugar.
3 Strain the saffron infusion; warm slightly. Add to the dry ingredients with the yeast liquid and beat well.
4 Turn the dough into the prepared tin, cover with a clean cloth and leave to rise in a warm place for about 1 hour until the dough comes to the top of the tin.
5 Bake in oven at 200°C (400°F) mark 6 for 30 minutes. Lower temperature to 180°C (350°F) mark 4 and bake for a further 30 minutes. Turn out on to a wire rack to cool.

FRUIT BRAZIL CAKE

MAKES ABOUT 12 SLICES

175 g (6 oz) butter	125 g (4 oz) no-soak dried apricots, chopped
175 g (6 oz) caster sugar	125 g (4 oz) sultanas
3 eggs, size 2, beaten	2 tablespoons apricot jam, sieved and melted
125 g (4 oz) plain white flour	
125 g (4 oz) self-raising flour	225 g (8 oz) marzipan
125 g (4 oz) Brazil nuts	few Brazil nuts, to decorate
50 g (2 oz) candied lemon peel, chopped	

1 Grease a deep 20 cm (8 inch) round cake tin or a 1.7 litre (3 pint) loaf tin and line with greaseproof paper.
2 Put the butter and sugar in a bowl and cream together until light and fluffy. Gradually beat in the eggs.
3 Sift the flours together and fold into the creamed mixture, followed by the chopped nuts, peel and fruit.
4 Spoon into the prepared tin, level surface and bake in the oven at 180°C (350°F) mark 4 for 1¼ hours. Leave in tin for 10 minutes, then turn out and cool on a wire rack.
5 Brush the top of the cake with the apricot jam. Roll out the marzipan to fit the cake and press on top. Crimp the edges and score the top in a diamond pattern. Decorate with the nuts. Grill the cake to brown the top.

FRUIT-CRUSTED CIDER CAKE

MAKES 8-10 SLICES

45 ml (3 tbsp) golden syrup	50 g (2 oz) cornflakes, crushed
150 g (5 oz) butter or margarine	125 g (4 oz) caster sugar
350 g (12 oz) cooking apples, peeled, cored and finely chopped	2 eggs, beaten
	125 g (4 oz) self-raising flour
45 ml (3 tbsp) mincemeat	45 ml (3 tbsp) dry cider

1 Line a 35 x 11 cm (14 x 4½ inch) tart frame with foil. Grease the foil.
2 Put the syrup into a pan with 25 g (1 oz) butter and heat until melted. Add the apple, mincemeat and cornflakes and mix together.
3 Put the remaining butter and the sugar into a bowl and beat together until pale and fluffy. Gradually beat in the eggs. Fold in the flour and cider.
4 Turn into the frame and level the surface. Spread the apple mixture on top.
5 Bake in the oven at 170°C (325°F) mark 3 for 45-50 minutes or until firm to the touch. Cool in the tin for 1 hour, then cut into bars.

COOK'S TIP

If you don't own a tart frame, use a 20 cm (8 inch) square cake tin instead.

FARMHOUSE SULTANA CAKE

MAKES ABOUT 16 SLICES

225 g (8 oz) plain white flour	175 g (6 oz) butter or block margarine
10 ml (2 level tsp) ground mixed spice	225 g (8 oz) soft brown sugar
5 ml (1 level tsp) bicarbonate of soda	225 g (8 oz) sultanas
	1 egg, beaten
225 g (8 oz) plain wholemeal flour	about 300 ml (½ pint) milk
	10 sugar cubes (optional)

1 Grease and base-line a 20 cm (8 inch) square cake tin.
2 Sift the plain flour with the spice and soda into a large mixing bowl; stir in the wholemeal flour.
3 Rub in the butter until the mixture resembles fine breadcrumbs, then stir in the sugar and sultanas.
4 Make a well in the centre of the dry ingredients and add the egg and milk. Beat gently until well mixed and of a soft dropping consistency, adding more milk if necessary. Turn into the prepared tin.
5 Roughly crush the sugar cubes with the end of a rolling pin and scatter over the cake, if liked.
6 Bake in the oven at 170°C (325°F) mark 3 for about 1 hour 40 minutes, until cooked. When a fine skewer is inserted into the centre, no traces of moist cake should remain. Turn out and cool on a wire rack.

HALF-POUND CAKE

MAKES ABOUT 16 SLICES

225 g (8 oz) butter or block margarine, softened	100 g (4 oz) glacé cherries, halved
225 g (8 oz) caster sugar	225 g (8 oz) plain flour
4 eggs, beaten	2.5 ml (½ level tsp) salt
225 g (8 oz) seedless raisins	2.5 ml (½ level tsp) ground mixed spice
225 g (8 oz) mixed currants and sultanas	15 ml (1 tbsp) brandy
	few walnut halves

1 Line a 20 cm (8 inch) round cake tin with greased greaseproof paper.
2 Cream the fat and sugar until pale and fluffy. Add the eggs, a little at a time, beating well after each addition.
3 Mix together the fruit, flour, salt and spice and fold into the creamed mixture, using a metal spoon. Add the brandy and mix to a soft dropping consistency.
4 Turn the mixture into the tin, level the top and arrange the nuts on top. Bake in the oven at 150°C (300°F) mark 2 for about 2½ hours, until a fine warmed skewer inserted in the centre comes out clean. Turn out and cool on a wire rack.

COOK'S TIP

This recipe is so named because the main ingredients are added in 225 g (8 oz) or half pound quantities, making it an easy one to remember.

DUNDEE CAKE

MAKES ABOUT 16 SLICES

100 g (4 oz) currants	225 g (8 oz) butter or block margarine, softened
100 g (4 oz) seedless raisins	225 g (8 oz) light soft brown sugar
50 g (2 oz) blanched almonds, chopped	finely grated rind of 1 lemon
100 g (4 oz) chopped mixed peel	4 eggs, beaten
275 g (10 oz) plain flour	25 g (1 oz) split almonds, to decorate

1 Line a 20 cm (8 inch) round cake tin with greased greaseproof paper. Combine the fruit, chopped nuts and mixed peel in a bowl. Sift in a little flour and stir until the fruit is evenly coated.
2 Cream the butter and sugar until pale and fluffy, then beat in the lemon rind. Add the eggs, a little at a time, beating well after each addition.
3 Sift the remaining flour over the mixture and fold in lightly with a metal spoon, then fold in the fruit and nut mixture.
4 Turn the mixture into the tin and make a slight hollow in the centre with the back of a metal spoon. Arrange the split almonds on top.
5 Bake in the oven at 170°C (325°F) mark 3 for about 2½ hours until a fine warmed skewer inserted in the centre comes out clean. Check near the end of the cooking time and cover with several layers of greaseproof paper if it is over-browning.
6 Cool in the tin for 15 minutes, before turning out on to a wire rack to cool completely for 2 hours. Wrap in greaseproof paper and foil and store in an airtight tin for at least 1 week to mature.

CHERRY AND COCONUT CAKE

MAKES ABOUT 10 SLICES

250 g (9 oz) self-raising white flour	125 g (4 oz) caster sugar
1.25 ml (¼ level tsp) salt	125 g (4 oz) glacé cherries, finely chopped
125 g (4 oz) butter or margarine	2 eggs, size 6, beaten
75 g (3 oz) desiccated coconut	225 ml (8 fl oz) milk
	25 g (1 oz) shredded coconut

1 Grease a 1.3 litre (2¼ pint) loaf tin. Line the base with greaseproof paper, grease the paper and dust with flour.
2 Put the flour and salt into a bowl and rub in the fat until the mixture resembles fine breadcrumbs. Stir in the desiccated coconut, sugar and cherries.
3 Whisk together the eggs and milk and beat into the dry ingredients. Turn the mixture into the tin, level the surface and scatter over the shredded coconut.
4 Bake in the oven at 180°C (350°F) mark 4 for 1½ hours until a fine warmed skewer inserted in the centre comes out clean. Check after 40 minutes and cover with greaseproof paper if overbrowning. Turn out on to a wire rack to cool.

COOK'S TIP

Wash any excess syrup from glacé cherries before use and dry thoroughly, then toss in a little flour.

CUT-AND-COME-AGAIN FRUIT CAKE

MAKES ABOUT 16 SLICES

100 g (4 oz) plain flour	175 g (6 oz) caster sugar
100 g (4 oz) self-raising flour	4 eggs, beaten
2.5 ml (½ level tsp) ground nutmeg	350 g (12 oz) mixed dried fruit
2.5 ml (½ level tsp) ground ginger	100 g (4 oz) glacé cherries, halved
finely grated rind of ½ lemon	15 ml (1 tbsp) milk
50 g (2 oz) ground almonds	25 g (1 oz) slivered almonds
175 g (6 oz) butter or margarine	

1 Grease and line a 20 cm (8 inch) round cake tin. Sift the flours, nutmeg and ginger into a bowl. Add the lemon rind and almonds and stir well to mix.
2 In a separate bowl, cream the butter and sugar together until pale and fluff. Add the eggs a little at a time, beating well after each addition. Fold in the flour mixture with a metal spoon, then the mixed dried fruit, halved glacé cherries and milk.
3 Turn the mixture into the prepared tin and make a slight hollow in the centre. Scatter the almonds on top.
4 Bake the cake in the oven at 180°C (350°F) mark 4 for 1 hour, then lower the temperature to 170°C (325°F) mark 3 and bake for a further 30 minutes.
5 Remove from the oven and allow to cool slightly for 15 minutes in the tin, then transfer to a wire rack to cool completely for at least 2 hours. Double wrap in greaseproof and foil and store in an airtight tin.

COOK'S TIP

This fruit cake improves with keeping and should be stored for at least 24 hours before being cut. It is perfect for teatime snacks or if visitors call unexpectedly, because it will keep for several months if wrapped in greaseproof paper and foil and stored in a tin.

MIXED FRUIT TEABREAD

MAKES 8-10 SLICES

175 g (6 oz) raisins	1 egg, beaten
125 g (4 oz) sultanas	225 g (8 oz) plain wholemeal flour
50 g (2 oz) currants	7.5 ml (1½ level tsp) baking powder
175 g (6 oz) soft brown sugar	
300 ml (½ pint) strained cold tea	2.5 ml (½ level tsp) ground mixed spice

1   Place the dried fruit and the sugar in a large bowl. Pour over the tea, stir well to mix and leave to soak overnight.
2   The next day, add the egg, flour, baking powder and mixed spice to the fruit and tea mixture. Beat thoroughly with a wooden spoon until all the ingredients are evenly combined.
3   Spoon the cake mixture into a greased and base-lined 900 g (2 lb) loaf tin. Level the surface.
4   Bake in the oven at 180°C (350°F) mark 4 for about 1¼ hours until the cake is well risen and a skewer inserted in the centre comes out clean.
5   Turn the cake out of the tin and leave on a wire rack until completely cold. Wrap in greaseproof paper and foil. Store in an airtight container for 1-2 days before slicing and eating.

SERVING SUGGESTION

Serve this moist, fruity teabread sliced and buttered at tea-time. Or serve with thin wedges of sharp Cheddar cheese for a snack at any time of day.

PRUNE AND NUT LOAF

MAKE 8-10 SLICES

275 g (10 oz) self-raising flour	1 egg
pinch of salt	100 ml (4 fl oz) milk
7.5 ml (1½ level tsp) ground cinnamon	50 g (2 oz) shelled walnuts, chopped
75 g (3 oz) butter or margarine	100 g (4 oz) no-soak prunes, chopped
75 g (3 oz) demerara sugar	15 ml (1 tbsp) clear honey

1   Grease a 2 litre (3½ pint) loaf tin, line with greaseproof paper and grease the paper.
2   Sift the flour and salt into a bowl and add the cinnamon. Rub in the fat until the mixture resembles fine breadcrumbs.
3   Stir in the sugar, and make a well in the centre. Add the egg and milk and gradually draw in the dry ingredients to form a smooth dough.
4   Using floured hands shape the mixture into sixteen even-sized rounds. Place eight in the base of the tin. Sprinkle over half of the nuts and all of the prunes.
5   Arrange the remaining dough rounds on top and sprinkle over the remaining chopped walnuts.
6   Bake in the oven at 190°C (375°F) mark 5 for about 50 minutes or until firm to the touch. Check near the end of the cooking time and cover with greaseproof paper if it is overbrowning.
7   Turn out on to a wire rack and leave to cool for 1 hour. When cold brush with the honey to glaze. Wrap and store for 1-2 days in an airtight tin before slicing and buttering.

COOK'S TIP

This fruity teabread improves as it matures, the flavour and moisture from the fruit penetrating the cake and mellowing it over a number of days.

WHOLEMEAL DATE AND BANANA BREAD

MAKES 10-12 SLICES

225 g (8 oz) stoned dates, roughly chopped	100 g (4 oz) butter or margarine
5 ml (1 level tsp) bicarbonate of soda	75 g (3 oz) shelled hazelnuts, chopped
300 ml (½ pint) milk	2 medium ripe bananas
275 g (10 oz) self-raising wholemeal flour	1 egg, beaten
	30 ml (2 tbsp) clear honey

1 Grease a 1.3 litre (2¼ pint) loaf tin and line with greaseproof paper.
2 Put the dates in a pan with the soda and milk. Bring slowly to boiling point, stirring, then remove from the heat and leave until cold.
3 Put the flour in a large bowl and rub in the butter. Stir in the hazelnuts, reserving 30 ml (2 tbsp) for the decoration.
4 Peel and mash the bananas, then add to the flour mixture with the dates and the egg. Beat well to mix.
5 Spoon the mixture into the prepared tin and bake in the oven at 180°C (350°F) mark 4 for 1-1¼ hours until a skewer inserted in the centre comes out clean.
6 Leave the loaf to cool in the tin for about 5 minutes. Turn out, peel off the lining paper and place on a wire rack.
7 Heat the honey gently, then brush over the top of the loaf. Sprinkle with the reserved hazelnuts and leave until cold.

COOK'S TIP

It may seem unusual to have a cake made entirely without sugar, but this is because of the high proportion of dates used in this recipe. Dates have the highest natural sugar content of all dried fruit and if used in cakes such as this one there is no need to add extra sugar.

BANANA AND BRAZIL NUT LOAF

MAKES 8-10 SLICES

75 g (3 oz) soft margarine	225 g (8 oz) self-raising flour
175 g (6 oz) caster sugar	Brazil nuts and icing sugar, to decorate
3 eggs	
450 g (1 lb) ripe bananas	
50 g (2 oz) Brazil nuts, roughly chopped	

1 Grease a 900 g (2 lb)/1.4 litre (2 pint) loaf tin and line the base with greaseproof paper.
2 Cream together the margarine and sugar until light and fluffy. Gradually add the eggs, beating well after each addition.
3 Peel and mash the bananas with a fork, then stir into the creamed mixture. Add the chopped nuts. Sift the flour over the mixture and fold in lightly. Turn the mixture into the prepared tin and smooth the surface. Decorate with a few Brazil nuts.
4 Bake at 180°C (350°F) mark 4 for about 1½ hours until golden brown, firm to the touch and cooked through. Cover with foil if the loaf becomes too brown. Leave to cool in the tin. Sift icing sugar over the loaf to decorate just before serving.

GINGER MARMALADE TEABREAD

MAKES 8-10 SLICES

200 g (7 oz) plain flour	60 ml (4 tbsp) ginger marmalade
5 ml (1 level tsp) ground ginger	1 egg, beaten
5 ml (1 level tsp) baking powder	60 ml (4 tbsp) milk
40 g (1½ oz) block margarine	40 g (1½ oz) stem ginger, chopped
65 g (2½ oz) light soft brown sugar	

1 Grease a 900 ml (1½ pint) loaf tin with melted lard. Base-line with greaseproof paper and grease the paper.
2 Put the flour, ginger and baking powder into a bowl and rub in the fat until the mixture resembles fine breadcrumbs. Stir in the sugar.
3 Mix together the marmalade, egg and most of the milk. Stir into the dry ingredients and add the rest of the milk, if necessary, to mix to a soft dough.
4 Turn the mixture into the prepared tin, level the surface and press pieces of ginger on top. Bake in the oven at 170°C (325°F) mark 3 for about 1 hour or until golden. Turn out on to a wire rack for 1 hour to cool.

VARIATION

Use coarse-cut orange marmalade instead of ginger marmalade, and replace the stem ginger with chopped candied orange peel.

MARBLED CHOCOLATE TEABREAD

MAKES ABOUT 10 SLICES

225 g (8 oz) butter	15 ml (1 tbsp) orange juice
225 g (8 oz) caster sugar	few drops of orange flower water (optional)
4 eggs, beaten	75 g (3 oz) plain chocolate
225 g (8 oz) self-raising flour	15 ml (1 level tbsp) cocoa powder
finely grated rind of 1 large orange	

1 Grease a 900 ml (2 pint) loaf tin and line the base and sides with greaseproof paper.
2 Cream the butter and sugar together until pale and fluffy, then gradually beat in the eggs, beating well after each addition. Fold in the flour.
3 Transfer half of the mixture to another bowl and beat in the orange rind, juice and orange flower water, if using.
4 Break the chocolate into pieces, put into a small bowl and place over a pan of simmering water. Stir until the chocolate melts. Stir into the remaining cake mixture with the cocoa powder.
5 Put alternate spoonfuls of the two mixtures into the prepared tin. Use a knife to swirl through the mixture to make a marbled effect, then level the surface.
6 Bake at 180°C (350°F) mark 4 for 1¼-1½ hours, until well risen and firm to the touch. Turn out on to a wire rack to cool. Serve cut in slices.

DATE AND ORANGE BARREL TEABREAD

MAKES 8-10 SLICES

200 g (7 oz) plain flour	75 g (3 oz) stoned dates, snipped
5 ml (1 level tsp) baking powder	finely grated rind of 1 orange
5 ml (1 level tsp) bicarbonate of soda	45 ml (3 tbsp) orange juice
65 g (2½ oz) butter or block margarine, cut into pieces	about 90 ml (6 tbsp) milk
65 g (2½ oz) light soft brown sugar	TO DECORATE
	½ quantity orange buttercream (see page 173)
	candied orange peel

1 Grease and flour a 25 cm (10 inch) Balmoral tin or a 900 ml (1½ pint) loaf tin.

2 Sift the flour, baking powder and bicarbonate of soda into a bowl. Rub in the butter until the mixture resembles fine breadcrumbs. Stir in the sugar and mix well until evenly incorporated.

3 Stir in the dates and orange rind. Add the orange juice and enough milk to make a soft dough.

4 Carefully turn the mixture into the prepared tin. Stand it on a baking sheet, grease another baking sheet and place it, greased side down, on top of the tin. Bake in the oven at 180°C (350°F) mark 4 for 1 hour or until a fine warmed skewer inserted in the centre comes out clean and dry.

5 Turn out on to a wire rack to cool for 1 hour. Wrap and store for 1 day in an airtight tin before eating. To serve, pipe buttercream along the top of the cake. Decorate with small diamonds of cut orange peel.

COOK'S TIP

You may think this is a strange way to bake a cake, covered with a baking sheet, but it achieves a special effect. Being totally surrounded by tin, the cake forms no crust and the inside stays particularly moist. A fluted Balmoral tin gives the full 'barrel' effect, but a loaf tin can be used instead.

PEANUT AND ORANGE TEABREAD

MAKES 12 SLICES

225 g (8 oz) chunky peanut butter	2 eggs
50 g (2 oz) butter or margarine	finely grated rind and juice of 1 orange
225 g (8 oz) self-raising flour	about 150 ml (¼ pint) milk
100 g (4 oz) light soft brown sugar	50 g (2 oz) unsalted peanuts

1 Grease a 1.7 litre (3 pint) loaf tin and line with greaseproof paper.

2 Put the peanut butter, fat, flour, salt, sugar, eggs and grated orange rind in a large bowl. Squeeze the juice from the orange and make up to 225 ml (8 fl oz) with milk. Add to the bowl and beat all together with a wooden spoon for about 3 minutes.

3 Turn into the prepared loaf tin. Level the surface, sprinkle with the peanuts and press them in lightly. Bake in the oven at 180°C (350°F) mark 4, for about 1¼ hours or until well risen and firm to the touch. Leave in the tin for 10 minutes before turning out to cool on a wire rack.

COOK'S TIP

Chunky peanut butter gives the best flavour and texture. If you only have the smooth variety, roughly chop a few nuts and stir into the cake mixture.

LARGE CAKES & SPONGES

There is nothing quite as tempting as a freshly baked cake and in this chapter you have a variety to choose from. Ideas range from classic sponges and spiced cakes to delicious moist cakes featuring fresh fruit, such as apples and pears. Irresistible chocolate cakes will satisfy all passionate chocolate lovers.

MADEIRA CAKE

MAKES ABOUT 12 SLICES

100 g (4 oz) plain flour	5 ml (1 tsp) vanilla flavouring
100 g (4 oz) self-raising flour	3 eggs, beaten
175 g (6 oz) butter or block margarine, softened	15-30 ml (1-2 tbsp) milk (optional)
175 g (6 oz) caster sugar	2-3 thin slices citron peel

1 Grease and line an 18 cm (7 inch) round cake tin with greaseproof paper.
2 Sift the plain and self-raising flours together. Cream the butter and the sugar together in a bowl until pale and fluffy, then beat in the vanilla flavouring. Add the eggs, a little at a time, beating well after each addition.
3 Fold in the sifted flour with a metal spoon, adding a little milk if necessary to give a dropping consistency.
4 Turn the mixture into the tin and bake in the oven at 180°C (350°F) mark 4 for 20 minutes.
5 Lay the citron peel on top of the cake, return it to the oven and bake for a further 40 minutes until firm. Turn out and cool on a wire rack.

VICTORIA SANDWICH CAKE

MAKES ABOUT 8 SLICES

175 g (6 oz) butter or block margarine, softened	175 g (6 oz) self-raising flour
175 g (6 oz) caster sugar	45-60 ml (3-4 level tbsp) jam
3 eggs, beaten	caster sugar, for sprinkling

1 Grease and base-line two 18 cm (7 inch) sandwich tins.
2 Beat the butter and sugar together until pale and fluffy. Add the eggs, a little at a time, beating well after each addition. Fold in half the flour, using a metal spoon, then fold in the rest.
3 Divide the mixture evenly between the tins and level with a knife. Bake in the oven at 190°C (375°F) mark 5 for about 20 minutes until they are well risen, firm to the touch and beginning to shrink away from the sides of the tins. Turn out and cool on a wire rack.
4 When the cakes are cool, sandwich them together with the jam and sprinkle the top with caster sugar.

VARIATION

Chocolate Sandwich Cake
Replace 45 ml (3 tbsp) flour with cocoa powder. Sandwich cakes together with buttercream (see page 173).

29

VICTORIAN SEED CAKE

MAKES 8-10 SLICES

175 g (6 oz) butter	110 g (4 oz) plain flour
175 g (6 oz) caster sugar	110 g (4 oz) self-raising flour
5 ml (1 tsp) vanilla flavouring	10 ml (2 level tsp) caraway seeds
3 eggs, beaten	15-30 ml (1-2 tbsp) milk (optional)

1 Grease an 18 cm (7 inch) round cake tin. Line with greaseproof paper and grease the paper.
2 Put the butter, sugar and vanilla flavouring into a bowl and beat until pale and fluffy. Beat in the eggs a little at a time.
3 Fold in the flours with the caraway seeds, adding a little milk if necessary to give a dropping consistency.
4 Turn the mixture into the prepared tin. Bake in the oven at 180°C (350°F) mark 4 for about 1 hour until firm to the touch. Turn out on to a wire rack to cool for 1-2 hours.

COOK'S TIP

Seed cake is one of the oldest traditional English cakes. It is said to have been made on the farms to celebrate the completion of sowing in the spring.

GUERNSEY APPLE CAKE

MAKES 8 SLICES

225 g (8 oz) wholemeal flour	125 g (4 oz) butter
10 ml (2 level tsp) freshly grated nutmeg	225 g (8 oz) dark soft brown sugar
5 ml (1 level tsp) ground cinnamon	2 eggs, beaten
10 ml (2 level tsp) baking powder	a little milk (optional)
225 g (8 oz) cooking apples, peeled, cored and chopped	15 ml (1 tbsp) clear honey
	15 ml (1 tbsp) demerara sugar

1 Grease an 18 cm (7 inch) deep round cake tin. Line with greaseproof paper and grease the paper.
2 Put the wholemeal flour, nutmeg, cinnamon and baking powder into a bowl and stir well. Mix in the chopped cooking apples.
3 Put the butter and sugar into a bowl and beat until pale and fluffy. Add the eggs, a little at a time, and continue to beat.
4 Fold the flour mixture into the creamed mixture with a little milk, if necessary, to give a dropping consistency.
5 Turn the mixture into the prepared tin. Bake in the oven at 170°C (325°F) mark 3 for about 1½ hours. Turn out on to a wire rack to cool for 1-2 hours. Brush with honey and sprinkle with the demerara sugar to decorate. Eat within 1-2 days.

GENOESE APPLE CAKE

MAKES 8-10 SLICES

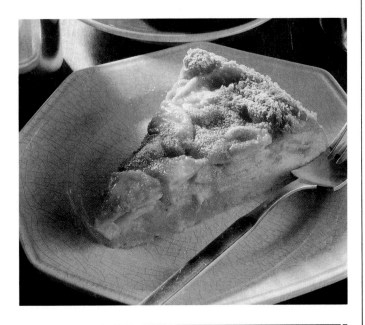

4 eggs	finely grated rind of 1 lemon
150 g (5 oz) caster sugar	700 g (1½ lb) Golden Delicious apples, peeled, cored and thinly sliced
150 g (5 oz) plain flour	
5 ml (1 tsp) baking powder	5-10 ml (1-2 tsp) vegetable oil
pinch of salt	
100 g (4 oz) butter, melted and cooled	15-30 ml (1-2 tbsp) dried breadcrumbs
90 ml (6 tbsp) milk	icing sugar, to finish

1 Put the eggs and sugar in a heatproof bowl standing over a pan of gently simmering water.
2 Whisk for 10-15 minutes until the mixture is thick and pale and holds a ribbon trail when the beaters are lifted. (Alternatively, if you have a table top electric mixer, this can be used instead of whisking over hot water.)
3 Remove the bowl from the heat and continue whisking until the mixture is cool.
4 Sift the flour with the baking powder and salt. Fold half of this mixture into the whisked eggs and sugar.
5 Slowly trickle the melted butter around the edge of the bowl and fold it in gently. Take care not to stir too heavily or the mixture will lose air.
6 Fold in the remaining flour mixture, then the milk and lemon rind. Fold in the apples.
7 Brush the inside of a 23 cm (9 inch) round cake tin with oil. Sprinkle with breadcrumbs, then shake off the excess.
8 Pour the cake mixture into the tin and bake in the oven at 180°C (350°F) mark 4 for about 40 minutes until a skewer inserted in the centre comes out clean.
9 Leave the cake to rest in the tin for about 5 minutes, then turn out on to a wire rack and leave for 2-3 hours to cool completely. Sift icing sugar over the top of the cake just before serving.

ORANGE-GLAZED GINGER CAKE

MAKES ABOUT 12 SLICES

125 g (4 oz) lard	5 ml (1 level tsp) ground ginger
125 g (4 oz) caster sugar	100 g (4 oz) golden syrup
1 egg, beaten	100 g (4 oz) black treacle
275 g (10 oz) plain white flour	FOR THE TOPPING
7.5 ml (1½ level tsp) bicarbonate of soda	pared rind and juice of 1 orange
2.5 ml (1½ level tsp) salt	100 g (4 oz) icing sugar
5 ml (1 level tsp) ground cinnamon	

1 Grease a deep 23 cm (9 inch) round cake tin. Line with greaseproof paper and then grease the paper.
2 Put the lard and sugar into a bowl and beat together until pale and fluffy. Beat in the egg, then the flour, bicarbonate of soda, salt and spices.
3 Put the golden syrup, black treacle and 225 ml (8 fl oz) water in a pan and bring to the boil. Stir into the lard mixture, beating all the time until completely incorporated.
4 Turn the mixture into the prepared tin. Bake in the oven at 180°C (350°F) mark 4 for about 50 minutes or until a fine warmed skewer inserted in the centre comes out clean. Cool in the tin for about 10 minutes before turning out on to a wire rack to cool completely. Wrap and store in an airtight tin for 2 days.
5 Cut the orange rind into strips, put into a pan and cover with water. Boil until tender, about 10 minutes, and drain well.
6 Make an orange glacé icing by sifting the icing sugar into a basin, then beating in enough orange juice to make a smooth, fairly thick icing.
7 Evenly coat the top of the cake with the orange icing and leave to set for 1 hour. Sprinkle the orange strips around the top to decorate.

SWEDISH GINGER CAKE

MAKES ABOUT 10 SLICES

100 g (4 oz) butter or margarine	5 ml (1 level tsp) ground mixed spice
175 g (6 oz) caster sugar	150 ml (¼ pint) soured cream
3 eggs, beaten	25 g (1 oz) stem ginger, chopped
200 g (7 oz) plain flour	
5 ml (1 level tsp) bicarbonate of soda	15 ml (1 tbsp) stem ginger syrup
7.5 ml (1½ level tsp) ground ginger	15 ml (1 tbsp) black treacle

1 Grease an 18 cm (7 inch) square cake tin, line with greaseproof paper and grease the paper.
2 Put the butter in a bowl and beat until soft. Gradually add the sugar and beat until fluffy. Add the eggs, a little at a time, beating well after each addition until thoroughly incorporated.
3 Sift together the flour, bicarbonate of soda, ground ginger and mixed spice. Fold half into the creamed mixture. Add the soured cream, stem ginger and syrup, black treacle and remaining flour. Fold in until well mixed.
4 Spoon the mixture into the prepared tin. Bake in the oven at 170°C (325°F) mark 3 for about 1¼ hours until the centre is firm to the touch.
5 Leave the cake to cool in the tin for about 15 minutes, then turn out on to a wire rack and leave to cool completely. Store in an airtight container for up to 2 weeks. Serve with butter.

SERVING SUGGESTION

Swedish Ginger Cake is moist, dark and spicy. Serve it with coffee and sherry when visitors call during the festive season.

GINGERBREAD SLAB CAKE

MAKES 20-24 SLICES

125 g (4 oz) black treacle	5 ml (1 level tsp) ground mixed spice
125 g (4 oz) golden syrup	
50 g (2 oz) butter or margarine	5 ml (1 level tsp) ground ginger
50 g (2 oz) lard	100 g (4 oz) dark soft brown sugar
225 g (8 oz) plain white flour	
1.25 ml (¼ level tsp) bicarbonate of soda	150 ml (¼ pint) milk

1 Grease a deep 18 cm (7 inch) square cake tin. Line with greaseproof paper and then grease the paper.
2 Put the black treacle, golden syrup, butter and lard into a saucepan and heat gently until melted.
3 Sift the flour, bicarbonate of soda and spices into a bowl and stir in the sugar. Make a well in the centre and pour in the milk and treacle mixture. Beat well until smooth and of a thick pouring consistency.
4 Pour into the prepared tin and bake in the oven at 170°C (325°F) mark 3 for 1-1¼ hours or until a fine warmed skewer inserted in the centre of the cake comes out clean. Cool in the tin for 1 hour then turn out and cool completely on a wire rack.
5 Wrap in greaseproof paper and foil and store in an airtight tin for 2 days before eating.

COOK'S TIP

Gingerbread should always be wrapped tightly in grease-proof paper and foil, then stored in an airtight tin for 2 days before eating. This allows the cake to mature and become moist and sticky.

APPLE GINGERBREAD

MAKES 12 SLICES

225 g (8 oz) plain flour	75 g (3 oz) butter or margarine
2.5 ml (½ level tsp) salt	75 g (3 oz) black treacle
15 ml (1 level tbsp) ground ginger	75 g (3 oz) golden syrup
7.5 ml (1½ level tsp) baking powder	150 ml (¼ pint) milk
7.5 ml (1½ level tsp) bicarbonate of soda	1 egg, size 4, beaten
100 g (4 oz) demerara sugar	1 eating apple, cored and roughly chopped

1 Grease and line a 900 g (2 lb) loaf tin. Sift the plain flour into a large bowl with the salt, ginger, baking powder and bicarbonate of soda.
2 Put the sugar, butter, treacle and syrup in a saucepan and warm gently over low heat until melted and well blended. Do not allow the mixture to boil. Remove from the heat and leave to cool slightly, until you can hold your hand comfortably against the side of the pan.
3 Mix in the milk and egg. Make a well in the centre of the dry ingredients, pour in the liquid and mix thoroughly. Stir in the chopped apple.
4 Turn into the tin and bake in the oven at 170°C (325°F) mark 3 for about 1½ hours, or until firm to the touch.
5 Turn out on to a wire rack to cool for at least 1 hour. Wrap in foil, then store in an airtight container for at least 2-3 days before eating.

SERVING SUGGESTION

Gingerbread can be served plain, but it tastes even better when spread with butter. It is the perfect cake to include in a lunch box because it keeps so well, and it tastes particularly good with cheese and apple.

LEMON SEED CAKE

MAKES 8-10 SLICES

325 g (11 oz) butter	250 g (9 oz) self-raising flour
175 g (6 oz) soft brown sugar	10 ml (2 level tsp) caraway seeds
finely grated rind and juice of 2 large lemons	175 g (6 oz) icing sugar, plus a little extra to decorate
3 eggs, separated	

1 Grease and base-line an 18 cm (7 inch) round cake tin. In a bowl, cream together 175 g (6 oz) butter, the brown sugar and the rind from one lemon, until fluffy.
2 Beat in the egg yolks, then stir in the flour, caraway seeds and 45 ml (3 tbsp) lemon juice.
3 Fold in the stiffly whisked egg whites. Turn into the prepared cake tin. Bake in the oven at 180°C (350°F) mark 4 for 1 hour. Turn out onto a wire rack and leave to cool for 1 hour.
4 To make the butter icing, cream the remaining butter until fluffy. Gradually sift in the icing sugar, beating until smooth. Beat in 15 ml (1 tbsp) lemon juice and the remaining grated lemon rind.
5 Use the lemon butter icing to completely coat the cake and then swirl using a small palette knife. Dust lightly with sifted icing sugar. This cake is best stored in an airtight tin and eaten the next day.

MARMALADE SPICE CAKE

MAKES ABOUT 12 SLICES

175 g (6 oz) butter or block margarine, at room temperature	5 ml (1 level tsp) grated nutmeg
120 ml (8 tbsp) golden syrup	5 ml (1 level tsp) ground cinnamon
2 eggs, size 2, beaten	1.25 ml (¼ level tsp) ground cloves
150 ml (10 tbsp) medium cut orange marmalade	about 150 ml (¼ pint) milk
350 g (12 oz) self-raising flour	50 g (2 oz) cornflakes
5 ml (1 level tsp) baking powder	

1 Grease and base-line a 20 cm (8 inch) square or 23 cm (9 inch) round cake tin.

2 In a bowl, beat the butter with 90 ml (6 tbsp) of the golden syrup until well mixed. Gradually beat in the eggs, keeping the mixture stiff.

3 Chop the marmalade and stir half into the cake mixture. Mix in the flour sifted with the baking powder and spices, adding sufficient milk to give a fairly stiff consistency. Turn into the prepared cake tin and level the surface.

4 Crush the cornflakes and mix with the remaining syrup and marmalade. Carefully spread over the cake mixture.

5 Bake in the oven at 180°C (350°F) mark 4 for about 1 hour until well risen and firm. Turn out and cool on a wire rack for 1-2 hours before serving.

MARZIPAN PINEAPPLE CAKE

MAKES 12-14 SLICES

175 g (6 oz) butter	50 g (2 oz) cornflour
150 g (5 oz) light soft brown sugar	pinch of salt
finely grated rind of 1 lemon plus 15 ml (1 tbsp) juice	75 g (3 oz) glacé pineapple, thinly sliced
finely grated rind of 1 orange plus 15 ml (1 tbsp) juice	75 g (3 oz) firm bought marzipan, cut into small cubes
2 eggs, size 2	FOR THE GLACÉ ICING
2 egg yolks	75 g (3 oz) icing sugar
125 g (4 oz) self-raising flour	15-30 ml (1-2 tbsp) lemon juice

1 Grease a 24 x 18 cm (9½ x 7inch) cake or roasting tin. Line with greaseproof paper and grease the paper.

2 Put the butter and sugar into a bowl and beat together until pale and fluffy. Stir in the lemon and orange rind.

3 Lightly beat in the whole eggs and the yolks. Lightly beat in the self-raising flour, cornflour and salt with the orange and lemon juice. Fold in the pineapple.

4 Turn the mixture into the prepared tin, level the surface and scatter with marzipan cubes.

5 Bake in the oven at 180°C (350°F) mark 4 for about 45 minutes or until a fine warmed skewer inserted in the centre comes out clean.

6 Meanwhile, make the glacé icing. Sift the icing sugar into a bowl and beat in enough lemon juice to make a smooth, fairly thick icing.

7 When the cake is baked, turn it out on to a wire rack and immediately coat the top with the glacé icing. Leave to cool completely for about 1 hour before serving.

HONEY CAKE

MAKES 12-16 SLICES

225 ml (8 fl oz) clear honey plus 45 ml (3 tbsp)	50 g (2 oz) glacé cherries, halved
75 g (3 oz) butter	50 g (2 oz) chopped mixed peel
350 g (12 oz) plain wholemeal flour	3 eggs
pinch of salt	45 ml (3 tbsp) milk
5 ml (1 level tsp) ground mixed spice	grated rind of 1 large lemon
5 ml (1 level tsp) bicarbonate of soda	25 g (1 oz) flaked almonds

1 Grease a 20 cm (8 inch) square cake tin and line the base and sides with greaseproof paper.
2 Put 225 ml (8 fl oz) honey in a saucepan, add the butter and heat gently, stirring, until smooth.
3 Sift the flour, salt, spice and bicarbonate of soda into a large bowl, stirring in any bran left in the sieve. Add the cherries and peel.
4 Beat the eggs and the milk together and stir into the honey mixture with the lemon rind. Pour gradually on to the dry ingredients, beating well after each addition, until well blended.
5 Turn the mixture into the prepared tin and sprinkle with flaked almonds. Bake at 170°C (325°F) mark 3 for about 1¼ hours, until the cake is firm to the touch or a skewer inserted in the centre of the cake comes out clean.
6 Using a skewer, prick the top of the cake all over and spoon over the remaining honey. Turn out and leave to cool on a wire rack. Do not remove the greaseproof lining paper until the cake is cold.

CARROT CAKE

MAKES 8 SLICES

225 g (8 oz) butter	50 g (2 oz) ground almonds
225 g (8 oz) light soft brown sugar	150 g (5 oz) walnut pieces, chopped
4 eggs, separated	350 g (12 oz) young carrots, peeled and grated
finely grated rind of ½ orange	225 g (8 oz) cream cheese
20 ml (4 tsp) lemon juice	10 ml (2 level tsp) clear honey
175 g (6 oz) self-raising flour	
5 ml (1 level tsp) baking powder	

1 Grease and line a deep 20 cm (8 inch) round cake tin.
2 Cream the butter and sugar together in a bowl until pale and fluffy. Beat in the egg yolks, then stir in the orange rind and 15 ml (3 tsp) of the lemon juice.
3 Sift in the flour and baking powder, then stir in the ground almonds and 125 g (4 oz) of the walnuts.
4 Whisk the egg whites until stiff, then fold into the cake mixture with the carrots. Pour into the prepared tin and hollow the centre slightly.
5 Bake at 180°C (350°F) mark 4 for about 1½ hours. Cover the top with foil after 1 hour if it starts to brown.
6 Leave to cool slightly, then turn out on to a wire rack and remove the lining paper. Leave to cool.
7 To make the topping, beat together the cream cheese, honey and remaining lemon juice and spread over the top of the cake. Sprinkle the topping with the remaining walnuts to decorate.

TODDY CAKE

MAKES 6-8 SLICES

225 g (8 oz) butter	60 ml (4 tbsp) whisky
175 g (6 oz) soft brown sugar	30 ml (2 level tbsp) thick honey
finely grated rind of 1 lemon	175 g (6 oz) icing sugar, sifted
3 eggs, beaten	
175 g (6 oz) self-raising flour, sifted	a few walnut halves

1 Butter and base-line two 18 cm (7 inch) straight-sided sandwich tins.

2 Beat 175 g (6 oz) of the butter until soft. Add the sugar and lemon rind. Continue to beat until pale and fluffy. Gradually beat in the eggs, keeping the mixture stiff.

3 Fold in half the sifted flour, then the whisky and lastly the remaining flour. Spoon into the prepared tins.

4 Bake in the oven at 190°C (375°F) mark 5 for 20-25 minutes. Turn out and cool on a wire rack.

5 Beat the remaining butter with the honey until smooth, then gradually work in the icing sugar and 15 ml (1 tbsp) lemon juice.

6 Sandwich the cake together with half the butter cream and swirl the rest over the top. Decorate with walnuts.

COOK'S TIP

To test whether the cake is cooked, press the centre very lightly with the fingertip. The cake should be spongy and should give only very slightly to pressure, then rise again immediately, retaining no impression.

BALMORAL ALMOND CAKE

MAKES ABOUT 8 SLICES

	FOR THE ICING AND DECORATION
125 g (4 oz) butter or margarine	
125 g (4 oz) caster sugar	50 g (2 oz) butter
almond flavouring	125 g (4 oz) icing sugar
2 eggs, beaten	almond flavouring
50 g (2 oz) ground almonds	toasted flaked almonds, to decorate
125 g (4 oz) self-raising flour	
30 ml (2 tbsp) milk	icing sugar, for dredging

1 Grease a 900 ml (1½ pint) Balmoral cake tin or use a 900 ml (1½ pint) loaf tin.

2 Cream together the butter and the caster sugar until light and fluffy. Add a few drops of almond flavouring. Beat in the eggs a little at a time. Fold in the ground almonds and flour with the milk. Spoon into the prepared tin and bake in the oven at 170°C (325°F) mark 3 for 45-50 minutes or until risen and firm to the touch. Turn out on to a wire rack to cool.

3 To make the icing, cream the butter and icing sugar together and flavour with one or two drops of almond flavouring. Pipe down the centre of the cake, decorate with the almonds and dust lightly with icing sugar.

PINEAPPLE AND CHERRY RING

MAKES 6-8 SLICES

175 g (6 oz) butter	25 g (1 oz) glacé pineapple, chopped
175 g (6 oz) caster sugar	
2 eggs, beaten	TO FINISH
225 g (8 oz) self-raising flour, sifted	1 quantity glacé icing (see page 173)
45 ml (3 tbsp) milk	8 pieces glacé pineapple
65 g (2½ oz) glacé cherries, quartered	8 glacé cherries

1   Butter and line a 1.4 litre (2½ pint) ring mould.
2   Beat together the butter and sugar in a bowl until pale and fluffy. Beat in the eggs, a little at a time, beating well after each addition, and add 15 ml (1 level tbsp) flour with last amount of egg. Fold the remaining flour into the mixture, then add the milk, cherries and pineapple.
3   Turn the mixture into the prepared tin and bake in the oven at 180°C (350°F) mark 4 for 55-60 minutes. Turn out and cool on a wire rack.
4   Spread a layer of glacé icing on top of the ring. Decorate with the pineapple and cherries, then trickle the remaining icing over the fruit, letting some run down the sides.

COOK'S TIP

Wash any excess syrup from glacé cherries before use and dry thoroughly, then toss in a little flour.

CHERRY AND ALMOND CAKE

MAKES ABOUT 12 SLICES

275 g (10 oz) glacé cherries	pinch of salt
225 g (8 oz) butter, softened	175 g (6 oz) ground almonds
225 g (8 oz) caster sugar	2.5 ml (½ tsp) almond flavouring
6 eggs, beaten	icing sugar, to decorate
65 g (2½ oz) self-raising flour	

1   Grease a deep 23 cm (9 inch) loose-bottomed round cake tin and line the base and sides with greaseproof paper. Grease the paper.
2   Arrange the cherries in the bottom of the tin.
3   Cream the butter and sugar together until pale and fluffy. Beat in the eggs a little at a time, adding a little of the flour if the mixture shows signs of curdling.
4   Sift in the remaining flour and salt, then add the ground almonds and almond flavouring.
5   Turn the mixture into the prepared tin and bake at 180°C (350°F) mark 4 for 1 hour, until firm to the touch. Cover with greaseproof paper if browning too quickly. Leave in the tin to cool.
6   When the cake is cold, remove from the tin and dredge the top with icing sugar to decorate.

COFFEE BATTENBERG

MAKES ABOUT 8 SLICES

175 g (6 oz) butter	150 ml (10 level tbsp) ginger marmalade or apricot jam
175 g (6 oz) caster sugar	450 g (1 lb) bought marzipan
3 eggs, beaten	
175 g (6 oz) self-raising flour	crystallised ginger, roughly chopped, to decorate (optional)
20 ml (4 tsp) coffee essence	
15 ml (1 tbsp) milk	

1   Butter a 20 cm (8 inch) square cake tin. Divide the tin in half by making a pleat, the height of the tin, in the centre of a piece of foil. Use the foil to base-line the tin, sliding a piece of cardboard inside the pleat to support it.

2   Cream the butter and sugar together in a bowl, then gradually beat in the eggs, keeping the mixture fairly stiff. Lightly fold in the flour.

3   Divide the mixture in half and fold the coffee essence into one portion and the milk into the other.

4   Spoon one flavour into each side of the tin and bake in the oven at 190°C (375°F) mark 5 for about 30 minutes. Turn out and cool on a wire rack.

5   Trim each piece of cake and divide in half lengthwise. Sandwich together alternately with half the marmalade or apricot jam.

6   Cut out a sheet of non-stick paper to exactly cover the cake, leaving the ends bare, and roll out the marzipan on top to just fit it. Spread the remaining jam over the marzipan and wrap closely around the Battenberg. Remove the paper. Crimp the top edges and press the roughly chopped ginger along the middle of the cake.

LEMON SWISS ROLL

MAKES 6-8 SLICES

3 eggs, size 2	about 275 g (10 oz) lemon curd
100 g (4 oz) caster sugar	
100 g (4 oz) plain flour	1 quantity glacé icing (see page 173)
150 ml (5 fl oz) double cream	

1   Grease a 33 x 23 cm (13 x 9 inch) Swiss roll tin. Line the base with greaseproof paper and grease the paper. Dust with caster sugar and flour.

2   Whisk the eggs and sugar in a bowl until thick enough to leave a trail on the surface when the whisk is lifted. Sift in the flour and fold gently through the mixture.

3   Turn the mixture into the prepared tin and level the surface. Bake in the oven at 200°C (400°F) mark 6 for 10-12 minutes or until the cake springs back when pressed lightly with a finger and has shrunk away a little from the sides of the tin.

4   Sprinkle a sheet of greaseproof paper with caster sugar and turn the cake out on to it. Roll up with the paper inside. Transfer to a wire rack and leave to cool for 30 minutes.

5   Whip the cream until it just holds its shape. Unroll the Swiss roll and spread with three quarters of the lemon curd. Top with cream then roll up again and place on a serving plate.

6   Spoon glacé icing on to the Swiss roll. Immediately, using the point of a teaspoon, draw rough lines of lemon curd across the icing and pull a skewer through to form a feather pattern. Leave to set, for about 1 hour.

WALNUT LAYER CAKE

MAKES 8 SLICES

4 eggs, separated	½ quantity coffee butter cream (see page 173)
100 g (4 oz) caster sugar	10 ml (2 tsp) coffee essence
75 g (3 oz) walnuts, finely chopped	1 quantity American frosting (see page 43)
25 g (1 oz) fresh brown breadcrumbs	walnut halves, to decorate
25 g (1 oz) plain flour	

1 Grease and base-line two 18 cm (7 inch) sandwich tins. Dust with caster sugar and flour.
2 Whisk together the egg yolks and caster sugar until very pale. Fold in the chopped walnuts, breadcrumbs and flour.
3 Whisk the egg whites until stiff. Stir one large spoonful into the egg yolk mixture, then fold in the remainder.
4 Divide the mixture equally between the tins and level the surface. Bake at 180°C (350°F) mark 4 for about 30 minutes. Turn out and cool on a wire rack.
5 When the cakes are cold, sandwich them together with the butter cream.
6 Coat the cake completely with the American frosting, working quickly to ensure an even glossy frosting. Decorate at once with the walnut halves.

FROSTED COCONUT CAKE

MAKES 8 SLICES

50 g (2 oz) shelled hazelnuts	125 g (4 oz) plain flour
225 g (8 oz) butter or block margarine, softened	125 g (4 oz) self-raising flour
225 g (8 oz) caster sugar	40 g (1½ oz) desiccated coconut
5 eggs	75 g (3 oz) icing sugar
2.5 ml (½ tsp) vanilla flavouring	shredded coconut, to decorate

1 Grease and base-line a 20 cm (8 inch) spring-release cake tin with greaseproof paper. Spread the hazelnuts in a grill pan and brown them under a hot grill. Place in a clean tea towel and rub off the skins. Leave to cool, then finely chop.
2 Cream the fat and sugar together until pale and fluffy. Whisk 4 whole eggs and 1 egg yolk together and gradually beat into the creamed mixture with the vanilla flavouring.
3 Sift the flours together into a large mixing bowl. Fold into the mixture with 25 g (1 oz) of the desiccated coconut, and half the nuts. Spoon into the prepared tin and bake in the oven at 180°C (350°F) mark 4 for 45 minutes.
4 Meanwhile, in a bowl whisk the egg white until stiff. Whisk in half the sifted icing sugar, then fold in the remaining icing sugar, desiccated coconut and hazelnuts.
5 Spoon the meringue topping on to the partially baked cake and scatter with shredded coconut.
6 Return to the oven for 20-30 minutes, or until a fine warmed skewer inserted in the centre comes out clean. Cover lightly with a double layer of greaseproof paper after 15 minutes if necessary. Cool on a wire rack.

SPICED
APPLE TORTE

MAKES 6 SLICES

175 g (6 oz) butter or margarine	finely grated rind of 1 lemon
175 g (6 oz) light soft brown sugar	45 ml (3 tbsp) lemon juice
	2 eggs, beaten
75 g (3 oz) oat flakes	125 g (4 oz) self-raising flour
5 ml (1 level tsp) ground cinnamon	5 ml (1 level tsp) ground mixed spice
450 g (1 lb) cooking apples	icing sugar, for dusting

1   Melt 50 g (2 oz) of the butter or margarine in a saucepan. Add 50 g (2 oz) of the sugar and the oats and cinnamon and fry gently stirring, until golden.
2   Spoon the mixture into a greased and lined 18 cm (7 inch) round cake tin.
3   Peel and core the apples, then slice them thinly into a bowl. Stir in the lemon rind and juice. Set aside.
4   Put the remaining butter or margarine in a separate bowl, add the remaining sugar and beat together until light and fluffy. Beat in the eggs gradually. Sift in the flour with the spice and stir in, followed by the apple mixture.
5   Spoon the mixture into the cake tin and level the surface. Bake in the oven at 180°C (350°F) mark 4 for about 50 minutes. Turn out on to a baking sheet lined with non-stick paper. Leave to cool completely for about 1 hour. Cover and chill until required or for up to 2 days.
6   Unwrap, cut into wedges and serve with single cream.

APPLE
HAZELNUT GENOESE

MAKES 6-8 SLICES

3 eggs	FOR THE FROSTING
100 g (4 oz) caster sugar	1 egg white
50 g (2 oz) plain flour	175 g (6 oz) caster sugar
15 ml (1 tbsp) cornflour	pinch of salt
25 g (1 oz) ground hazelnuts	pinch of cream of tartar
75 g (3 oz) butter, melted and cooled	FOR THE FILLING AND DECORATION
90 ml (6 tbsp) apple jelly or purée	30 ml (2 tbsp) thick apple purée
	about 12 hazelnuts

1   Grease two 18 cm (7 inch) sandwich tins, line the bases with greaseproof paper and grease the paper.
2   Whisk the eggs and sugar together in a bowl until very thick. Sift in the flour and cornflour. Add the hazelnuts, then fold in the butter. Turn the mixture into the prepared cake tins.
3   Bake in the oven at 180°C (350°F) mark 4 for about 25 minutes or until the sponge springs back when pressed lightly with a finger and has shrunk away a little from the tins. Turn out on to a wire rack and leave to cool for 1-2 hours.
4   Sandwich the layers together with apple jelly. To prepare the seven-minute frosting put all the ingredients into a bowl and whisk lightly. Place the bowl over a pan of hot water and heat, whisking continuously, until the mixture thickens sufficiently to stand in peaks. This will take about 7 minutes.
5   Cover the cake with the frosting, peaking up the surface and decorate with hazelnuts. Leave for 2-3 hours before serving to allow the frosting to firm up.

COOK'S TIP

Home-made apple jelly or purée gives the best flavour, but do not add too much sugar; the frosting is very sweet.

PEAR SPONGE

MAKES ABOUT 12 SLICES

1¼ quantity shortcrust pastry (see page 172)	100 g (4 oz) self-raising flour
FOR THE FILLING	75 g (3 oz) cornflour
150 g (5 oz) butter or margarine	5 ml (1 level tsp) baking powder
150 g (5 oz) caster sugar	75 g (3 oz) ground almonds
few drops of almond flavouring	30 ml (2 tbsp) milk
	3 small ripe, even-sized pears
3 eggs	icing sugar, for dusting

1 Grease a 24 cm (9½ inch) round spring-release cake tin.
2 Roll out the pastry and use to line the tin. Chill.
3 To make the filling, cream the butter and sugar together in a bowl until pale and fluffy. Beat in a few drops of almond flavouring, then add the eggs, one at a time. Fold in the flours, baking powder and ground almonds, then fold in the milk. Spoon the mixture into the pastry case and level the surface.
4 Peel, core and halve the pears. Make a series of parallel cuts across the width of each pear half, but do not cut right through. Arrange the pear halves, rounded sides up, on top of the filling.
5 Bake in the oven at 190°C (375°F) mark 5 for 1¼ hours or until a skewer inserted into the centre comes out clean. Cool in the tin for 15 minutes, then carefully remove the sides of the tin. Serve the sponge flan warm or cold, dusted with icing sugar.

COOK'S TIP

Make sure you use ripe even-sized pears or the appearance of the finished flan will be spoilt.

CARAMEL BANANA TORTE

MAKES 8 SLICES

175 g (6 oz) self-raising flour	TO FINISH
1.25 ml (¼ level tsp) each baking powder and bicarbonate of soda	75 g (3 oz) sugar
	175 g (6 oz) full-fat soft cheese
50 g (2 oz) butter, in pieces	30 ml (2 tbsp) lemon juice
150 g (5 oz) caster sugar	30 ml (2 level tbsp) icing sugar
175 g (6 oz) ripe bananas	
2.5 ml (½ level tsp) freshly grated nutmeg	175 g (6 oz) ripe bananas
45 ml (3 tbsp) milk	50 g (2 oz) flaked almonds, toasted
1 egg, beaten	

1 Grease a 20 cm (8 inch) round cake tin, line the base with greaseproof paper and grease the paper.
2 Sift the flour, baking powder and bicarbonate of soda into a bowl. Rub in the butter until the mixture resembles fine breadcrumbs, then stir in the caster sugar.
3 Peel the bananas and mash them in a bowl, then beat in the nutmeg, milk and egg. Stir the banana mixture into the dry ingredients.
4 Turn into the prepared tin and level the surface. Bake in the oven at 180°C (350°F) mark 4 for about 40 minutes. Leave in the tin for 5 minutes before turning out on to a wire rack to cool. Cut the cake in half horizontally.
5 To make the caramel, dissolve the sugar in a small saucepan without stirring, over gentle heat, then boil until a rich brown colour. Immediately pour on to the cake and spread with an oiled knife to cover the top. Mark into 8 portions.
6 Beat the cheese, lemon juice and icing sugar together. Peel and chop the bananas; add to half of the cheese mixture. Use this to sandwich the cakes together.
7 Use remaining cheese mixture to coat sides and decorate top. Finish with the almonds.

MARBLED
CHOCOLATE CAKE

MAKES ABOUT 8 SLICES

50 g (2 oz) plain chocolate	10 ml (2 level tsp) baking powder
5 ml (1 tsp) vanilla flavouring	50 g (2 oz) ground almonds
225 g (8 oz) butter or block margarine	30 ml (2 tbsp) milk
225 g (8 oz) caster sugar	FOR THE FROSTING
4 eggs, beaten	150 g (5 oz) plain chocolate
225 g (8 oz) plain flour	100 g (4 oz) butter

1   Grease a 1.7 litre (3 pint) ring mould. Melt the chocolate with the vanilla flavouring and 15 ml (1 tbsp) water in a bowl placed over a pan of simmering water. Remove from the heat.

2   Cream together the fat and caster sugar until pale and fluffy. Add the eggs, a little at a time, beating well after each addition.

3   Fold the flour, baking powder and ground almonds into the creamed mixture. Stir in the milk. Spoon half the mixture evenly into the base of the prepared tin.

4   Stir the cooled but still soft chocolate into the remaining mixture. Spoon into the tin. Draw a knife through the cake mixture in a spiral. Level the surface.

5   Bake in the oven at 180°C (350°F) mark 4 for about 55 minutes, until well risen, firm to touch and beginning to shrink from sides of tin. Turn out and cool on a wire rack.

6   To make the chocolate frosting, melt the chocolate and butter with 30 ml (2 tbsp) water in a bowl over a pan of hot water. Stir until smooth, then pour over the cooled cake, working quickly to coat top and sides. Leave to set.

COOK'S TIP

For a decorative finish, drizzle a little melted chocolate over the top of the ring cake.

CHOCOLATE
BISCUIT CAKE

MAKES ABOUT 8 SLICES

125 g (4 oz) plain chocolate or plain chocolate flavoured cake covering	25 g (1 oz) seedless raisins
15 ml (1 tbsp) golden syrup	25g (1 oz) glacé cherries, halved
125 g (4 oz) butter or block margarine	50 g (2 oz) flaked almonds, toasted
125 g (4 oz) digestive biscuits, broken up	

1   Grease a loose-based 18 cm (7 inch) flan tin.

2   Break the chocolate into a bowl and place over a pan of simmering water. Add the syrup and butter and stir until the chocolate and butter have melted. Remove from the heat and cool slightly.

3   Mix the biscuits, fruit and almonds into the chocolate mixture. Turn the mixture into the tin, lightly level the top, then chill for at least 1 hour before serving.

VARIATION

Vary this simple no-bake cake by using different biscuits, such as petit beurre biscuits or ratafias.

RICH CHOCOLATE CAKE

MAKES 6-8 SLICES

100 g (4 oz) plain flour	150 g (5 oz) butter or margarine
45 ml (3 level tbsp) cocoa powder	75 g (3 oz) light soft brown sugar
2.5 ml (¼ level tsp) baking powder	1 egg, size 4, beaten
large pinch of bicarbonate of soda	75 ml (5 tbsp) natural yogurt
large pinch of salt	few drops of vanilla flavouring
100 g (4 oz) plain chocolate, in pieces	150 g (5 oz) icing sugar

1 Grease and line a 15 cm (6 inch) round cake tin with greaseproof paper.
2 Sift the flour into a bowl with 15 ml (1 tbsp) of the cocoa powder, the baking powder, bicarbonate of soda and salt.
3 Put half of the chocolate in a bowl with 15 ml (1 tbsp) water. Place over a pan of hot water and heat gently, stirring, until melted. Remove and cool.
4 Put 50 g (2 oz) of the butter in a separate bowl. Add the brown sugar and beat until fluffy. Beat in the egg, then fold in the melted chocolate, yogurt, vanilla flavouring and the sifted ingredients.
5 Turn the mixture into the prepared tin and level the surface. Bake in the oven at 190°C (375°F) mark 5 for 45 minutes until risen and firm to the touch. Turn out on to a wire rack and leave to cool for at least 1 hour.
6 To make the chocolate frosting, cream the remaining butter with the sifted icing sugar and remaining cocoa powder. Melt the remaining chocolate in a small bowl over a pan of hot water, leave to cool, then beat into the creamed mixture until evenly mixed.
7 Split the cake into two halves. Use half the frosting to sandwich the cakes together and smooth the remainder over the top. Allow to set for at least 30 minutes.

DEVIL'S FOOD CAKE

MAKES 8 SLICES

75 g (3 oz) plain chocolate	175 g (6 oz) plain flour
250 g (9 oz) light soft brown sugar	3.75 ml (¾ level tsp) bicarbonate of soda
200 ml (7 fl oz) milk	FOR THE AMERICAN FROSTING
75 g (3 oz) butter or block margarine, softened	450 g (1 lb) caster sugar
2 eggs, beaten	2 egg whites

1 Grease and base-line two 19 cm (7½ inch) sandwich tins. Grease the paper and dust with caster sugar and flour.
2 Break the chocolate into a small saucepan, add 75 g (3 oz) brown sugar and the milk and heat very gently, stirring. Remove from the heat and leave to cool.
3 Cream the butter with the remaining brown sugar. Gradually beat in the eggs, then slowly pour in the chocolate mixture and beat until well combined.
4 Sift together the flour and bicarbonate of soda and gently fold into the cake mixture, using a metal spoon.
5 Turn the mixture into the prepared tins and tilt to spread evenly. Bake in the oven at 180°C (350°F) mark 4 for about 35 minutes, until the cakes spring back when lightly pressed. Turn out on to a wire rack to cool.
6 Meanwhile, make the frosting. Place sugar in a large heavy-based saucepan with 135 ml (4½ fl oz) water and heat gently until dissolved. Bring to the boil and boil to 115°C (240°F) as registered on a sugar thermometer.
7 Meanwhile, whisk the egg whites in a large deep bowl until stiff. Allow the bubbles to settle, then slowly pour the hot syrup on to the egg whites, whisking constantly. When all the sugar syrup is added, continue whisking until the mixture stands in peaks and just starts to become matt around the edges. The icing sets quickly, so work rapidly.
8 Sandwich cakes together with frosting; spread remainder over top and sides using a palette knife and pull up into peaks. Leave to set in a cool place, not the refrigerator.

CHOCOLATE BRAZIL CAKE

MAKES 8 SLICES

100 g (4 oz) plus a knob of butter	30 ml (2 tbsp) cornflour
300 g (11 oz) plain chocolate	175 g (6 oz) Brazil nuts, ground
100 g (4 oz) caster sugar	100 g (4 oz) icing sugar
4 eggs, separated	chocolate caraque, to decorate

1 Grease a 1.7 litre (3 pint) ring tin. Dust with flour.
2 Break 200 g (7 oz) chocolate into a small bowl. Add 30 ml (2 tbsp) water. Place over a saucepan of gently simmering water until melted. Remove from the heat and stir until smooth.
3 Cream 100 g (4 oz) of the butter with the caster sugar until pale and fluffy. Gradually beat in the egg yolks and cornflour. Fold in the melted chocolate and nuts.
4 Whisk the egg whites until stiff but not dry. Stir one spoonful of egg white into the mixture to loosen it. Gently fold in the remainder. Spoon into the tin.
5 Bake in the oven at 170°C (325°F) mark 3 for about 1 hour 20 minutes or until a skewer inserted into the centre comes out clean. Leave to cool in the tin for 5 minutes before turning out on to a wire rack to finish cooling.
6 Place the remaining chocolate in a bowl with the knob of butter and 60 ml (4 tbsp) water. Melt over a saucepan of simmering water as in stage 2. Beat in the sifted icing sugar until smooth. Cool, then chill in the refrigerator for about 15 minutes until the consistency of lightly whipped cream.
7 Place the cake on its rack over a baking sheet. Spread over the chocolate icing until thinly coated. Decorate with chocolate caraque. Leave to set.

COOK'S TIP

To make chocolate caraque, spread the melted chocolate thinly on a cold surface. When it is just on the point of setting, shave it off in curls, with a thin, sharp knife.

CHOCOLATE FUDGE CAKE

MAKES ABOUT 8 SLICES

325 g (12 oz) plain chocolate flavoured cake covering	10 ml (2 tsp) vanilla flavouring
275 g (10 oz) butter	100 g (4 oz) icing sugar, sifted
175 g (6 oz) caster sugar	10-15 ml (2-3 tsp) coffee essence
4 eggs, size 2, beaten	toasted almonds, half dipped in melted chocolate, to decorate
175 g (6 oz) self-raising flour	
50 g (2 oz) ground rice	

1 Grease and line a 23 cm (9 inch) round cake tin with greaseproof paper. Melt half the chocolate cake covering in a bowl over a pan of hot water.
2 Whisk 225 g (8 oz) butter and caster sugar together in a bowl until pale and fluffy then gradually beat in the eggs, keeping the mixture stiff. Lightly beat in the flour with the ground rice, vanilla and cool, but still liquid, chocolate cake covering.
3 Turn the mixture into the cake tin. Bake in the oven at 180°C (350°F) mark 4 for about 1¼ hours. Cool in the tin for 30 minutes before turning out on to a wire rack.
4 Melt the remaining chocolate cake covering and use to coat the top and sides of the cake.
5 Cream the remaining butter in a bowl, then beat in the icing sugar and coffee essence. Pipe around the top of the cake, using a piping bag fitted with a 1 cm (½ inch) star nozzle. Decorate with chocolate toasted almonds.

SPECIAL OCCASION CAKES

You will find plenty of ideas for special occasion baking in this chapter. Sumptuous cream filled gâteaux flavoured with summer fruits contrast with wickedly rich chocolate and coffee concoctions. Festive and celebration cakes – such as Simnel cake, stollen and traditional Christmas cakes – are included, too.

CHOCOLATE AND ORANGE GATEAU

SERVES 6-8

100 g (4 oz) butter	175 ml (6 fl oz) milk
100 g (4 oz) sugar	300 ml (10 fl oz) whipping cream
1 egg, beaten	
175 g (6 oz) self-raising flour	10 ml (2 tsp) orange-flavoured liqueur
30 ml (2 tbsp) cocoa powder	finely pared rind and segments of 1 orange
5 ml (1 level tsp) bicarbonate of soda	

1 Lightly grease two 15 cm (6 inch) cake tins. Melt the butter and sugar in a saucepan over a low heat. Leave to cool for 2 minutes. Add the egg and beat well. Fold in the flour and cocoa powder. Mix the bicarbonate of soda and milk together, then slowly add to the mixture.
2 Pour into the prepared cake tins and bake at 180°C (350°F) mark 4 for 25 minutes, until cooked and risen.
3 Leave in the tins for 2 minutes, then turn out and leave to cool on a wire rack.
4 Whip the cream stiffly, then fold in the liqueur. Use to sandwich the cakes together, reserving some for the top. Decorate with the remaining cream mixture, orange rind and orange segments.

STRAWBERRY GATEAU

SERVES 12-16

225 g (8 oz) butter	300 ml (10 fl oz) double cream
225 g (8 oz) caster sugar	225 g (8 oz) strawberries, sliced
4 eggs, beaten	
350 g (12 oz) self-raising flour	icing sugar, to decorate
30-45 ml (2-3 tbsp) milk	

1 Grease and line the bases of three 18 cm (7 inch) round cake tins.
2 Cream the butter and the sugar together until pale and fluffy. Gradually add the eggs, a little at a time, beating well after each addition. Fold in the flour, then add enough milk to give a soft dropping consistency.
3 Divide the mixture evenly between the prepared tins and bake at 190°C (375°F) mark 5 for 25-30 minutes, until well risen and firm to the touch, swapping the position of the top and bottom cakes halfway through cooking. Turn out and leave to cool on a wire rack.
4 Whip the cream until it just holds its shape. Sandwich the cakes together with the cream and the strawberries, reserving a few for decoration. Dredge the top with icing sugar and decorate with the reserved strawberries.

CHOCOLATE COFFEE REFRIGERATOR SLICE

SERVES 6

30 ml (2 tbsp) instant coffee granules	2 egg yolks
45 ml (3 tbsp) brandy	300 ml (½ pint) whipping cream
100 g (4 oz) plain chocolate	50 g (2 oz) chopped almonds, toasted
50 g (2 oz) icing sugar	about 30 sponge fingers
100 g (4 oz) unsalted butter, softened	coffee beans, to decorate

1 Grease a 22 x 11.5 cm (8½ x 4½ inch) top measurement loaf tin and line the base with greaseproof paper. Grease the paper.
2 Make up the coffee granules with 250 ml (8 fl oz) boiling water and stir in the brandy. Set aside to cool for 15 minutes.
3 Break the chocolate into small pieces. Place in a heatproof bowl with 15 ml (1 tbsp) water. Stand the bowl over a pan of simmering water and heat gently until the chocolate melts. (Alternatively microwave on LOW for 4-5 minutes or until melted, stirring occasionally.) Remove from the heat and leave to cool for about 5 minutes.
4 Sift the icing sugar into a bowl. Add the butter and beat together until pale and fluffy. Add the egg yolks, beating well.
5 Lightly whip the cream and chill half of it. Stir the remaining cream, the cooled chocolate and the nuts into the butter and egg yolk mixture.
6 Line the bottom of the prepared tin with sponge fingers, cutting to fit if necessary. Spoon over one third of the coffee and brandy mixture.
7 Layer the chocolate mixture and sponge fingers in the tin, soaking each layer with coffee and ending with soaked sponge fingers. Weight down lightly and chill for 3-4 hours until set.
8 Turn out, remove the paper and decorate with the reserved whipped cream and the coffee beans.

BLACK FOREST GATEAU

SERVES 10

100 g (4 oz) butter	two 425 g (15 oz) cans stoned black cherries, drained and syrup reserved
6 eggs	
225 g (8 oz) caster sugar	60 ml (4 tbsp) kirsch
75 g (3 oz) plain flour	600 ml (20 fl oz) whipping cream, whipped
50 g (2 oz) cocoa powder	chocolate caraque
2.5 ml (½ tsp) vanilla flavouring	5 ml (1 level tsp) arrowroot

1 Grease and base-line a 23 cm (9 inch) round cake tin. Beat butter in a bowl over a pan of warm water until soft.
2 Put the eggs and sugar in a large bowl over a pan of hot water and whisk until pale and creamy and thick enough to leave a trail on the surface when the whisk is lifted.
3 Sift the flour and cocoa together, then lightly fold into the mixture. Fold in the vanilla and softened butter.
4 Turn mixture into the tin and tilt to spread evenly. Bake in the oven at 180°C (350°F) mark 4 for about 40 minutes, until well risen, firm to the touch and beginning to shrink away from sides of tin. Turn out and cool on a wire rack.
5 Cut the cake into three horizontally. Place a layer on a flat plate. Mix together 75 ml (5 tbsp) cherry syrup and the kirsch. Spoon 45 ml (3 tbsp) over the cake. Spread with a thin layer of cream. Reserve a quarter of the cherries for decoration; scatter half the remainder over the cream.
6 Repeat layers of sponge, syrup, cream and cherries. Top with the third cake round and spoon over remaining kirsch-flavoured syrup. Spread a thin layer of cream around side of cake and coat with chocolate caraque.
7 Decorate top edge with cream whirls and caraque. Fill the centre with the reserved cherries. Blend the arrowroot with 45 ml (3 tbsp) cherry syrup, place in a small saucepan, bring to the boil and boil, stirring, for a few minutes until the mixture is thickened and clear. Brush the glaze over the cherries.

DOBOS TORTE

SERVES 8

4 eggs	FOR THE FILLING
275 g (10 oz) caster sugar	3 egg whites
150 g (5 oz) plain flour	175 g (6 oz) icing sugar
100 g (4 oz) chopped nuts, for coating	225 g (8 oz) butter
	100 g (4 oz) plain chocolate, melted

1 Line 2 baking sheets with non-stick baking parchment.
2 Whisk the eggs and 175 g (6 oz) of the caster sugar in a bowl standing over a pan of hot water. Whisk until the mixture is thick enough to leave a trail on the surface when the whisk is lifted. Remove from the heat.
3 Sift half the flour over the mixture and fold in lightly with a metal spoon. Add the remaining flour in the same way. Carefully spread some of the mixture into 20 cm (8 inch) rounds on the prepared baking sheets.
4 Bake in the oven at 190°C (375°F) mark 5 for 7-10 minutes until golden brown. Loosen from baking sheets and trim to neaten. Transfer to wire racks to cool.
5 Repeat to make six or seven rounds. Select the round with the best surface and lay it on an oiled baking sheet.
6 Dissolve the remaining caster sugar in a small, heavy-based saucepan, without stirring, over a gentle heat, then boil steadily to a rich brown. Pour over the round on the baking sheet, spreading it with a knife brushed with oil. Mark into eight sections and trim round the edge.
7 To make the filling, whisk egg whites and sifted icing sugar in a heatproof bowl standing over a pan of simmering water until very thick, then remove from heat.
8 Put the butter into a bowl and beat until pale and soft. Gradually beat in the egg and sugar mixture, then stir in the melted chocolate.
9 Sandwich the remaining biscuit rounds together with some of filling and put the caramel-covered one on top.
10 Spread the sides of the torte with the remaining filling and press the chopped nuts round the sides.

WHITE CHOCOLATE GATE

SERVES 12-16

23 cm (9 inch) Genoese cake (see page 171)	300 ml (½ pint) double cream
FOR THE FILLING	5 ml (1 level tsp) powdered gelatine
175 g (6 oz) plain chocolate, in pieces	TO DECORATE
30 ml (2 tbsp) brandy	275 g (10 oz) white chocolate
2 eggs, separated	150 ml (¼ pint) double cream
	icing sugar, for dusting

1 To make the filling, put the chocolate into a heatproof bowl standing over a pan of simmering water and heat gently until the chocolate melts. Remove from the heat and stir in the brandy and egg yolks. Whip cream until it stands in soft peaks, then fold into the mixture.
2 Sprinkle the gelatine over 15 ml (1 tbsp) water in a small bowl; soak for 2-3 minutes. Place bowl over a pan of simmering water until dissolved. Cool, then stir into the chocolate mixture. Whisk egg whites until stiff, then fold in.
3 Cut the cake into two layers. Put one piece of sponge back in the tin. Pour the mousse filling on top. Put the second piece of sponge on top. Leave to set.
4 While the filling is setting, make the decoration. Melt the white chocolate as in step 1. Spread out thinly on a marble slab or a clean, smooth work surface. Leave until set. When the chocolate is set, push a clean stripping knife (see below) across the chocolate at an angle of about 25° to create large thick chocolate curls. Chill until required.
5 When mousse is set, whip cream until it holds its shape. Ease cake out of tin and cover with cream. Coat with the chocolate curls and dust lightly with icing sugar.

COOK'S TIP

A stripping knife is a decorator's tool used for scraping off wallpaper! It has a sharp flexible blade and is ideal for making large chocolate curls. Buy one and keep it specifically for this purpose.

CHOCOLATE AND HAZELNUT GATEAU

SERVES 10

275 g (10 oz) unsalted butter, softened	100 g (4 oz) plain chocolate, finely grated
225 g (8 oz) soft light brown sugar	225 g (8 oz) icing sugar
4 eggs, separated	50 g (2 oz) cocoa powder
100 g (4 oz) self-raising flour	30 ml (2 tbsp) milk
pinch of salt	25 g (1 oz) chopped hazel-nuts, to decorate
100 g (4 oz) ground hazel-nuts	

1 Grease and line a 23 cm (9 inch) round cake tin. Put 225 g (8 oz) of the butter and the sugar into a bowl and beat together until pale and fluffy. Beat in the egg yolks one at a time, then fold in the flour and salt. Stir in the hazelnuts and chocolate.
2 Whisk the egg whites until stiff, then fold into the cake mixture. Pour into the prepared tin and bake in the oven at 170°C (325°F) mark 3 for 1-1¼ hours or until a fine warmed skewer inserted in the centre comes out clean. Leave to cool in the tin for 45 minutes.
3 Make the fudge icing. Sift the icing sugar and cocoa powder together, then put into a heavy-based pan with the remaining butter and the milk. Heat gently until the butter has melted; beat until smooth. Remove from heat.
4 Cut the cake in half horizontally. Spread a little icing over one half, then top with the other. Swirl remaining icing over and sprinkle with nuts.

CHOCOLATE MOUSSE CAKE

SERVES 8

450 g (1 lb) plain chocolate	100 g (4 oz) unsalted butter, softened
45 ml (3 tbsp) orange-flavoured liqueur	TO DECORATE
9 eggs, 5 of them separated	blanched julienne strips of orange rind
150 g (5 oz) caster sugar	

1 Grease a 20 cm (8 inch) spring-release cake tin, line with greaseproof paper and grease the paper.
2 Break 225 g (8 oz) of the chocolate into small pieces. Place in a heatproof bowl standing over a pan of simmering water and heat gently until the chocolate melts. Stir in 15 ml (1 tbsp) of the liqueur, then remove from the heat.
3 Using an electric whisk, whisk 5 egg yolks and the sugar together in a bowl until thick and creamy. Beat in the butter, a little at a time, until smooth. Beat in the melted chocolate until smooth.
4 Whisk the 5 egg whites until stiff, then fold into the chocolate mixture. Turn into the prepared tin.
5 Bake in the oven at 180°C (350°F) mark 4 for 40 minutes until risen and firm. Leave to cool in the tin for 1 hour.
6 To make the top layer, melt the remaining chocolate as before, then stir in the remaining liqueur. Remove from the heat and cool for 1-2 minutes. Separate the remaining eggs and beat the egg yolks into the chocolate mixture. Whisk the egg whites until stiff, then fold into the chocolate mixture.
7 Press the crust down on the baked cake with your fingers and pour the top layer over it. Chill overnight.
8 The next day, remove the cake carefully from the tin and put on to a serving plate. Arrange strips of orange rind around the edge to decorate.

DARK AND SINFUL CHOCOLATE CAKE

SERVES 8

	FOR THE ICING
125 g (4 oz) unsalted butter	175 g (6 oz) plain chocolate, broken into pieces
3 eggs, separated	25 g (1 oz) unsalted butter
125 g (4 oz) dark soft brown sugar	175 g (6 oz) icing sugar, sifted
50 ml (2 fl oz) brandy	45 ml (3 tbsp) warm water
2.5 ml (½ tsp) vanilla flavouring	TO DECORATE
200 g (7 oz) plain chocolate, melted	300 ml (½ pint) double cream, stiffly whipped
75 g (3 oz) plain flour	grated chocolate
50 g (2 oz) ground almonds	

1 Grease and flour a deep 20 cm (8 inch) round cake tin and line the base with greaseproof paper.
2 Whisk the egg yolks and sugar in a large bowl over a pan of hot water until very pale and creamy and thick enough to leave a trail on the surface when the whisk is lifted. Remove from the heat and whisk until cool.
3 Add the brandy and vanilla flavouring and whisk in the melted chocolate and butter mixture. Add the sifted flour and the ground almonds and fold in gently using a metal spoon. Whisk the egg whites until stiff then lightly fold into the mixture, a little at a time.
4 Pour into the tin and bake at 180°C (350°F) mark 4 for 45-50 minutes or until firm to the touch. Leave in the tin for 10 minutes, then turn out onto a wire rack to cool.
5 To make the icing, melt chocolate and butter in a bowl over a pan of hot water. Remove from heat and gradually stir in the icing sugar and water to make a thick icing.
6 Cut the cake in half and spread one third of the icing over one half; cool, then top with one third of the whipped cream. Put the remaining cake on top. Spoon the rest of the icing over the cake and swirl quickly with a knife to completely coat the top and sides. Leave to set.
7 Decorate with cream and grated chocolate.

CHOCOLATE-WRAPPED ORANGE GATEAU

SERVES 12

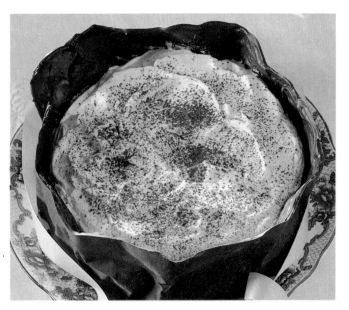

	FOR THE LIQUEUR SYRUP
200 g (7 oz) self-raising flour	100 g (4 oz) granulated sugar
50 g (2 oz) cornflour	finely grated rind and juice of 1 orange
7.5 ml (1½ level tsp) baking powder	45 ml (3 tbsp) orange-flavoured liqueur
175 g (6 oz) caster sugar	TO DECORATE
3 eggs, separated	2 large oranges, peeled segmented and chopped
finely grated rind and juice of 1 small orange	300 ml (½ pint) whipped cream
105 ml (7 tbsp) oil	225 g (8 oz) plain chocolate, melted
45 ml (3 tbsp) milk	cocoa powder, for dusting

1 Grease a deep 22 cm (8½ inch) spring-release cake tin and line the base with greaseproof paper.
2 To make the sponge, mix the flours, baking powder and sugar together in a bowl. Blend the egg yolks with the orange rind and juice, oil and milk, then mix into the dry ingredients. Beat thoroughly to a smooth batter. Whisk the egg whites until stiff, then fold in. Pour into the tin.
3 Bake in the oven at 180°C (350°F) mark 4 for about 55 minutes or until well risen and firm to the touch.
4 Meanwhile to make the syrup, gently heat the sugar, orange rind and juice and 60 ml (4 tbsp) water in a heavy-based saucepan until the sugar has dissolved. Bring to the boil and boil rapidly for 2 minutes. Stir in the liqueur.
5 Prick the hot cake all over, then spoon over the hot syrup. Leave to cool, then top with the oranges. Spread the cream over the top and sides.
6 Meanwhile, spread the melted chocolate over a strip of greaseproof paper, long enough to go round the side and wide enough to extend above the cake. Leave until setting, then wrap around the gâteau. Dust the top with cocoa.

CHOCOLATE MACAROON LOG

SERVES 10

FOR THE MACAROONS	300 ml (½ pint) double cream
3 egg whites, size 6	45 ml (3 tbsp) almond-flavoured liqueur
175 g (6 oz) ground almonds	TO DECORATE
275 g (10 oz) caster sugar	icing sugar, for dusting
7.5 ml (1½ tsp) almond flavouring	cocoa powder, for dusting
FOR THE FILLING	chocolate leaves or curls
100 g (4 oz) hazelnuts	hazelnuts
100 g (4 oz) plain chocolate, in pieces	

1   To make the macaroons, line two baking sheets with non-stick baking paper. Whisk the egg whites in a bowl until stiff, then fold in the ground almonds, sugar and almond flavouring.

2   Spoon the mixture into a piping bag fitted with a 1 cm (½ inch) plain nozzle and pipe 30 small rounds on to the prepared baking sheets, allowing room for spreading.

3   Bake in the oven at 180°C (350°F) mark 4 for about 20 minutes. Transfer to a wire rack to cool for 20 minutes.

4   To make filling, spread the nuts on a baking sheet. Brown in the oven at 200°C (400°F) mark 6 for 5-10 minutes. Tip on to a cloth and rub off skins. Chop finely.

5   Place the chocolate in a heatproof bowl standing over a pan of simmering water and heat gently until melted. Leave to cool for 5 minutes.

6   Whip the cream until it holds its shape. Gradually beat in the cooled chocolate, nuts and liqueur.

7   Use some of the chocolate cream to sandwich the macaroons together. Place side by side on a serving plate to form a double log. Spread chocolate cream on top and add a further layer of macaroons. Spread remaining chocolate cream over the top and sides. Chill overnight.

8   To serve, dust with icing sugar and cocoa, then decorate with chocolate leaves or curls and whole hazelnuts.

CINNAMON CHOCOLATE TORTE

SERVES 6-8

175 g (6 oz) plain chocolate	75 g (3 oz) ground almonds
175 g (6 oz) butter	FOR THE FILLING
200 g (7 oz) caster sugar	90 ml (6 tbsp) apricot jam
5 eggs, separated	30 ml (2 tbsp) lemon juice
150 g (5 oz) plain flour	300 ml (½ pint) whipping cream, whipped
15 ml (3 level tsp) ground cinnamon	icing sugar, for dusting

1   Grease and line two 19 cm (7½ inch) sandwich tins.

2   To make the cake, first break the chocolate into small pieces. Place in a heatproof bowl with 45 ml (3 tbsp) water. Stand the bowl over a pan of simmering water and heat gently until the chocolate melts. Leave to cool.

3   Cream the butter and sugar together in a bowl until light. Beat in the egg yolks. Add the cooled chocolate, mixing well.

4   Whisk the egg whites. Sift the flour with 10 ml (2 tsp) of the cinnamon and fold into the creamed mixture with the ground almonds and egg whites. Spoon the mixture into the prepared tins.

5   Bake in the oven at 190°C (375°F) mark 5 for 35-40 minutes or until a skewer inserted into the centre comes out clean. Turn out on to a wire rack and leave to cool for about 2 hours. Cut each cake into two layers.

6   To make the filling, put the apricot jam in a small pan with the lemon juice and remaining cinnamon, then heat gently. Cool and spread on the cakes. Layer up with cream and dust the top with icing sugar before serving.

COOK'S TIP

Use quality French, Swiss or Belgian chocolate, available from most supermarkets and delicatessens.

SACHERTORTE

SERVES 8-10

150 g (5 oz) plain chocolate, in pieces	50 g (2 oz) fresh brown breadcrumbs
100 g (4 oz) unsalted butter or margarine, softened	30 ml (2 level tbsp) apricot jam, melted
100 g (4 oz) caster sugar	FOR THE ICING
100 g (4 oz) ground almonds	200 g (7 oz) plain chocolate, in pieces
4 eggs, separated	200 ml (7 fl oz) double cream

1 Grease a 23 cm (9 inch) spring-release cake tin, line with greaseproof paper and grease the paper.
2 Melt the chocolate in a heatproof bowl over a pan of simmering water. Remove from the heat.
3 Cream the butter and sugar together in a bowl until pale and fluffy. Stir in the ground almonds, egg yolks, breadcrumbs and melted chocolate, then beat until well combined.
4 Whisk the egg whites until stiff and fold half into the chocolate mixture, then fold in the other half. Pour the mixture into the prepared tin and level the surface.
5 Bake in the oven at 180°C (350°F) mark 4 for 40-45 minutes until firm to the touch.
6 Cover with a damp tea towel, leave for 5 minutes to cool slightly, then transfer on to a wire rack to cool. When cold, brush the top with the melted apricot jam.
7 To make the icing, place the chocolate in a heatproof bowl with the cream. Stand the bowl over a pan of simmering water and heat until the chocolate melts and blends with the cream. Cool for a few minutes until the icing just coats the back of a spoon.
8 Stand the cake on the wire rack on a baking sheet and pour over the icing. Gently shake the cake to spread the icing evenly and use a palette knife, if necessary to ensure that the sides are completely covered. Leave in a cool place, but not the refrigerator, to set.

RASPBERRY TORTE

SERVES 12

1½ quantity Genoese sponge mixture (see page 171)	225 ml (8 fl oz) milk
1 quantity pâte sucrée (see page 172)	300 ml (½ pint) double cream
15 ml (1 tbsp) raspberry conserve, sieved	30 ml (2 tbsp) icing sugar
	225 g (8 oz) raspberries, sieved
FOR THE BAVAROIS	TO DECORATE
20 ml (4 level tsp) gelatine	450 ml (¾ pint) double cream, whipped
4 egg yolks	toasted flaked almonds
25 g (1 oz) caster sugar	few raspberries

1 Grease and line a 25 cm (10 inch) round cake tin. Turn the genoese into the prepared tin and bake in the oven at 180°C (350°F) mark 4 for 30-35 minutes until well risen and firm to the touch. Turn out and cool on a wire rack.
2 Roll out pastry on a baking sheet and trim to a 25 cm (10 inch) round. Prick all over and chill for 30 minutes. Bake in the oven at 220°C (425°F) mark 7 for 20 minutes.
3 To make the bavarois, soak gelatine in 45 ml (3 tbsp) water. Lightly whisk egg yolks and caster sugar together. Heat milk until almost boiling, then whisk into the egg yolks. Stir over a pan of hot water until custard is thick enough to coat back of spoon. Strain into a bowl, add gelatine and stir until dissolved. Cool, stirring often.
4 Softly whip cream with icing sugar. Mix custard and raspberry purée together, then fold in the cream.
5 Cut the sponge into two layers. Place pastry base on a plate, then spread with the raspberry conserve. Cover with a layer of sponge. Trim pastry base to the same size as the sponge and place a torten ring or a length of flexible card around them to fit snugly. Pour bavarois on to sponge, then chill until beginning to set. Place the other sponge layer on top and chill until very firm. Remove ring or card. Coat with a layer of cream, then cover sides with almonds. Decorate with remaining cream and raspberries.

PINEAPPLE GRIESTORTE

SERVES 6-8

3 eggs, separated	75 g (3 oz) semolina
125 g (4 oz) caster sugar	300 ml (10 fl oz) whipping cream
376 g (13¼ oz) can pineapple pieces, drained and juice reserved	100 g (4 oz) chopped mixed nuts, toasted

1 Grease a 20 cm (8 inch) round cake tin. Base-line with greaseproof paper and grease the paper.
2 Whisk the egg yolks and sugar in a bowl until pale and really thick. Stir in 30 ml (2 tbsp) of the reserved pineapple juice together with the semolina.
3 Whisk the egg whites until stiff, then gently fold into the yolks and sugar mixture.
4 Turn into the prepared tin. Bake in the oven at 180°C (350°F) mark 4 for about 40 minutes or until the sponge springs back when pressed lightly with a finger and has shrunk away a little from the tin. Turn out on to a wire rack and leave for 30 minutes to cool.
5 Roughly chop the pineapple pieces. Lightly whip the cream. Split the cake in half and fill with half the cream and half the pineapple. Spread a little of the cream around the sides and top of the cake and press the nuts on the side. Pipe the remaining cream in whirls on top of the cake and decorate with the remaining nuts and pineapple.

LEMON AND PASSION FRUIT GATEAU

SERVES 8-10

50 g (2 oz) butter	50 g (2 oz) icing sugar
4 eggs	3 passion fruit
125 g (4 oz) caster sugar	150 ml (5 fl oz) whipping cream
finely grated rind and juice of 1 lemon	150 ml (5 fl oz) soured cream
125 g (4 oz) plain flour	lemon slice and strawberry, to decorate
225 g (8 oz) strawberries, hulled and thinly sliced	

1 Grease a deep 20 cm (8 inch) round cake tin. Base-line with greaseproof paper. Grease paper, then dust with sugar and flour.
2 Melt the butter in a small saucepan, remove from the heat and cool for 10 minutes.
3 In another bowl, whisk together the eggs, caster sugar and lemon rind until very pale and thick enough to leave a trail. Sift the flour over the egg mixture.
4 Drizzle over the butter. Fold in thoroughly. Turn the mixture into the prepared tin.
5 Bake in the oven at 190°C (375°F) mark 5 for 35-40 minutes or until a fine warmed skewer inserted in the centre comes out clean. Turn out on to a wire rack and cool for 1-2 hours.
6 Meanwhile, put the strawberries into a bowl with the lemon juice and 25 g (1 oz) icing sugar and leave to macerate for 2-3 hours. When the cake is cold, split in half and drizzle both halves with the juices from the fruit.
7 Using a sharp knife, cut the passion fruit in half and scoop out the pulp. Discard the skin. Lightly whip the cream, fold in the soured cream and passion fruit seeds.
8 Sandwich the cakes together with the strawberries and cream mixture and dust the top with the remaining icing sugar. Decorate with a lemon slice and a strawberry.

CHOCOLATE AND COCONUT ROULADE

SERVES 8

165 g (5½ oz) plain chocolate, broken into pieces	caster sugar, for dusting
5 eggs, separated	300 ml (½ pint) double cream
175 g (6 oz) caster sugar	50 g (2 oz) creamed coconut, grated or finely chopped
15 ml (1 tbsp) water	25 g (1 oz) flaked or shredded coconut, toasted
15 g (½ oz) cocoa powder, sifted	

1 Grease a 33 x 23 cm (13 x 9 inch) Swiss roll tin and line with greased greaseproof paper.
2 Melt 125 g (4 oz) chocolate in a heatproof bowl set over a saucepan of hot water. Leave the chocolate to cool.
3 Whisk the egg yolks with the sugar until pale and fluffy. Add the water, melted chocolate and cocoa and whisk well to combine.
4 Stiffly whisk the egg whites and lightly fold into the mixture. Turn the mixture into the prepared tin and level the surface.
5 Bake at 180°C (350°F) mark 4 for 20 minutes until well risen and firm to the touch. Remove from the oven, but do not turn out of the tin. Cover with a sheet of greaseproof paper and a damp tea towel and leave at room temperature overnight.
6 The next day, have ready a large sheet of greaseproof paper dusted with caster sugar. Turn the cake out on to the paper and remove the lining paper.
7 Stiffly whip the cream and fold in the creamed coconut. Spread half of the cream over the chocolate mixture and roll up, like a Swiss roll. (Don't worry when it cracks during rolling, as this won't show once the roll is complete).
8 Cover the roll with the remaining coconut cream and arrange the toasted coconut down the centre. Melt the remaining chocolate and drizzle over the roll. Leave to set before serving.

COFFEE PRALINE GATEAU

SERVES 8

75 g (3 oz) caster sugar	PRALINE
3 eggs	50 g (2 oz) unblanched almonds
100 g (3½ oz) plain flour	50 g (2 oz) caster sugar
1½ quantity coffee butter cream (see page 173)	

1 Grease a 33 x 23 cm (13 x 9 inch) Swiss roll tin and line the base and sides with greaseproof paper.
2 To make the sponge, whisk the sugar and eggs in a bowl over a pan of hot water, using an electric whisk until pale and creamy and thick enough to leave a trail on the surface when the whisk is lifted. Remove the bowl from the heat and whisk until cool.
3 Sift the flour over the mixture and fold in lightly using a metal spoon. Turn the mixture into the prepared tin and gently level the surface.
4 Bake in the oven at 190°C (375°F) mark 5 for 10-12 minutes until well risen and golden brown. Have ready a large sheet of greaseproof paper, sprinkled with a little caster sugar. Turn the sponge out on to the paper, remove the lining paper and leave to cool.
5 To make the praline, gently heat the almonds and sugar in a non-stick frying pan until the sugar melts and turns a rich dark golden brown. Carefully pour on to a well-buttered baking sheet. Quickly coat and separate 8 almonds and leave to one side to set individually; leave the rest of the praline to cool and set.
6 Roughly crush the praline in a blender, or between two sheets of greaseproof paper with a rolling pin.
7 Cut sponge crossways into 3 equal strips. Sandwich together with half of the butter cream. Spread remainder over the top and sides of the gâteau. Cover sides with the crushed praline. Put the remaining butter cream in a piping bag fitted with a small star nozzle and pipe on top of the gâteau. Decorate with the caramel coated almonds.

GATEAU AMANDINE

MAKES ABOUT 8 SLICES

3 large eggs	30 ml (2 tbsp) almond-flavoured liqueur
125 g (4 oz) caster sugar	
75 g (3 oz) plain flour	30 ml (2 level tbsp) icing sugar
FOR THE FILLING AND DECORATION	100 g (4 oz) flaked and toasted almonds
300 ml (½ pint) double cream	

1 Grease a moule à manque cake tin measuring 24 cm (9½ inches) across the top. Line the base with greaseproof paper.

2 Put the eggs and sugar in a bowl, stand it over a pan of hot water and whisk until thick, creamy and pale in colour. The mixture should be stiff enough to leave a trail when the whisk is lifted. Remove from the heat and continue whisking until cool.

3 Sift the flour over the surface and lightly fold in with a metal spoon.

4 Turn the mixture into the prepared tin and bake in the oven at 190°C (375°F) mark 5 for about 30 minutes, until well risen and golden brown. Turn out and cool on a wire rack.

5 Whip the cream with the liqueur and icing sugar, until it stands in soft peaks. Spread the cream all over the cake so that it is completely covered. Sprinkle over the nuts. Dust lightly with icing sugar and chill before serving.

COOK'S TIP

A moule à manque cake tin is a deep sandwich tin which has sloping sides.

COFFEE CREAM GATEAU

SERVES 6

2 eggs	25 g (1 oz) blanched almonds
75 g (3 oz) caster sugar	FOR THE FILLING
50 g (2 oz) plain flour	150 ml (¼ pint) double cream
15 ml (1 tbsp) coffee flavouring	30 ml (2 tbsp) coffee-flavoured liqueur
PRALINE	icing sugar, for dusting
25 g (1 oz) caster sugar	

1 Grease a 20 cm (8 inch) round cake tin, line the base with greaseproof paper and grease the paper. Dust with caster sugar and flour.

2 To make the sponge, put the eggs and sugar in a large heatproof bowl standing over a pan of hot water. Whisk until pale and creamy and thick enough to leave a trail on the surface when the whisk is lifted. Remove from the heat and whisk until cool.

3 Sift the flour evenly over the surface of the mixture and fold in lightly, using a large metal spoon. Lightly fold in the coffee flavouring. Turn into the prepared tin.

4 Bake in the oven at 180°C (350°F) mark 4 for about 30 minutes or until the sponge springs back when pressed lightly with a finger and has shrunk away a little from the sides of the tin. Turn out on to a wire rack to cool.

5 Meanwhile to make the praline, oil a baking sheet. Put the caster sugar and almonds into a small frying pan and heat gently, shaking the pan occasionally, until the sugar dissolves and caramelizes to a rich brown colour.

6 Pour the mixture on to the baking sheet and leave for 10-15 minutes to cool and harden. When cold, grind or crush with the end of a rolling pin in a strong bowl.

7 To make filling, whip cream until it holds its shape; whisk in the liqueur. Fold in three quarters of the praline.

8 Cut the sponge into two layers and sandwich together with the cream. Dust the top with icing sugar and decorate with the remaining praline. Chill for 1-2 hours.

CELEBRATION CAKE

MAKES 20-24 SLICES

225 g (8 oz) butter or margarine	three 225 g (8 oz) packets ready-to-roll fondant icing
225 g (8 oz) caster sugar	300 ml (10 fl oz) double cream
4 eggs, beaten	120 ml (8 level tbsp) black cherry conserve or 50 g (2 oz) sliced strawberries
225 g (8 oz) self-raising flour	
grated rind and juice of 1 lemon	icing sugar for dusting
red, blue or yellow edible food colouring	fresh flowers and ribbon, to decorate

1 Grease and base-line a 23 cm (9 inch) round cake tin.

2 Cream the butter and sugar together until pale and fluffy. Add the eggs a little at a time, beating well after each addition.

3 Sift the flour and fold into the mixture with the grated lemon rind and juice. Spoon into the prepared tin and level the surface.

4 Bake in the oven at 180°C (350°F) mark 4 for about 1-1½ hours or until golden and firm to the touch. Cover the top with greaseproof paper, if necessary, towards the end of cooking time. Turn out on to a wire rack to cool.

5 Meanwhile tint the ready-to-roll icing a pale shade by kneading in a little colouring until evenly blended. Wrap tightly in greaseproof paper.

6 Split the cake in half horizontally. Whip the cream until it just holds its shape. Sandwich the cake layers together with jam or fruit and all but 45 ml (3 level tbsp) cream. Place on a serving plate. Spread the reserved cream thinly around the sides and over the top of the cake.

7 Dust the work surface lightly with icing sugar and roll out the icing large enough to cover the cake completely. Fold icing over a rolling pin and carefully lift it onto the cake; gently smooth the sides. Trim excess icing from base.

8 Decorate with a broad ribbon and fresh flowers just before serving.

SIMNEL CAKE

MAKES ABOUT 20 SLICES

175 g (6 oz) butter	100 g (4 oz) sultanas
175 g (6 oz) caster sugar	50 g (2 oz) chopped mixed peel
3 whole eggs and 1 egg white	100 g (4 oz) glacé cherries, quartered
225 g (8 oz) plain flour	
pinch of salt	finely grated rind of 1 lemon
2.5 ml (½ level tsp) each ground cinnamon and grated nutmeg	15-30 ml (1-2 tbsp) milk
	450 g (1 lb) almond paste
250 g (9 oz) currants	glacé icing (see page 173)

1 Grease an 18 cm (7 inch) round cake tin. Line with greaseproof paper and grease the paper.

2 Cream the butter and sugar until pale and fluffy. Gradually beat in the lightly whisked whole eggs.

3 Sift the flour, salt and spices over the surface and fold into the mixture with a metal spoon. Fold in the fruit, peel, lemon rind and milk to give a dropping consistency.

4 Divide the almond paste in half and roll out one half to a 16 cm (6½ inch) circle on a sugared surface.

5 Spoon half the cake mixture into the prepared tin. Place the round of almond paste on top and cover with the remaining cake mixture. Level the surface.

6 Tie a double thickness of brown paper round the outside of the tin. Bake in the oven at 170°C (325°F) mark 3 for 1 hour, then lower the heat to 150°C (300°F) mark 2 and bake for a further 2 hours. Leave in the tin for about 1 hour, then turn out and cool on a wire rack.

7 Divide remaining almond paste in two. Roll out one half to an 18 cm (7 inch) circle and the rest into 11 small balls and a rope edging. Brush the top of the cake with lightly beaten egg white. Place the circle on top and apply the edging and balls, securing with a little egg white.

8 Brush the almond paste with egg white and place under a hot grill for 1-2 minutes until browned. Coat the top of the cake with glacé icing and apply any decorations.

TRADITIONAL CHRISTMAS CAKE

MAKES ABOUT 25 SLICES

225 g (8 oz) currants	2.5 ml (½ level tsp) ground cinnamon
225 g (8 oz) sultanas	225 g (8 oz) butter
225 g (8 oz) seedless raisins, chopped	225 g (8 oz) dark brown soft sugar
100 g (4 oz) glacé cherries, halved	finely grated rind of 1 lemon
100 g (4 oz) chopped mixed peel	4 eggs, beaten
50 g (2 oz) nibbed almonds	30 ml (2 tbsp) brandy
225 g (8 oz) plain white flour	60 ml (4 tbsp) apricot glaze (see page 173)
pinch of salt	900 g (2 lb) almond paste
2.5 ml (½ level tsp) ground mace	900 g (2 lb) royal icing (see page 173)

1 Grease a 20 cm (8 inch) round cake tin. Line with a double thickness of greaseproof paper, and tie a double band of brown paper round the outside.
2 Mix together the fruit, peel and almonds. Sift the flour, salt and spices together.
3 Cream the butter, sugar and lemon rind together until pale and fluffy. Beat in the eggs, a little at a time. Fold in half the flour, then fold in the rest with the brandy. Finally, fold in the fruit.
4 Spread in the tin, stand on a layer of brown paper and bake at 150°C (300°F) mark 2 for about 3¾ hours; cover with greaseproof paper after 1½ hours.
5 Cool in the tin, then turn out. Wrap in greaseproof paper, then in foil and store in an airtight tin for 1 month.
6 About 14 days before required, transfer cake to a board, brush with apricot glaze, then cover with almond paste. Leave to dry in a cool dry place for 4-5 days.
7 Flat ice the cake with royal icing and pipe decorative borders on the top and bottom. Finish with a ribbon and almond paste holly leaves or Christmas trees.

CHRISTMAS CAKE WITH GLACE FRUIT

MAKES ABOUT 10 SLICES

225 g (8 oz) butter or margarine	45 ml (3 tbsp) apricot glaze (see page 173)
225 g (8 oz) caster sugar	50 g (2 oz) glace cherries, halved
4 eggs, beaten	50 g (2 oz) blanched almonds
100 g (4 oz) ground almonds	25-40 g (1-1½ oz) angelica, cut into diamonds
125 g (4 oz) self-raising flour, sifted with a pinch of salt	
225 g (8 oz) can pineapple slices, drained and roughly chopped	

1 Grease and base line a deep 20 cm (8 inch) loose-bottomed round cake tin. Tie a double thickness of brown paper round the outside.
2 Cream the butter and sugar together until light and fluffy. Beat in the eggs a little at a time. Fold in the ground almonds and flour.
3 Fold in the pineapple, then add 15-30 ml (1-2 tbsp) warm water to give a soft dropping consistency. Spread in the prepared cake tin.
4 Bake in the oven at 170°C (325°F) mark 3 for 1½ hours, covering the top with a double thickness of greaseproof paper after 1 hour to prevent overbrowning.
5 Leave in the tin for 5-10 minutes, then turn out and stand on a wire rack. Brush the top with apricot glaze while still warm and press on the cherries, nuts and angelica in a decorative design. Glaze the decoration.
6 Finish with festive ribbon. Store in an airtight tin for up to 2 weeks.

YULE LOG

MAKES 8-10 SLICES

3 eggs	caster sugar, to dredge
100 g (4 oz) caster sugar	1 quantity chocolate butter cream (see page 173)
100 g (4 oz) plain flour	icing sugar, to decorate

1   Grease a 30 x 20 cm (12 x 8 inch) Swiss roll tin. Line with greaseproof paper and grease the paper. Dust with caster sugar and flour.

2   Put the eggs and sugar in a large bowl, place over a pan of hot water and whisk until pale and creamy and thick enough to leave a trail on the surface of the mixture when the whisk is lifted.

3   Sift half the flour over the mixture and fold in very lightly with a metal spoon. Sift and fold in the remaining flour, then lightly stir in 15 ml (1 tbsp) hot water.

4   Pour the mixture into the prepared tin. Bake in the oven at 220°C (425°F) mark 7 for 8-12 minutes until golden brown, well risen and firm to the touch.

5   Meanwhile, place a sheet of greaseproof paper over a damp tea towel. Dredge the paper with a little caster sugar.

6   Quickly turn out the cake on to the paper, trim off the crusty edges and roll up with the paper inside. Leave to cool on a wire rack.

7   When cold, unroll and remove the paper. Spread one third of the butter cream over the surface and re-roll. Refrigerate for 30 minutes until the roll is firm.

8   Coat with the remaining butter cream and mark lines with a fork to resemble tree bark.

9   Chill for 1 hour before serving. Dust lightly with icing sugar and decorate with a sprig of real or artificial holly.

STOLLEN

MAKES 12 SLICES

15 g (1½ oz) fresh yeast or 7.5 ml (1½ tsp) dried plus a pinch of sugar	grated rind of 1 small lemon
100 ml (4 fl oz) tepid milk	50 g (2 oz) chopped mixed peel
225 g (8 oz) strong plain flour	50 g (2 oz) currants
1.25 ml (¼ level tsp) salt	50 g (2 oz) sultanas
25 g (1 oz) butter or margarine	25 g (1 oz) blanched almonds, chopped
	½ a beaten egg
	icing sugar, to dredge

1   Grease a large baking sheet.

2   Crumble the fresh yeast into a bowl and cream with the milk until smooth. If using dried yeast, sprinkle on to the milk with the sugar and leave in a warm place for 15 minutes or until the surface is frothy.

3   Put the flour and salt into a bowl and rub in the butter. Add the lemon rind, peel, fruit and nuts. Add the yeast mixture and the egg and mix thoroughly to a soft dough.

4   Turn on to a lightly floured working surface and knead for about 10 minutes until smooth. Cover with a clean cloth and leave to rise in a warm place for about 1 hour until doubled in size.

5   Knead the dough for 2-3 minutes, then roll into an oval shape measuring about 23 x 18 cm (9 x 7 inches). Mark a line lengthways with the rolling pin.

6   Carefully fold the dough in half along the marked line. Place on the baking sheet, cover with a clean cloth and leave in a warm place for about 40 minutes until doubled in size.

7   Bake in the oven at 200°C (400°F) mark 6 for about 30 minutes until well risen and golden brown. Transfer to a wire rack to cool. When cold, dredge the stollen all over with icing sugar to serve.

PANETTONE

MAKES ABOUT 10 SLICES

350 g (12 oz) plain white flour	50 g (2 oz) caster sugar
20 g (¾ oz) fresh yeast or 15 g (2¼ tsp) dried	75 g (3 oz) candied peel, chopped
225 ml (8 fl oz) tepid milk	50 g (2 oz) sultanas
100 g (4 oz) butter, softened	pinch of grated nutmeg
2 egg yolks	egg yolk, to glaze

1 Sift the flour into a large bowl and make a well in the centre. Blend the fresh yeast with the milk. If using dried yeast, sprinkle it on to the milk and leave in a warm place for 15 minutes or until frothy. Add the yeast liquid to the flour and mix well together, gradually drawing in the flour from the sides of the bowl. Leave to stand in a warm place for 45 minutes or until doubled in size.

2 Add the softened butter to the dough with the egg yolks, sugar, candied peel, sultanas and nutmeg. Mix well together. Leave to stand again in a warm place for a further 45 minutes or until doubled in bulk.

3 Meanwhile, cut 3 strips of baking parchment, each one measuring 56 x 25 cm (22 x 10 inches). Fold each piece over lengthways.

4 Stand the 3 pieces of parchment together on a greased baking sheet to make a 17 cm (6½ inch) circle and secure with staples. Place the dough inside the paper and leave in a warm place for about 1 hour or until risen to the top of the paper.

5 Cut the top of the dough in the shape of a cross, then brush with egg yolk, to glaze. Bake on the lowest shelf of the oven at 200°C (400°F) mark 6 for 20 minutes, then lower the temperature to 180°C (350°F) mark 4 for a further 40 minutes or until a fine warmed skewer inserted in the centre comes out clean. Leave to cool in the paper. Panettone may be stored in an airtight tin for a maximum of 1 week.

SCOTTISH BLACK BUN

MAKES ABOUT 12 SLICES

1 quantity shortcrust pastry (see page 172)	450 g (1 lb) seedless raisins
FOR THE FILLING	450 g (1 lb) currants
225 g (8 oz) plain flour	50 g (2 oz) chopped mixed peel
5 ml (1 level tsp) ground cinnamon	100 g (4 oz) chopped almonds
5 ml (1 level tsp) ground ginger	100 g (4 oz) dark brown soft sugar
5 ml (1 level tsp) ground allspice	1 egg, beaten
5 ml (1 level tsp) cream of tartar	150 ml (¼ pint) whisky
5 ml (1 level tsp) bicarbonate of soda	about 60 ml (4 tbsp) milk
	beaten egg, to glaze

1 Grease a deep 20 cm (8 inch) round cake tin.

2 Roll out two thirds of the pastry on a lightly floured surface to a round, 35 cm (14 inches) in diameter. Line the tin with the pastry, making sure it overhangs the sides.

3 Sift together the flour, spices, cream of tartar and bicarbonate of soda. Mix in the raisins, currants, peel, almonds and sugar.

4 Add the egg, whisky and milk and stir until the mixture is evenly moistened. Pack the filling into the pastry case and fold the top of the pastry over the filling.

5 On a lightly floured surface, roll out the remaining dough to a 20 cm (8 inch) round. Moisten the edges of the pastry case, put the pastry round on top and seal firmly.

6 With a skewer, make four or five holes right down to the bottom of the cake, then prick all over the top with a fork and brush with egg.

7 Bake in the oven at 180°C (350°F) mark 4 for 2½-3 hours or until a fine warmed skewer inserted in the centre comes out clean. Cover with greaseproof paper if it is becoming too brown. Turn out on to a wire rack to cool.

CHEESECAKES

Few can resist a creamy rich, velvety smooth cheesecake, and there is a wide
variety to choose from in this chapter. From traditional baked cheesecakes to
light gelatine-set cheesecakes with tangy citrus and berry fruit toppings,
you will find a recipe to suit everyone.

RICOTTA CHEESECAKE

SERVES 4

350 g (12 oz) Ricotta or curd cheese	50 g (2 oz) ground almonds
3 egg yolks, beaten	40 g (1½ oz) chopped candied peel
100 g (4 oz) sugar	grated rind of 1 lemon
50 ml (2 fl oz) rum or brandy	caster sugar, to decorate

1 Grease and flour a 20 cm (8 inch) cake tin and set aside
until required.
2 Push the Ricotta or curd cheese through a sieve into a
bowl and beat in the egg yolks and sugar.
3 Add the rum, beat well, then fold in the ground
almonds, candied peel and lemon rind.
4 Pour into the prepared tin and bake in the oven at
180°C (350°F) mark 4 for 30-40 minutes or until firm and
slightly shrunken from the sides of the tin.
5 Open the door of the oven and switch off. Leave the
cheesecake inside the oven for about 2-3 hours to cool
with the door ajar.
6 To serve, carefully remove the cheesecake from the tin
and dredge with sugar.

CALCIONI ALL'ASCOLANA

SERVES 16

225 g (8 oz) plain flour	25 g (1 oz) caster sugar
pinch of salt	1 egg yolk
2 eggs, beaten	finely grated rind of 1 lemon
30 ml (2 tbsp) olive oil	50 g (2 oz) candied peel, finely chopped
FOR THE FILLING	
225 g (8 oz) ricotta cheese	beaten egg, to glaze
50 g (2 oz) ground almonds	icing sugar, for dusting

1 To make the pastry, put the flour and salt in a bowl.
Make a well in the centre and stir in the eggs and olive oil.
Using your fingertips, knead to a smooth dough.
2 Turn out on to a floured work surface and knead for
about 5 minutes. Wrap and chill for 30 minutes.
3 To make the filling, mix the ingredients together.
4 Roll out the pastry very thinly on a lightly floured
surface and cut out sixteen 10 cm (4 inch) rounds.
5 Divide filling between pastry rounds. Brush edges
with beaten egg, then fold in half to enclose the filling.
Brush with beaten egg to glaze. Transfer to baking sheets.
6 Bake in the oven at 190°C (375°F) mark 5 for 25-30
minutes. Serve cold, dusted with icing sugar.

CHEESECAKE WITH RED FRUIT SAUCE

SERVES 8

175 g (6 oz) digestive biscuits, crushed	grated rind and juice of 3 lemons
50 g (2 oz) ground almonds	100 g (4 oz) caster sugar
75 g (3 oz) butter, melted	FOR THE SAUCE
FOR THE FILLING	350 g (12 oz) strawberries
225 g (8 oz) full fat soft cheese	350 g (12 oz) raspberries
225 g (8 oz) cottage cheese	40 g (½ oz) icing sugar
60 ml (4 tbsp) double cream	90 ml (6 tbsp) orange-flavoured liqueur
2 eggs, separated	TO DECORATE
1 egg yolk	whipped cream
15 ml (1 tbsp) cornflour	icing sugar, for dusting

1 Grease the base and sides of a 20 cm (8 inch) spring-release cake tin and line with greaseproof paper.
2 To make the base, stir the crushed biscuits and ground almonds into the melted butter and blend well. Press half the mixture into the base of the prepared tin.
3 To make the filling, blend the cheeses, double cream, egg yolks, cornflour, lemon rind and 60 ml (4 tbsp) lemon juice together in a blender or food processor.
4 Whisk the egg whites until stiff but not dry. Whisk in 30 ml (2 tbsp) of the caster sugar, then whisk again until stiff and shiny. Fold in the remaining caster sugar. Gently fold the egg whites into the cheese mixture. Spoon into the tin. Sprinkle the remaining biscuit mixture on top.
5 Bake in the oven at 200°C (400°F) mark 6 for 30 minutes. Reduce temperature to 180°C (350°F) mark 4, cover with foil and bake for a further 45 minutes. Cool in the tin. Chill for at least 1 hour.
6 To make the sauce, blend the strawberries, raspberries, icing sugar and liqueur together in a blender or food processor. Sieve to remove pips. Chill.
7 Carefully remove cheesecake from tin. Decorate with cream. Dust with icing sugar and serve with the sauce.

RUM AND RAISIN CHEESECAKE

SERVES 8

FOR THE PASTRY	FOR THE FILLING
225 g (8 oz) self raising flour	75 g (3 oz) raisins
5 ml (1 level tsp) bicarbonate of soda	75 ml (5 tbsp) dark rum
5 ml (1 level tsp) cream of tartar	100 g (4 oz) cottage cheese
75 g (3 oz) butter	100 g (4 oz) full fat soft cheese
finely grated rind of 1 lemon	2 eggs, separated
150 ml (¼ pint) soured cream	50 g (2 oz) caster sugar
	150 ml (¼ pint) double cream
	15 ml (1 tbsp) icing sugar, for dusting

1 Grease a 25 cm (10 inch) flan dish.
2 To make the filling, put the raisins and rum in a saucepan and bring to the boil. Remove from the heat and leave to cool for 15 minutes.
3 Meanwhile, to make the pastry, sift the flour, bicarbonate of soda and cream of tartar into a bowl. Rub in the butter until the mixture resembles fine breadcrumbs. Add the lemon rind. Bind to a smooth dough with the soured cream. Roll out and use to line the prepared dish.
4 Beat the cottage and cream cheeses together in a bowl. Stir in the rum and raisins.
5 In a separate bowl, whisk the egg yolks and caster sugar together until pale and fluffy. Whisk in the double cream, and continue whisking until the mixture is the consistency of lightly whipped cream. Fold into the cheese, rum and raisin mixture. Whisk the egg whites until stiff, then fold into the mixture. Pour into the pastry case.
6 Bake in the oven at 180°C (350°F) mark 4 for about 1 hour. Turn off the heat and leave to cool in the oven for 15 minutes. Remove from the oven and cool for a further 45 minutes. Dust with icing sugar.

TRADITIONAL BAKED CHEESECAKE

SERVES 8

FOR THE BASE	225 g (8 oz) caster sugar
50 g (2 oz) self-raising flour	450 g (1 lb) full fat soft cheese
2.5 ml (½ level tsp) baking powder	40 g (1½ oz) plain flour
50 g (2 oz) butter, softened	grated rind and juice of 1 lemon
50 g (2 oz) caster sugar	300 ml (½ pint) soured cream
1 egg	75 g (3 oz) sultanas
FOR THE FILLING	pinch of grated nutmeg
4 eggs, separated	

1 Grease a 20 cm (8 inch) round spring-release cake tin and line the base with greaseproof paper; grease the paper.
2 To make the base, sift the self-raising flour and baking powder into a bowl. Add the butter, sugar and egg. Mix well and beat for 2-3 minutes. Spread the mixture evenly over the bottom of the prepared tin.
3 To make the filling, whisk the egg yolks with the sugar until the mixture is thick and creamy.
4 Beat the soft cheese lightly in a bowl. Add the whisked egg mixture and mix until smooth. Sift in the plain flour and stir in. Add the lemon rind and juice, 150 ml (¼ pint) of the soured cream and the sultanas.
5 Whisk the egg whites until stiff, then fold into the mixture. Pour on to the mixture in the tin.
6 Bake in the oven at 170°C (325°F) mark 3 for 1 hour or until firm but still spongy to the touch. Turn off the heat and leave in the oven for 1 hour with the door ajar.
7 Remove from the oven and cool for 2-3 hours. Carefully remove cheesecake from tin. To serve, spread the remaining cream over the top and sprinkle with nutmeg.

COOK'S TIP

Bake cheesecakes in spring-release cake tins to make turning out easy. If you do not own a spring-release tin, a cake tin with a loose base works almost as well.

EASTER CHEESECAKE

SERVES 8

FOR THE PASTRY	2.5 ml (½ tsp) vanilla flavouring
225 g (8 oz) plain flour	200 ml (7 fl oz) double cream
125 g (4 oz) butter	150 ml (5 fl oz) soured cream
45 ml (3 tbsp) caster sugar	50 g (2 oz) caster sugar
FOR THE FILLING	1 ripe pear (optional)
400 g (14 oz) full fat soft cheese	icing sugar, for dusting
2 eggs, separated	crystallized primroses, to decorate (optional)

1 To make the pastry, sift the flour into a bowl. Rub in the butter until the mixture resembles fine bread-crumbs. Stir in the caster sugar. Bind to a dough with about 60 ml (4 tbsp) water. Roll out on a lightly floured surface and use to line a 22 cm (8½ inch) deep, fluted loose bottomed flan tin. Chill for 15 minutes then bake blind at 200°C (400°F) mark 6 for 20-25 minutes or until pale golden brown and cooked through.
2 Beat together the soft cheese, egg yolks and vanilla flavouring. Gradually beat in the double and soured creams until thoroughly combined.
3 Whisk the egg whites until they just hold their shape. Fold in 25 g (1 oz) caster sugar and continue whisking until stiff. Whisk in a further 25 g (1 oz) sugar. Fold into the cheese mixture.
4 Peel, core and thinly slice the pear into the prepared flan case if using. Spoon over the cheese mixture. Place the tin on a baking sheet and bake at 220°C (425°F) mark 7 for 20 minutes. Reduce the oven temperature to 180°C (350°F) mark 4 and bake for a further 35-40 minutes or until the cheesecake is golden brown and just set. Cool in the tin.
5 Serve the cheesecake warm, dusted with icing sugar and decorated with crystallized primroses, if desired.

HOT CHOCOLATE CHEESECAKE

SERVES 10-12

FROSTED MINT CHEESECAKE

SERVES 6

FOR THE CHOCOLATE PASTRY	FOR THE FILLING
150 g (5 oz) plain flour	2 eggs, separated
75 g (3 oz) butter or margarine	75 g (3 oz) caster sugar
30 ml (2 level tbsp) cocoa powder, sifted	350 g (12 oz) curd cheese
30 ml (2 level tbsp) caster sugar	40 g (1½ oz) ground hazelnuts
25 g (1 oz) ground hazelnuts	150 ml (¼ pint) double cream
1 egg yolk	25 g (1 oz) cocoa powder, sifted
	10 ml (2 tsp) dark rum
	icing sugar, for dusting

1   Grease a 20 cm (8 inch) round loose-based cake tin.

2   To make the chocolate pastry, put the flour in a bowl and rub in the butter until the mixture resembles fine breadcrumbs. Stir in the cocoa powder, sugar and hazelnuts. Add the egg yolk and sufficient water to give a soft dough.

3   Roll out the pastry on a lightly floured work surface and use to line the prepared tin. Chill while making the filling.

4   To make the filling, whisk the egg yolks and sugar together in a bowl until thick enough to leave a trail on the surface when the whisk is lifted. Whisk in the curd cheese, nuts, cream, cocoa powder and rum until blended.

5   Whisk the egg whites until stiff, then fold into the cheese mixture. Pour into the pastry case and fold the edges of the pastry over the filling.

6   Bake in the oven at 170°C (325°F) mark 3 for 1½ hours until risen and just firm to the touch. Carefully remove from the tin and dust the top with icing sugar. Serve the cheesecake while it is still hot.

75 g (3 oz) butter or margarine	7.5 ml (1½ tbsp) mint-flavoured liqueur
150 g (5 oz) caster sugar	30 ml (2 tbsp) water
100 g (4 oz) plain flour	7.5 ml (1½ level tsp) powdered gelatine
225 g (8 oz) full fat soft cheese	1 egg white
150 ml (5 fl oz) natural yogurt	mint sprigs, to decorate

1   To make the shortbread base, cream the butter with 50 g (2 oz) caster sugar until smooth. Stir in the flour and knead the mixture until it is smooth.

2   Press the shortbread mixture into the base of a 20 cm (8 inch) flan ring, placed on a foil-lined baking sheet. Bake in the oven at 180°C (350°F) mark 4 for 18-20 minutes; cool in the ring.

3   Meanwhile, beat the cheese with a wooden spoon until smooth, then gradually whisk in the yogurt, 25 g (1 oz) sugar and the mint-flavoured liqueur.

4   Place the water in a bowl and sprinkle in the gelatine. Stand the bowl over a saucepan of hot water and heat gently until dissolved. Leave to cool slightly, then stir into the cheese mixture. Whisk the egg white until stiff, then fold into the cheesecake mixture.

5   Pour the mixture over the shortbread base. Open freeze for about 8 hours or overnight, then ease off the flan ring. Wrap in foil when firm and return to the freezer until required.

6   About 1 hour before serving, remove the cheesecake from the freezer, and place on a serving plate.

7   Warm the remaining sugar until it caramelises, then pour over the cheesecake in a lattice pattern. Place in the refrigerator for 45 minutes before serving. Decorate the cheesecake with mint sprigs.

GINGER AND BANANA CHEESECAKE

SERVES 6-8

FOR THE BASE	30 ml (2 tbsp) clear honey
225 g (8 oz) ginger biscuits, crushed	15 ml (1 tbsp) chopped preserved ginger (with syrup)
100 g (4 oz) unsalted butter, melted and cooled	15 ml (1 level tbsp) powdered gelatine
FOR THE FILLING	60 ml (4 tbsp) lemon juice
225 g (8 oz) full fat soft cheese	TO DECORATE
150 ml (¼ pint) soured cream	banana slices
3 bananas	preserved ginger slices

1 To make the base, mix the biscuits and melted butter together. Press the mixture over the base of a 20 cm (8 inch) spring-release tin or deep cake tin with a removable base. Chill for about 30 minutes.
2 To make the filling, beat the cheese and cream together in a bowl until well mixed. Peel and mash the bananas, then beat into the cheese mixture with the honey and ginger.
3 Sprinkle the gelatine over the lemon juice in a small bowl and leave to soak for 2-3 minutes. Place the bowl over a pan of simmering water and stir until dissolved.
4 Stir the dissolved gelatine slowly into the cheesecake mixture. Spoon on to the biscuit base. Chill for about 3-4 hours until the cheesecake is set.
5 To serve, remove the cheesecake carefully from the tin and place on a serving plate. Decorate around the edge with banana and ginger slices. Serve as soon as possible or the banana will discolour.

VARIATION

Use chocolate digestive biscuits for the base of this cheesecake instead of ginger biscuits, and omit the preserved ginger from the filling. Decorate the top with bananas slices arranged alternately with chocolate buttons.

COFFEE CHEESECAKE

SERVES 8

FOR THE BASE	30 ml (2 tbsp) coffee-flavoured liqueur
50 g (2 oz) butter, melted	150 g (5 oz) light brown soft sugar
175 g (6 oz) gingernut biscuits, finely crushed	450 g (1 lb) curd cheese
FOR THE FILLING	300 ml (½ pint) whipping cream
15 ml (1 level tbsp) powdered gelatine	coffee beans, to decorate
15 ml (1 level tbsp) instant coffee powder	

1 Lightly oil a 20 cm (8 inch) loose-based deep cake tin or spring-release cake tin.
2 To make the base, stir the butter and crushed biscuits together. Press firmly into the base of the prepared tin. Chill for 30 minutes until set.
3 To make the filling, sprinkle the gelatine over 45 ml (3 tbsp) water in a small bowl and leave to soak for 10 minutes. Place the bowl over a pan of simmering water and stir until dissolved. (Alternatively, microwave on HIGH for 30 seconds or until dissolved.)
4 Stir the coffee and coffee liqueur into 300 ml (½ pint) boiling water. Stir in the gelatine, then the sugar.
5 Put the coffee mixture and curd cheese into a blender or food processor and work until just smooth. Leave until beginning to set. Lightly whip the cream and fold half into the cheese mixture.
6 Turn the mixture into the prepared tin and chill for 2-3 hours or until set.
7 When set, carefully remove the cheesecake from the tin. Pipe whirls of the remaining cream around the cheesecake and decorate with coffee beans.

COOK'S TIP

If you can find them use sugar coffee beans, available from high class confectioners, to decorate.

LEMON CHEESECAKE

SERVES 6

FOR THE BASE	225 g (8 oz) cottage cheese, sieved
75 g (3 oz) butter or margarine	150 ml (5 fl oz) soured cream
175 g (6 oz) digestive biscuits, finely crushed	75 g (3 oz) caster sugar
FOR THE FILLING	2 eggs, separated
15 ml (1 level tbsp) powdered gelatine	TO DECORATE
finely grated rind and juice of 1 lemon	sliced strawberries or lemon slices

1 Melt the butter in a saucepan and mix in the biscuit crumbs. Press into the base of a 20 cm (8 inch) loose-bottomed or spring-release cake tin. Chill in the refrigerator for 30 minutes.
2 Sprinkle the gelatine in 60 ml (4 tbsp) water in a small bowl. Place over a pan of simmering water and stir until dissolved. Cool slightly.
3 Put the lemon rind, juice and cottage cheese into a bowl, then add the soured cream and sugar and mix well together. Stir in the egg yolks and gelatine.
4 Whisk the egg whites until stiff, then fold lightly into the mixture. Carefully pour into the tin and chill for several hours, preferably overnight until firm.
5 Remove the cheesecake from the tin and place on a flat serving plate. Decorate with strawberries or lemon slices.

VARIATION

Set the cheesecake in an oiled 25 cm (10 inch) fluted savarin mould as for Cranberry Cheesecake (opposite). Set the filling in the tin first, then cover with the base. Turn out to serve.

MINI GRAPE CHEESECAKES

SERVES 24

FOR THE PASTRY	2 eggs, beaten
275 g (10 oz) plain flour	25 g (1 oz) caster sugar
pinch of salt	10 ml (2 level tsp) plain flour
175 g (6 oz) butter or margarine, cut into pieces	finely grated rind and juice of ½ lemon
50 g (2 oz) caster sugar	TO DECORATE
FOR THE FILLING	175 g (6 oz) grapes, halved and seeded
225 g (8 oz) full fat soft cheese	150 ml (¼ pint) whipping cream, whipped

1 To make the pastry, put the flour and salt into a bowl. Rub in the butter until the mixture resembles breadcrumbs. Stir in the sugar and add sufficient water, about 60 ml (4 tbsp), to mix to a smooth dough.
2 Roll out the pastry on a lightly floured work surface and cut out twelve 7.5 cm (3 inch) rounds, using a fluted pastry cutter. Use to line 24 deep patty tins.
3 Bake blind in the oven at 200°C (400°F) mark 6 for 10 minutes. Remove the foil and baking beans, then return to the oven for a further 5 minutes.
4 Meanwhile to make the filling, beat the soft cheese, eggs, sugar, flour and lemon rind and juice together in a bowl until evenly mixed. Pour the filling into the pastry cases.
5 Lower the oven temperature to 150°C (300°F) mark 2 and bake the cheesecakes for 15 minutes until the fillings are set. Leave to cool on a wire rack for 30 minutes, then refrigerate the cheesecakes for at least 1 hour before serving.
6 Just before serving, decorate the top of each cheesecake with the grapes and piped whipped cream.

CRANBERRY CHEESECAKE

SERVES 10

FOR THE FILLING	300 ml (½ pint) double cream
225 g (8 oz) full fat soft cheese	15 ml (1 level tbsp) powdered gelatine
2 eggs, separated	225 g (8 oz) cranberries
finely grated rind and juice of 2 lemons	10 ml (2 level tsp) arrowroot
225 g (8 oz) caster sugar	FOR THE BASE
	175 g (6 oz) digestive biscuits, crushed
300 ml (½ pint) natural yogurt	75 g (3 oz) butter, melted

1   Lightly oil a 25 cm (10 inch) fluted savarin spring release tin.

2   For the filling, beat the cheese, egg yolks, lemon rind, 50 g (2 oz) of the sugar and the yogurt together in a bowl. Whip the cream lightly and fold into the cheese mixture.

3   In a small bowl, mix 75 ml (5 tbsp) lemon juice with 30 ml (2 tbsp) water. Sprinkle in the gelatine and leave to soak for 2-3 minutes. Place the bowl over a pan simmering water and stir until dissolved. Stir into the cheese mixture and leave to cool.

4   Whisk the egg whites until standing in soft peaks, then fold into the cheese mixture until evenly incorporated. Pour the mixture into the prepared tin. Chill for 3-4 hours until completely set.

5   To make the base, mix the biscuits and melted butter together. Spoon the mixture over the set cheesecake and pat down firmly. Chill again for 1 hour until set.

6   Cook the cranberries with the remaining sugar and 150 ml (¼ pint) water in a pan for about 10 minutes until soft but still whole. Blend a little water with the arrowroot, stir into the cranberry mixture and slowly bring to boiling point. Cook for 2-3 minutes, then leave to cool for 30 minutes.

7   Invert the cheesecake on to a flat serving plate. Spoon the cranberry mixture into the centre before serving.

INDIVIDUAL RASPBERRY CHEESECAKES

SERVES 2

50 g (2 oz) cream cheese	15 g (½ oz) butter
5 ml (1 level tsp) caster sugar	2 digestive biscuits, finely crushed
75 g (3 oz) fresh or frozen raspberries, thawed	raspberries, to decorate
120 ml (4 fl oz) double cream	

1   In a small bowl, beat the cream cheese and 2.5 ml (½ tsp) of the sugar together until smooth. Add the raspberries and mix well.

2   Whip the cream until it just holds its shape, then fold into the cheese mixture until evenly incorporated.

3   Wet the insides of 2 ramekin dishes, to ensure that the mixture will turn out easily. Spoon in the cheese mixture, levelling it evenly.

4   Melt the butter in a saucepan and stir in the biscuits and remaining sugar.

5   Press the biscuit mixture on top of the cheese mixture and level the top. Chill in the refrigerator for at least 2 hours before serving.

6   To serve, loosen around the edges of the ramekins with a knife and turn the cheesecakes out on to serving plates. Decorate with raspberries and serve chilled.

SERVING SUGGESTION

Light and creamy, these cheesecakes make perfect summer desserts. Serve with crisp biscuits.

GOOSEBERRY CHEESECAKE

SERVES 6

450 g (1 lb) gooseberries, topped and tailed	125 g (4 oz) cottage cheese
75 ml (5 tbsp) water	225 g (8 oz) full fat soft cheese
125 g (4 oz) caster sugar	150 ml (5 fl oz) double cream
75 g (3 oz) shelled hazelnuts	2 eggs, separated
75 g (3 oz) butter	15 ml (1 tbsp) lemon juice
175 g (6 oz) digestive biscuits, finely crushed	7.5 ml (1½ level tsp) powdered gelatine

1 Put the gooseberries into a pan with 60 ml (4 tbsp) water and 75 g (3 oz) caster sugar. Cover and cook slowly for 20 minutes until mushy. Press through a nylon sieve into a bowl and let cool for 30 minutes.

2 Roughly chop 50 g (2 oz) hazelnuts and fry gently in the butter until golden. Stir in the crushed digestive biscuits. Press into the base of a 24 cm (9½ inch) deep fluted flan dish. Refrigerate to set.

3 Sieve the cottage cheese into a large bowl. Beat in the soft cheese, then the cream.

4 Whisk the egg yolks and remaining caster sugar until thick enough to leave a trail on the surface when the whisk is lifted. Stir into the cheese mixture.

5 Put the lemon juice in a small bowl with 15 ml (1 tbsp) water and sprinkle in the gelatine. Leave to soak for 10 minutes. Stand the bowl over a pan of gently simmering water until the gelatine dissolves, then stir into the cheese mixture with half the fruit purée.

6 Whisk one egg white until stiff and fold into the mixture then spoon into the lined flan dish. Refrigerate for 1-2 hours.

7 Spread remaining nuts on a baking sheet and brown in the oven at 200°C (400°F) mark 6 for 5-10 minutes. Put into a tea towel and rub off skins, then chop roughly.

8 Decorate the cheesecake with the nuts and remaining gooseberry pureé.

QUICK CHERRY CHEESECAKE

SERVES 4-6

65 g (2½ oz) unsalted butter, melted	60 ml (4 tbsp) icing sugar, sifted
150 g (5 oz) digestive biscuits, crushed	300 ml (10 fl oz) double cream
225 g (8 oz) full fat soft cheese	400 g (14 oz) can cherry pie filling
2.5 ml (½ tsp) vanilla flavouring	

1 Stir the melted butter into the crushed biscuits and mix well, then press into the base and sides of a 22 cm (8½ inch) fluted flan dish. Refrigerate for 30 minutes.

2 Put the cheese into a bowl and beat until soft and creamy, then beat in the vanilla flavouring and icing sugar.

3 Whip the cream until it holds its shape, then fold into the cheese mixture until evenly blended.

4 Spoon the mixture into the biscuit base and level the surface. Refrigerate for 30 minutes.

5 Spoon the pie filling over the top of the cheesecake. Refrigerate for 2-3 hours to set.

VARIATION

Use blackcurrant instead of cherry pie filling.

LEMON
MUESLI CHEESECAKE

SERVES 6

FOR THE BASE	225 g (8 oz) low fat soft cheese
175 g (6 oz) muesli	150 ml (¼ pint) natural yogurt
75 g (3 oz) butter or margarine, melted	60 ml (4 tbsp) clear honey
FOR THE FILLING	2 egg whites
3 lemons	
15 ml (1 level tbsp) powdered gelatine	

1 Grease a 20 cm (8 inch) spring-release cake tin.
2 To make the base, mix the muesli and melted butter together. Press the mixture over the base of the prepared tin, using the back of a metal spoon. Chill to set while making the filling.
3 To make the filling, finely grate the rind of 2 of the lemons; set aside. Squeeze the juice from the 2 lemons and make up to 150 ml (¼ pint) with water.
4 Sprinkle the gelatine over the lemon juice and water in a bowl and leave to soak for 2-3 minutes. Place the bowl over a pan of simmering water and stir until dissolved. (Alternatively, microwave on HIGH for 30 seconds or until dissolved.) Leave to cool slightly.
5 Whisk the cheese, yogurt and honey together in a separate bowl. Stir in the grated lemon rind and dissolved gelatine until evenly incorporated. Whisk the egg whites until standing in stiff peaks. Fold into the cheesecake mixture until evenly incorporated. Spoon the mixture into the prepared tin and level the surface. Chill for at least 4 hours until set.
6 Coarsely grate the rind from the remaining lemon over the centre of the cheesecake, to decorate. As an alternative, slice the lemon thinly and arrange on top of the cheesecake. Remove the cheesecake from the tin and place on a serving plate. Serve chilled.

RASPBERRY
RIPPLE CHEESECAKE

SERVES 12

FOR THE BASE	300 ml (½ pint) Greek yogurt
25 g (1 oz) blanched almonds	150 g (5 oz) low fat soft cheese
225 g (8 oz) almond butter biscuits, crushed	15 ml (1 level tbsp) powdered gelatine
100 g (4 oz) butter or margarine, melted	2 egg whites
few drops of almond flavouring	50 g (2 oz) icing sugar
FOR THE FILLING	mint leaves, to decorate
450 g (1 lb) raspberries	

1 Grease a 2.3 litre (4 pint) loose-based cake tin or spring-release cake tin.
2 To make the base, lightly toast the almonds, then finely chop. Mix with the biscuits and butter. Add a few drops of almond flavouring. Spoon the mixture into the base of the prepared tin and pack down with the back of a metal spoon. Chill while making the filling.
3 To make the filling, purée 225 g (8 oz) of the raspberries in a blender or food processor, then press through a sieve. Pour three-quarters of the purée into a bowl and reserve. Add the yogurt and cheese to the purée remaining in the blender and process until well blended.
4 Sprinkle the gelatine over 30 ml (2 tbsp) water in a small bowl and leave to soak for 2-3 minutes. Place the bowl over a pan of simmering water and stir until dissolved. Leave to cool, then add to the cheese mixture.
5 Whisk the egg whites with the icing sugar until very thick and shiny. Fold into the cheese mixture.
6 Arrange 100 g (4 oz) of the reserved raspberries over the biscuit base. Pour the cheese mixture into the tin. Sprinkle with the remaining raspberries. Spoon in the reserved purée and mark in a swirl with a knife to make a marbled pattern. Chill for 3-4 hours or until set.
7 To serve, unmould and decorate with mint leaves.

PINEAPPLE CHEESECAKE

SERVES 10

FOR THE BASE	150 ml (5 fl oz) soured cream
75 g (3 oz) butter	3 eggs separated
175 g (6 oz) plain chocolate wholewheat biscuits, roughly crushed	50 g (2 oz) caster sugar
	15 ml (3 level tsp) powdered gelatine
FOR THE FILLING	two 432 g (14½ oz) cans sliced pineapple, with juice
225 g (8 oz) cottage cheese	
100 g (4 oz) full fat soft cheese	60 ml (4 level tbsp) sieved apricot jam
pared rind and juice of 1 large lemon	

1 Melt the butter in a pan. Stir the biscuits into the butter. Press the crumb mixture on to the base and sides of a 23 cm (9 inch) spring-release cake tin and refrigerate to set.
2 Place the cottage and full fat soft cheeses, lemon rind, 45 ml (3 tbsp) lemon juice and the soured cream in a blender or food processor and work until smooth.
3 Whisk the egg yolks and sugar until thick. Soak the gelatine in 45 ml (3 tbsp) of water in a small bowl. Dissolve by standing the bowl in a pan of simmering water. Whisk the gelatine into the egg yolks with the cheese mixture.
4 Drain and roughly chop three-quarters of the pineapple, reserving the juice. Whisk the egg whites until stiff. Fold the egg whites into the setting cheese mixture with the chopped pineapple. Pour into the biscuit crust and refrigerate until set.
5 Carefully remove the sides of the cake tin then, using a fish slice, lift and slide the cheesecake off the base on to a serving plate.
6 Decorate with the reserved pineapple. Put the reserved juice in a saucepan with the jam and simmer to reduce to a thick glaze; cool, then spoon over the pineapple.

CHERRY AND LEMON CHEESECAKE

SERVES 10

75 g (3 oz) butter	150 ml (5 fl oz) soured cream
125 g (4 oz) caster sugar	300 ml (10 fl oz) double cream
150 g (5 oz) plain flour	
1 egg yolk	15 ml (1 level tbsp) powdered gelatine
225 g (8 oz) full fat soft cheese	45 ml (3 tbsp) water
225 g (8 oz) cottage cheese, sieved	225 g (8 oz) fresh red cherries, halved and stoned, or 213 g (7½ oz) can cherries, drained
2 eggs, separated	
finely grated rind and juice of 2 lemons	angelica, to decorate

1 Cream the butter with 75 g (3 oz) of the sugar. Mix to a firm dough with the flour and 1 egg yolk. Roll out half to fit the base of a 20 cm (8 inch) spring-release cake tin, and the other half to fit a 20 cm (8 inch) plain flan ring.
2 Bake both in the oven at 180°C (350°F) mark 4 for about 15 minutes. Cut the flan ring round into 10 wedges and cool on a wire rack. Leave the other round in the tin.
3 With an electric mixer beat together the cheeses, 2 egg yolks, lemon rind, 75 ml (5 tbsp) lemon juice, remaining sugar and soured cream. Stir in half the double cream.
4 Soak the gelatine in the water in a small bowl. Dissolve by standing the bowl in a pan of simmering water. Stir into the cheese mixture. Refrigerate for 2-3 hours until beginning to set.
5 Whisk the egg whites until stiff. Fold the cherries and egg whites into the cheese mixture, then turn into the tin. Refrigerate until firm.
6 Carefully unmould the cheesecake. Place the pastry wedges on top and decorate with angelica and the remaining double cream.

TROPICAL CHEESECAKE

SERVES 8

REDCURRANT CHEESECAKE

SERVES 4-6

FOR THE BASE	150 ml (¼ pint) orange juice
75 g (3 oz) butter, melted	350 g (12 oz) full fat soft cheese
175 g (6 oz) plain chocolate digestive biscuits, finely crushed	100 g (4 oz) caster sugar
50 g (2 oz) desiccated coconut	2 eggs, separated
FOR THE FILLING	30 ml (2 tbsp) lemon juice
2 medium mangoes	300 ml (½ pint) double cream
30 ml (2 level tbsp) powdered gelatine	3 kiwi fruit, peeled and sliced, to decorate

65 g (2½ oz) butter, melted	40 g (1½ oz) caster sugar
150 g (5 oz) wheatmeal biscuits, finely crushed	150 ml (5 fl oz) natural yogurt
175 g (6 oz) redcurrants	150 ml (5 fl oz) double cream
15 ml (1 level tbsp) powdered gelatine	15 ml (1 level tbsp) redcurrant jelly
125 g (4 oz) cottage cheese	redcurrants, to decorate
1 egg, separated	

1 Lightly oil a 22 cm (8½ inch) spring-release cake tin. Line the base with greaseproof paper and grease the paper.
2 To make the base, stir the melted butter into the biscuit crumbs and coconut. Mix well together. Press over the base of the prepared tin. Chill for 30 minutes.
3 To make the filling, peel the mangoes and cut the flesh from the stone. Discard the stone. Roughly chop or mash the flesh.
4 Sprinkle the gelatine over the orange juice in a bowl and leave to soak for 2-3 minutes. Place the bowl over a pan of simmering water and stir until dissolved. Leave the gelatine to cool for 5 minutes.
5 Beat the soft cheese and sugar together in a bowl until smooth, then beat in the egg yolks and lemon juice. Stir in the mango flesh and dissolved gelatine. Lightly whip the cream and fold into the mixture.
6 Whisk the egg whites until stiff, then carefully fold into the cheese mixture. Pour on to the biscuit base. Chill for 3-4 hours until firm. Carefully remove the cheesecake from the tin. Decorate with the kiwi fruit.

COOK'S TIP

Once the cheesecake has set, remove it from the tin to prevent any reaction between the metal tin and the acid in the cheesecake causing discolouration.

1 Mix together the butter and biscuit crumbs. Press the mixture into a 20 cm (8 inch) round loose-bottomed cake tin to line the base.
2 Put the redcurrants in a medium saucepan with 45 ml (3 tbsp) water and simmer gently for 5-6 minutes, until soft. Allow to cool.
3 Sprinkle the gelatine in 45 ml (3 tbsp) water in a small bowl and leave to soak. Place the bowl over a saucepan of simmering water and stir until dissolved. Leave until lukewarm.
4 Put the cottage cheese, egg yolk, sugar and yogurt in a food processor or blender and work together until smooth. Whip the cream until it just holds its shape. Fold the cooked redcurrants, redcurrant jelly, gelatine and most of the cream into the cheese mixture. Whisk the egg white until stiff and fold into the mixture.
5 Pour the mixture on to the biscuit base and chill in the refrigerator until set.
6 Carefully remove the cheesecake from the tin and decorate with the remaining whipped cream and sprigs of redcurrants to serve.

PIES, FLANS & PASTRIES

Traditional fruit pies, colourful glazed fruit and nut flans, and crisp light-textured pastries are featured here. Remember, the secret to successful pastry making is to keep everything cool – the kitchen, work surface, utensils, ingredients and yourself!

BAKEWELL PUDDING

SERVES 4

212 g (7½ oz) packet frozen puff pastry, thawed	100 g (4 oz) butter or margarine, melted
FOR THE FILLING	100 g (4 oz) caster sugar
2 eggs	50 g (2 oz) ground almonds
2 egg yolks	30 ml (2 level tbsp) raspberry jam

1 Roll out the pastry on a floured surface and use to line an 18 cm (7 inch) pie plate or loose-based flan tin.
2 Beat the eggs and extra yolks together, add the butter, sugar and ground almonds and mix well.
3 Spread the bottom of the pastry case with the jam and pour on the egg mixture.
4 Bake in the oven at 200°C (400°F) mark 6 for 30 minutes, until the filling is firm to the touch. Serve warm or cold, with cream or custard.

DEEP-DISH APPLE FLAN

SERVES 8

1½ quantity flan pastry (see page 172)	1 cinnamon stick
FOR THE FILLING	75 g (3 oz) caster sugar
1.4 kg (3 lb) cooking apples	beaten egg, for glazing
50 g (2 oz) butter	flaked almonds
5 ml (1 level tsp) ground mixed spice	demerara sugar
	icing sugar, for dusting

1 Roll out the pastry and use to line a deep 22 cm (8½ inch) loose-based fluted flan tin. Chill the trimmings.
2 To make the filling, peel, quarter, core and thickly slice the apples. Put half in a saucepan with the butter, mixed spice, cinnamon and caster sugar. Cook, stirring, over a high heat until the apples are soft. Off the heat, remove cinnamon, then add the remaining apples. Cool slightly.
3 Spoon the apple mixture into the pastry case. Make pastry leaves from the trimmings. Arrange attractively interlocking over the apple filling and brush lightly with beaten egg. Sprinkle with almonds and demerara sugar.
4 Bake in the oven at 180°C (350°F) mark 4 for 35 minutes or until golden and crisp. Leave for 10 minutes before removing from tin. Serve warm dusted with icing sugar.

BANBURY APPLE PIE

SERVES 6

350 g (12 oz) plain flour	75 g (3 oz) soft brown sugar
pinch of salt	pinch of ground cinnamon
175 g (6 oz) butter	pinch of freshly grated nutmeg
15 ml (1 tbsp) caster sugar	grated rind and juice of 1 orange
1 egg, lightly beaten	milk, to glaze
700 g (1½ lb) cooking apples	caster sugar for sprinkling
juice of ½ lemon	
100 g (4 oz) sultanas	

1 To make the pastry, put the flour and salt in a bowl and rub in the butter until the mixture resembles fine breadcrumbs. Stir in the caster sugar, then stir in the egg and enough water to bind the mixture together.
2 Knead lightly on a lightly floured surface, then roll out two-thirds of the pastry and use to line a shallow 900 ml (1½ pint) pie dish.
3 Peel, core and thinly slice the apples. Put in a bowl and sprinkle with lemon juice.
4 Layer the apples, sultanas, brown sugar, spices and orange rind in the pie dish. Sprinkle with the orange juice.
5 Roll out the remaining pastry to form a lid, pressing the edges together. Scallop the edges, then make a slit in the centre of the pie.
6 Brush the top with milk to glaze, then bake at 200°C (400°F) mark 6 for 30 minutes, until golden brown. Sprinkle the top with caster sugar and serve hot or cold.

COOK'S TIP

Despite the mystique attached to making pastry, the only secrets to success are patience, practice and care. Unless making choux or filo (strudel) pastry, the golden rule is keep everything cool – kitchen, work surface, utensils, ingredients and yourself.

TARTE TATIN

SERVES 8

150 g (5 oz) butter or block margarine	1 egg yolk
175 g (6 oz) plain flour	15 ml (1 tbsp) water
65 g (2½ oz) caster sugar	450 g (1 lb) crisp eating apples

1 Rub 125 g (4 oz) fat into the flour until the mixture resembles fine breadcrumbs. Add 15 g (½ oz) caster sugar. Blend the egg yolk with the water and stir into the mixture. Knead the dough lightly, then refrigerate while making the filling.
2 In a saucepan, melt the remaining fat and add the remaining caster sugar. Heat until caramelised and golden brown. Remove from the heat and pour into a 20 cm (8 inch) round sandwich tin.
3 Peel, core and halve the apples and slice them into 1 cm (½ inch) pieces. Pack them tightly to fill the bottom of the tin, leaving no gaps.
4 Roll out the pastry on a floured work surface to a round slightly larger than the tin. Place on top of the apples and tuck in around the edges of the tin. Refrigerate for 30 minutes.
5 Place the tin on a baking sheet and bake in the oven at 200°C (400°F) mark 6 for 30-35 minutes until the pastry is golden. Turn out, apple side uppermost, on to a serving dish. Serve hot, with cream.

COOK'S NOTE

Correctly called Tarte des Demoiselles Tatin in French, this famous upside-down apple tart is named after the sisters Tatin, hoteliers in the nineteenth century who originated the recipe. There are now numerous versions of the original recipe, which has become something of a classic in French cookery. Most recipes use shortcrust pastry as here, although some use puff. In all versions the pastry is baked on the top so that the apples are completely sealed in with their juices, then the tart turned out upside down for serving.

PEACH PIE

SERVES 6

FOR THE PASTRY	2 egg yolks
225 g (8 oz) plain flour	FOR THE FILLING
50 g (2 oz) walnuts, finely chopped	900 g (2 lb) peaches
100 g (4 oz) softened butter or margarine, cut into pieces	1 egg white, for glazing
	caster sugar, for dredging
75 g (3 oz) caster sugar	

1 To make the pastry, place the flour on a work surface and sprinkle the walnuts over the top. Make a well in the centre and add the butter, sugar, egg yolks and 30 ml (2 tbsp) water.
2 Using the fingertips of one hand only, work the well ingredients together until evenly blended. Using a palette knife, gradually draw in the flour, then knead lightly until just smooth.
3 Roll out two thirds of the pastry on a floured work surface and use to line a 23 cm (9 inch) loose-based fluted flan tin. Chill for 30 minutes.
4 To make the filling, quarter the peaches and easy away from the stone. Peel off the skins carefully and divide each quarter in two lengthways.
5 Arrange the peaches in the pastry case. Roll out the remaining pastry and use to cover the pie, sealing well. Make a small hole in the centre to let steam escape.
6 Bake in the oven at 200°C (400°F) mark 6 for about 20-25 minutes or until just beginning to brown.
7 Brush the top of the pie with lightly beaten egg white and dredge with caster sugar. Return to the oven for a further 10 minutes or until well browned and crisp. Cool for 15 minutes in the tin before removing. Serve while still slightly warm, with cream.

VARIATION

Use firm, ripe nectarines in place of the peaches.

APRICOT AND CARDAMOM FLAN

SERVES 6

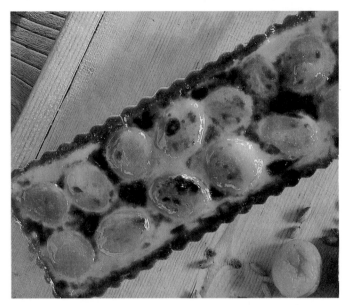

100 g (4 oz) no-soak dried apricots	150 ml (¼ pint) single cream
6 green cardamom pods, split	1 egg
	1 egg yolk
2 bay leaves	25 g (1 oz) caster sugar
1½ quantity pâte sucrée (see page 172)	60 ml (4 level tbsp) apricot jam

1 Place the apricots, cardamoms and bay leaves in a medium bowl. Completely cover with cold water and leave to soak overnight in the refrigerator.
2 Roll out the pastry on a lightly floured work surface and use to line a 34 x 11 cm (13½ x 4½ inch) loose-based fluted tranche tin. Chill for 10-15 minutes. Place on a flat baking sheet.
3 Bake blind in the oven at 190°C (375°F) mark 5 for about 20 minutes.
4 Drain the apricots, discard the bay leaves and cardamoms. Cut the apricots in half and pat dry with absorbent kitchen paper.
5 Whisk the cream, eggs and sugar together. Arrange the apricots, cut-side down, in the pastry case. Pour over the cream mixture.
6 Reduce the oven temperature to 180°C (350°F) mark 4 and bake for 35 minutes or until just set. Brown under the grill. Cool before removing the flan case.
7 Melt the apricot jam with 15 ml (1 tbsp) water over a gentle heat in a pan. Bring to the boil. Brush evenly over the warm flan. Serve warm or cold.

COOK'S TIP

Soaking the apricots with cardamoms and bay leaves gives them a delicious aromatic flavour.

72

FRENCH APPLE FLAN

SERVES 6

2 x quantity flan pastry (see page 172)	finely grated rind of ½ lemon
900 g (2 lb) cooking apples	30 ml (2 tbsp) Calvados or brandy
50 g (2 oz) butter or margarine	225 g (8 oz) eating apples
120 ml (9 level tbsp) apricot jam	about 30 ml (2 tbsp) lemon juice
50 g (2 oz) sugar	5 ml (1 level tsp) caster sugar

1 Roll out the pastry on a floured surface and use to line a 20 cm (8 inch) loose-based fluted flan tin placed on a baking sheet. Chill in the refrigerator for 30 minutes.
2 Bake blind in the oven at 200°C (400°F) mark 6 for 10-15 minutes, then remove paper and beans and bake for a further 5 minutes until the base is set.
3 Cut the cooking apples into quarters, core and roughly chop the flesh. Melt the butter in a saucepan and add the apples with 30 ml (2 tbsp) water. Cover the pan tightly and cook gently for about 15 minutes until soft and mushy.
4 Rub the apples through a sieve into a large clean pan. Add half the apricot jam with the sugar, lemon rind and brandy. Cook over a high heat for about 15 minutes, stirring, until all excess liquid has evaporated and the mixture is thickened.
5 Spoon the thick apple purée into the flan case and smooth the surface. Peel, quarter, core and slice the dessert apples very thinly. Arrange in an overlapping circle over the apple purée. Brush lightly with lemon juice; sprinkle with the caster sugar.
6 Return the flan to the oven and bake for a further 25-30 minutes, or until the pastry and apples are lightly coloured. Transfer to a plate. Cool for 10 minutes.
7 Gently warm the remaining jam with 15 ml (1 tbsp) lemon juice, then sieve. Brush over the top and sides of the flan. Serve warm or cold.

GLAZED NUT FLAN

SERVES 6-8

1 quantity pâte sucrée (see page 172)	25 g (1 oz) butter, melted
	pinch of grated nutmeg
FOR THE FILLING	60 ml (4 level tbsp) golden syrup
50 g (2 oz) hazelnuts	15 ml (1 level tbsp) plain flour
25 g (1 oz) pistachio nuts	
1 egg	75 g (3 oz) walnut pieces
25 g (1 oz) caster sugar	75 g (3 oz) Brazil nuts
grated rind and juice of 1 lemon	50 g (2 oz) pecan nuts

1 Roll out the pastry on a floured surface and use to line a 22 cm (8½ inch) loose-based fluted flan tin. Chill for 15 minutes.
2 Bake blind in the oven at 200°C (400°F) mark 6 for 10-12 minutes. Remove the beans and paper, then reduce the oven temperature to 180°C (350°F) mark 4 and bake for a further 10 minutes until pale golden.
3 Meanwhile to make the filling, brown the hazelnuts under a hot grill. Place in a clean tea towel and rub well to remove the skins. Dip the shelled pistachio nuts in boiling water for 1 minute. Drain and remove the skins.
4 Using an electric whisk, beat the egg and sugar together in a bowl until very thick and pale – about 5 minutes. Quickly stir in the lemon rind, melted butter, nutmeg and 30 ml (2 tbsp) of the golden syrup. Fold in the flour and finally all the nuts.
5 Spoon the nut mixture into the pastry case. Bake in the oven at 180°C (350°F) mark 4 for about 35 minutes or until golden brown and firm to the touch. Leave to cool for 10-15 minutes.
6 Heat the remaining golden syrup and 30 ml (2 tbsp) lemon juice together in a pan. Boil for 2-3 minutes until syrupy. Brush over the warm flan. Leave in the tin for 10-15 minutes before removing to a wire rack to cool. Serve warm or cold.

RHUBARB AND ORANGE CHIFFON PIE

SERVES 6

175 g (6 oz) digestive biscuits, crushed	finely grated rind and juice of 1 large orange
50 g (2 oz) demerara sugar	2 eggs, separated
75 g (3 oz) unsalted butter, melted	50 g (2 oz) caster sugar
450 g (1 lb) fresh rhubarb, trimmed and cut into 2.5 cm (1 inch) lengths	30 ml (2 level tbsp) cornflour
	2.5 ml (½ level tsp) ground ginger
	orange slices, to decorate

1 In a bowl, mix together the biscuits and demerara sugar, then stir in the butter.
2 Press evenly over the base and up the sides of a 20 cm (8 inch) fluted flan dish. Chill in the refrigerator while preparing the filling.
3 Cook the rhubarb with 45 ml (3 tbsp) water in a covered pan until soft and pulpy, stirring occasionally.
4 Purée the rhubarb in a blender or food processor, then pour into a bowl. Put the orange rind and juice into a heavy-based saucepan. Add the egg yolks, caster sugar, cornflour and ginger. Heat gently, stirring, until thick. Stir into the rhubarb purée.
5 Whisk the egg whites until stiff. Fold into the rhubarb custard, then spoon the mixture into the biscuit crust. Chill in the refrigerator for at least 4 hours, or overnight. Decorate with orange slices just before serving.

RASPBERRY ALMOND FLAN

SERVES 8

225 g (8 oz) plain flour	125 g (4 oz) self-raising flour
225 g (8 oz) butter or margarine	75 g (3 oz) ground almonds
125 g (4 oz) light soft brown sugar	60 ml (4 tbsp) milk
2 eggs, separated	225 g (8 oz) raspberries
	150 ml (¼ pint) whipping cream, to serve

1 Sift the plain flour into a bowl. Rub in half the fat until the mixture resembles fine breadcrumbs. Bind to a firm dough with 60 ml (4 tbsp) water.
2 Knead the dough lightly on a floured surface, then roll out and use to line a 25 cm (10 inch) loose-based fluted flan tin.
3 Bake blind in the oven at 200°C (400°F) mark 6 for 15-20 minutes until set but not browned. Remove the paper and beans.
4 Meanwhile beat the remaining fat with the sugar until light and fluffy. Gradually beat in the egg yolks. Gently stir in the self-raising flour, ground almonds and milk. Whisk the egg whites until stiff, then fold into the mixture.
5 Spoon the cake mixture into the baked flan case and level the surface. Sprinkle over the raspberries, reserving a few for decoration.
6 Bake in the oven at 180°C (350°F) mark 4 for 40-45 minutes or until the flan is golden brown and firm to the touch. Cool.
7 Whip the cream until thick, then use to decorate the flan, with the reserved raspberries. Cut the flan into large wedges to serve.

FUDGY NUT PIE

SERVES 8

225 g (8 oz) shortcrust pastry (see page 172)	100 ml (4 fl oz) milk
FOR THE FILLING	75 g (3 oz) corn syrup or golden syrup
50 g (2 oz) plain chocolate, broken into small pieces	5 ml (1 tsp) vanilla flavouring
50 g (2 oz) butter or margarine	1.25 ml (¼ tsp) salt
175 g (6 oz) caster sugar	3 eggs
75 g (3 oz) light soft brown sugar	100 g (4 oz) chopped mixed nuts
	icing sugar, to decorate

1 Roll out the pastry on a floured work surface and use to line a 23 cm (9 inch) flan dish or fluted flan ring placed on a baking sheet. Bake blind in the oven at 200°C (400°F) mark 6 for 10-15 minutes until set. Set aside to cool.

2 While the pastry case is cooling, put the chocolate and fat in a large heatproof bowl standing over a pan of simmering water. Heat gently until melted.

3 Remove the bowl from the pan and add the remaining ingredients, except the chopped nuts. Beat with a wooden spoon until well mixed, then stir in the nuts.

4 Pour the filling into the pastry case and bake in the oven at 180°C (350°F) mark 4 for 45-60 minutes or until puffy and golden. Dredge with icing sugar. Serve hot or cold, with ice cream.

COOK'S NOTE

Rich and nutty, this pie has a definite 'American' flavour. Corn syrup is a popular ingredient in American pies and desserts. A by-product of sweetcorn, it is similar to golden syrup but has a thinner consistency and lighter flavour. Look for it in delicatessens and large supermarkets if you want to give your pie an authentic flavour.

RIPE CHERRY TART

SERVES 8

225 g (8 oz) plain flour	FOR THE FILLING
pinch of salt	450 g (1 lb) cherries, stoned
25 g (1 oz) cornflour	2 eggs
100 g (4 oz) plus 10 ml (2 tsp) icing sugar	75 g (3 oz) ground almonds
100 g (4 oz) butter	few drops of almond flavouring
1 egg yolk	

1 Sift the flour, salt, cornflour and 10 ml (2 tsp) icing sugar into a bowl, then rub in the butter until the mixture resembles fine breadcrumbs. Add the egg yolk and 30 ml (2 tbsp) cold water and stir to bind together.

2 Knead lightly on a lightly floured surface, then roll out. Use to line a 23 cm (9 inch) fluted flan tin. Bake blind in the oven at 200°C (400°F) mark 6 for 10-15 minutes, until set.

3 Arrange the cherries in the flan case. Mix 100 g (4 oz) icing sugar with the eggs, almonds and flavouring, then pour over cherries.

4 Bake at 170°C (325°F) mark 3 for 50-60 minutes, until the top is firm and golden. Serve hot or cold.

COOK'S TIP

Baking Blind is the term used to describe the cooking of pastry cases without any filling. The pastry may be partially prebaked to be cooked for a further period when filled, or completely cooked if the filling requires no further cooking.

Cut out a piece of greaseproof paper or foil larger than the pastry case. Prick the pastry base, lay the paper or foil in the pastry case and fill with baking beans.

For partially prebaked cases, bake in the oven at 200°C (400°F) mark 6 for 10-15 minutes until the pastry is just 'set'. Remove the paper and beans, then bake for a further 5 minutes until lightly coloured. Pastry cases which need complete baking should be returned to the oven for a further 15 minutes or until pale golden brown.

YORKSHIRE CURD TART

SERVES 8-10

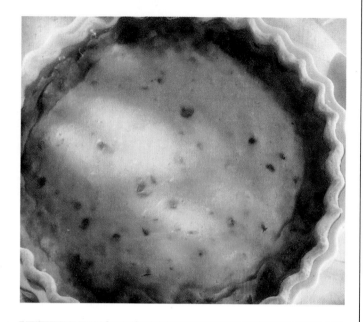

FOR THE PASTRY	FOR THE FILLING
225 g (8 oz) plain flour	450 g (1 lb) curd cheese
pinch of salt	3 eggs, beaten
150 g (5 oz) butter or block margarine	75 g (3 oz) currants
1 egg yolk	100 g (4 oz) demerara sugar
about 30 ml (2 tbsp) cold water	finely grated rind of 1 lemon

1 To make the pastry, place the flour and salt in a bowl, add 125 g (4 oz) of the fat and rub in until the mixture resembles fine breadcrumbs. Stir in the egg yolk and enough water to bind the mixture together. Form into a ball.
2 Roll out the pastry on a floured work surface. Use to line a 20 cm (8 inch) fluted flan dish or sandwich tin, then refrigerate while making the curd cheese filling.
3 Put the curd cheese in a bowl and stir in the eggs, followed by the currants, sugar and lemon rind. Melt the remaining fat and stir in until evenly mixed.
4 Pour the filling into the pastry case, place on a preheated baking sheet and bake in the oven at 190°C (375°F) mark 5 for 45 minutes or until the filling is golden and set. Serve the tart warm or cold.

OLD-FASHIONED TREACLE TART

SERVES 4-6

¾ quantity shortcrust pastry (see page 172)	finely grated rind and juice of 1 lemon
FOR THE FILLING	75 g (3 oz) fresh breadcrumbs
225 g (8 oz) golden syrup	beaten egg, to glaze

1 Roll out the pastry on a floured surface and use to line a 20 cm (8 inch) fluted flan dish. Reserve trimmings. Chill for 30 minutes.
2 Meanwhile, to make the filling, warm the golden syrup in a saucepan with the lemon rind and juice. Sprinkle the breadcrumbs evenly over the pastry base, then slowly pour in the syrup.
3 Make strips from the reserved pastry trimmings and place these over the tart in a lattice pattern, brushing the ends with water to stick them to the pastry case. Glaze with a little egg.
4 Bake in the oven at 190°C (375°F) mark 5 for about 25 minutes until the filling is just set. Serve warm.

COOK'S TIP

You may wonder why recipes for treacle tart always contain golden syrup rather than treacle. The explanation is quite simple. Treacle is the syrup which is left in the sugar refining process when the sugar has been crystallized. In the seventeenth century, when West Indian sugar cane was first refined to make sugar, treacle was unrefined and recipes for treacle tart such as this one would have used black treacle rather than syrup. It was not until the late nineteenth century that treacle was refined to make the golden syrup which is so popular today. As tastes changed, recipes which originally used treacle began to specify syrup instead.

FRESH PEAR SHORTCAKE

SERVES 6

FOR THE SHORTCAKE	FOR THE FILLING
150 g (5 oz) self-raising flour	3 ripe large, even-sized pears, about 450 g (1 lb) total weight
25 g (1 oz) ground rice	
grated rind of 1 lemon	125 g (4 oz) full fat soft cheese
50 g (2 oz) dark soft brown sugar	1 egg
150 g (5 oz) butter or block margarine	few drops of almond flavouring

1 Lightly grease a 20 cm (8 inch) loose-based fluted flan tin and set aside. In a mixing bowl, stir together the flour, ground rice and lemon rind. Sieve the sugar into the bowl.

2 Rub in the butter and continue lightly kneading the mixture until it forms a dough.

3 Press the dough into the prepared tin with floured fingertips. Mark into six portions and prick well with a fork.

4 Bake in the oven at 190°C (375°F) mark 5 for 30-35 minutes until golden brown and cooked through. Leave in the tin to cool slightly.

5 Using a sharp knife, peel and halve the pears. Scoop out the cores using a teaspoon or corer.

6 Cut each pear half crossways into 3 mm (⅛ inch) slices, keeping them together at one edge. Place a sliced pear half on each portion of shortcake, fanning out the slices a little.

7 Beat together the soft cheese, egg and almond flavouring until smooth, then spoon over the pears, completely covering fruit and shortcake.

8 Bake in the oven at 180°C (350°F) mark 4 for about 40 minutes until golden. Ease the shortcake out of the tin and serve warm or cold.

WALNUT AND HONEY TART

SERVES 6

FOR THE PASTRY	FOR THE FILLING
175 g (6 oz) plain wholemeal flour	60 ml (4 tbsp) clear honey
pinch of salt	75 g (3 oz) fresh wholemeal breadcrumbs
75 g (3 oz) butter	45 ml (3 tbsp) dark soft brown sugar
finely grated rind and juice of 1 orange	3 eggs
	100 g (4 oz) walnut pieces, roughly chopped

1 To make the pastry, put the flour and salt in a bowl and rub in the butter until the mixture resembles fine breadcrumbs. Stir in the orange rind and enough orange juice to bind the mixture together.

2 Roll out the pastry on a lightly floured surface and use to line a 20 cm (8 inch) fluted flan dish or tin. Bake blind at 200°C (400°F) mark 6 for 10-15 minutes, until set.

3 Mix the honey, breadcrumbs and the sugar together. Gradually beat in the eggs, one at a time, and any remaining orange juice.

4 Sprinkle the walnuts in the bottom of the pastry case and pour over the filling. Bake at 200°C (400°F) mark 6 for 20-25 minutes, until set. Cover the tart with greaseproof paper if it browns too quickly. Serve warm or cold with clotted or double cream.

BUTTERSCOTCH CREAM PIE

SERVES 6

175 g (6 oz) plain flour	150 ml (¼ pint) milk
1.25 ml (¼ tsp) salt	170 ml (6 fl oz) evaporated milk
165 g (5½ oz) butter or block margarine	50 g (2 oz) dark soft brown sugar
10 ml (2 tsp) caster sugar	15 ml (1 tbsp) cornflour
5 egg yolks and 1 egg white	150 ml (5 fl oz) double cream

1 Put the flour into a bowl with half the salt. Add 100 g (4 oz) fat in pieces and rub in with the fingertips until the mixture resembles fine breadcrumbs.

2 Stir in the sugar and 1 egg yolk and draw the dough together to form a ball. Add a few drops of cold water if the dough is too dry.

3 Press the dough gently into a 20 cm (8 inch) loose-bottomed fluted flan tin or ring placed on a baking sheet. Refrigerate for 30 minutes.

4 Prick the base of the pastry case and bake blind in the oven at 200°C (400°F) mark 6 for 10 minutes. Remove the foil and beans, brush the pastry with the egg white, then return to the oven and bake for a further 10 minutes until crisp and lightly coloured. Leave to cool.

5 To make the filling, put the milk and evaporated milk in a saucepan and bring to boiling point. Put the brown sugar, cornflour, remaining butter, egg yolks and salt in a saucepan. Heat gently until the butter has melted and sugar dissolved, then gradually stir in the scalded milk.

6 Cook over gentle heat, whisking constantly until the custard is thick. Don't worry if the mixture is lumpy at first – keep whisking vigorously with a balloon whisk and it will become smooth.

7 Remove from the heat and cool slightly, then pour into the baked pastry case. Leave until cold.

8 To serve, whip the cream until stiff, then pipe on top of the pie. Chill before serving.

OLDE ENGLISH EGG-NOG PIE

SERVES 6

175 g (6 oz) flour	1.25 ml (¼ level tsp) ground nutmeg
125 g (4 oz) butter	2 eggs separated
45 ml (3 level tbsp) ground almonds	15 ml (3 level tsp) powdered gelatine
90 ml (6 level tbsp) caster sugar	45 ml (3 tbsp) rum
300 ml (½ pint) milk plus 30 ml (2 tbsp)	90 ml (6 tbsp) double cream
	grated chocolate, to decorate

1 Put the flour into a bowl. Rub the butter into the flour, then stir in the ground almonds with 45 ml (3 level tbsp) sugar. Add about 30 ml (2 tbsp) milk to bind the mixture to a soft dough.

2 Roll out the pastry and use to line a deep 20 cm (8 inch) loose-bottomed flan tin. Bake blind in the oven at 200°C (400°F) mark 6 for 10-15 minutes. Leave to cool.

3 Gently heat the milk and nutmeg in a saucepan. Beat the egg yolks, 1 egg white and remaining sugar together. Pour on the heated milk, return to the pan and cook gently, stirring, until it thickens. Do not allow the mixture to boil.

4 Soak the gelatine in the rum. Stir into the hot custard to dissolve. Allow to cool until beginning to set.

5 Whip the cream until softly stiff. Whisk the remaining egg white until stiff. Fold the cream, then the egg white into the cool, half-set custard. Turn into a flan case and refrigerate to set.

6 Remove from the flan tin and leave for 30 minutes at room temperature. Decorate with grated chocolate.

PANADE

SERVES 6-8

175 g (6 oz) butter or margarine	700 g (1½ lb) ripe pears
225 g (8 oz) plain flour	grated rind and juice of 1 large orange
large pinch of ground cinnamon	beaten egg and caster sugar, for glazing
700 g (1½ lb) sweet eating apples	

1   Rub 125 g (4 oz) butter into the flour and cinnamon until the mixture resembles fine breadcrumbs. Add enough chilled water, about 90 ml (6 tbsp), to bind to a soft paste. Wrap and refrigerate for 10 minutes.

2   On a lightly floured surface, roll the dough out thinly and line a 24 cm (9½ inch) loose-based fluted flan tin. Re-roll the excess pastry and cut into 1 cm (½ inch) wide strips. Cover and chill until required. Bake the flan blind in the oven at 200°C (400°F) mark 6 for about 20 minutes.

3   Meanwhile, peel, core and grate the apples and pears. Melt the remaining butter in a large non-stick frying pan and stir in the grated apples and pears, the grated orange rind and 45 ml (3 tbsp) orange juice.

4   Cook over a high heat, stirring constantly, until all excess moisture has evaporated and the mixture is quite dry. Spoon into the warm flan case.

5   Quickly lattice the pastry strips over the fruit mixture. Brush with beaten egg and dust with caster sugar. Bake at 200°C (400°F) mark 6 for about 20 minutes, or until golden brown and crisp.

COOK'S NOTE

The boulangeries of Provence provide wonderful fruit tarts but there are local specialities to make at home too. Panade is unusual: apples and pears are grated, cooked together with orange juice, then enclosed in pastry or dough. The origins of this recipe are not hard to trace, with so many fruit trees covering the valleys.

ROLY-POLY WITH HOT JAM SAUCE

SERVES 4

FOR THE SUETCRUST PASTRY	little milk, for brushing
175 g (6 oz) self-raising flour	FOR THE SAUCE
1.25 ml (½ level tsp) salt	45 ml (3 level tbsp) red jam
75 g (3 oz) shredded suet	finely grated rind of 1 orange
about 100 ml (32 fl oz) chilled water	10 ml (2 tsp) arrowroot
FOR THE FILLING	150 ml (¼ pint) fresh orange juice
90 ml (6 tbsp) red jam	

1   To make the suetcrust pastry, mix the flour, salt and suet together in a bowl. Using a round-bladed knife, stir in enough water to give a light elastic dough. Knead lightly until smooth.

2   Roll out the pastry on a floured work surface to a 25 x 20 cm (10 x 8 inch) oblong. Spread the jam over the pastry to 5 mm (¼ inch) of the edges. Brush edges with milk.

3   Roll up the pastry evenly like a Swiss roll, starting from one short side.

4   Place the roll, seam side down, on a sheet of greased foil measuring at least 30 x 23 cm (12 x 9 inches). Wrap the foil loosely around the roll to allow room for expansion during cooking. Seal well.

5   Place the roly-poly in the top of a steamer over a pan of boiling water and steam for 1½-2 hours, topping up the water as necessary.

6   Just before serving, make the sauce. Put the jam and orange rind in a heavy-based saucepan. Mix the arrowroot to a paste with a little of the orange juice, then stir the remaining orange juice into the pan. Heat gently until the jam has melted, then stir in the arrowroot paste and bring to the boil. Simmer until thickened, stirring constantly.

7   Unwrap the roly-poly and place on a warmed serving plate. Pour over the hot jam sauce and serve immediately.

APPLE AND BLACKBERRY TART

SERVES 6

½ quantity shortcrust pastry (see page 172)	25 g (1 oz) sultanas
450 g (1 lb) cooking apples, peeled, cored and sliced	225 g (8 oz) blackberries, or 200 g (7 oz) can blackberries, drained
50 g (2 oz) butter	2.5 ml (½ level tsp) ground cinnamon
1 egg, separated	150 ml (5 fl oz) double cream
50 g (2 oz) soft brown sugar	

1 Roll out the pastry on a lightly floured surface and use to line a 20 cm (8 inch) flan ring. Arrange the apples in the flan case.

2 Melt the butter, remove from heat and cool. Beat in the egg yolk and add the sugar, sultanas, blackberries, cinnamon and butter. Mix well together and place in the flan case.

3 Bake in the oven at 200°C (400°F) mark 6 for 30-35 minutes. Allow to cool.

4 Whip the cream until softly stiff. Whip the egg white until stiff and fold into the cream. Pile on top of the tart to serve.

SERVING SUGGESTION

Apples and blackberries are two delicious fruits which are traditionally cooked together in old-fashioned tarts and pies. Topped with a delicious creamy swirl, this lovely pudding, with a hint of cinnamon, makes a mouthwatering end to a late summer or early autumn meal.

LIME MERINGUE PIE

SERVES 6

1 quantity shortcrust pastry (see page 172)	45 ml (3 tbsp) cornflour
finely grated rind and juice of 2 limes	2 eggs, separated
	knob of butter
75 g (3 oz) granulated sugar	125 g (4 oz) caster sugar
	lime slices, to decorate

1 Roll out the pastry on a lightly floured work surface and use to line a 20 cm (8 inch) flan ring. Refrigerate for 30 minutes.

2 Bake blind in the oven at 200°C (400°F) mark 6 for 10-15 minutes.

3 Put the lime rind into a small saucepan. Strain the juice, make up to 300 ml (½ pint) with water and add to the pan with the granulated sugar. Heat gently to dissolve the sugar.

4 Blend the cornflour with 30 ml (2 tbsp) water to a smooth paste. Add some of the heated liquid and stir. Return to the pan and boil for 2 minutes, stirring all the time. Cool slightly, then beat in the egg yolks and butter. Pour into the warm pastry case.

5 Whisk the egg whites until stiff, then fold in the caster sugar. Spread a thin layer of meringue over the pie, then pipe the rest around the edge.

6 Bake in the oven at 150°C (300°F) mark 2 for about 45 minutes until the meringue is crisp and lightly browned.

7 Decorate with lime slices. Serve warm, with cream.

PINEAPPLE TARTE TATIN

SERVES 6

50 g (2 oz) caster sugar	60 ml (4 tbsp) double cream
175 g (6 oz) butter or margarine	900 g (2 lb) pineapple, peeled, cored and thinly sliced
2 egg yolks	15 ml (1 tbsp) kirsch (optional)
125 g (4 oz) self-raising flour	mint sprigs, to decorate
125 g (4 oz) granulated sugar	

1   Beat the caster sugar with 50 g (2 oz) of the butter until pale and light. Beat in the egg yolks, then fold in the flour and knead lightly together to form a smooth dough. Wrap and chill in the refrigerator for 30 minutes.

2   Melt the remaining 125 g (4 oz) butter with the granulated sugar in a small saucepan over a low heat. Bring to the boil, then simmer for 3-4 minutes, beating continuously until the mixture is smooth, dark and fudge-like. (Do not worry if the mixture separates at this stage.)

3   Take off the heat, allow to cool for 1 minute, then stir in the cream, beating until smooth. If necessary, warm gently, stirring, until completely smooth. Spoon into a shallow 22 cm (8½ inch) round non-stick sandwich tin.

4   Arrange the pineapple neatly in overlapping circles on the fudge mixture. Drizzle over the kirsch if wished.

5   Roll out the prepared pastry to a 25 cm (10 inch) round. Place over the pineapple, tucking and pushing the edges down the side of the tin. Trim off any excess pastry. Stand the tin on a baking sheet.

6   Bake in the oven at 200°C (400°F) mark 6 for about 20 minutes or until the pastry is a deep golden brown. Run the blade of a knife around the edge of the tin to loosen the pastry. Leave to cool for 2-3 minutes, then turn out onto a heatproof serving dish and place under a hot grill for 2-3 minutes to caramelize the top.

7   Decorate with mint sprigs and serve with thick yogurt, or cream.

LEMON MERINGUE PIE

SERVES 4-6

¾ quantity shortcrust pastry (see page 172)	125 g (4 oz) granulated sugar
finely grated rind and juice of 2 lemons	75 ml (5 level tbsp) cornflour
	2 eggs, separated
	75 g (3 oz) caster sugar

1   Roll out the pastry on a floured surface and use to line a 20 cm (8 inch) loose-based flan tin or fluted flan dish. Chill in the refrigerator for 30 minutes.

2   Bake blind in the oven at 200°C (400°F) mark 6 for 10-15 minutes, then remove the paper and beans and bake for a further 5 minutes until the base is firm.

3   Put the lemon rind and juice, granulated sugar and 300 ml (½ pint) water in a saucepan. Heat gently until the sugar dissolves.

4   Mix the cornflour to a smooth paste with 90 ml (6 tbsp) water and stir into the saucepan until well blended. Bring to the boil, stirring and cook for 1 minute, until thickened.

5   Cool slightly, then beat in the egg yolks, one at a time.

6   Pour the warm lemon filling into the pastry case, levelling the surface.

7   Whisk the egg whites until stiff. Whisk in half the caster sugar a little at a time, then carefully fold in the remainder.

8   Spoon the meringue on to the filling and swirl with a palette knife. The filling must be completely covered, but the meringue should not overlap the edge of the flan tin. Bake in the oven at 150°C (300°F) mark 2 for about 35 minutes. Allow to cool before serving.

RASPBERRY AND APPLE TORTE

SERVES 8

450 g (1 lb) eating apples	225 g (8 oz) plain flour
150 g (5 oz) butter or block margarine	10 ml (2 level tsp) ground cinnamon
450 g (1 lb) raspberries, hulled	25 g (1 oz) icing sugar
	1 egg, separated
65 g (2½ oz) demerara sugar	45 ml (3 tbsp) water
5 ml (1 tsp) lemon juice	few raspberries (optional)

1 Peel, core and roughly chop the apples. Melt 25 g (1 oz) butter in a medium saucepan, then add the apples, raspberries and 50 g (2 oz) demerara sugar. Heat gently until the sugar dissolves. Increase the heat and cook, stirring, for about 10 minutes or until the apples are soft.

2 Turn the mixture into a bowl, stir in the lemon juice and cool for 30 minutes.

3 Meanwhile, sift the flour and cinnamon into a mixing bowl. Rub in the remaining butter until the mixture resembles fine breadcrumbs. Stir in the icing sugar. Mix the egg yolk with the water and stir into the pastry mixture; knead lightly.

4 Roll out two-thirds of the pastry and use to line a 23 cm (9 inch) fluted flan dish. Spoon in the raspberry and apple mixture.

5 Roll out the remaining pastry and cut into 1 cm (½ inch) wide strips long enough to make a lattice. Place over the filling and trim to fit.

6 Place on a baking sheet and bake in the oven at 200°C (400°F) mark 6 for about 15 minutes or until the pastry is set but not browned.

7 Lightly whisk the egg white and brush over the lattice; sprinkle with remaining demerara sugar.

8 Return to the oven for a further 15-20 minutes or until browned. Chill for 2-3 hours before serving. Decorate with a few raspberries, if wished.

PLUM AND ALMOND TORTE

SERVES 8

1 quantity shortcrust pastry (see page 172)	2. 5 ml (½ tsp) almond flavouring
125 g (4 oz) butter	125 g (4 oz) self-raising flour
125 g (4 oz) caster sugar	30 ml (2 tbsp) lemon juice
1 egg, separated, plus 1 egg yolk	30 ml (2 tbsp) milk
	90 ml (6 level tbsp) plum jam
25 g (1 oz) ground almonds	25 g (1 oz) flaked almonds

1 Base-line a 22 cm (8½ inch) straight-sided sandwich tin with greaseproof paper. Roll out the pastry and use to line the tin; prick well with a fork. Bake blind in the oven at 200°C (400°F) mark 6 for 10-15 minutes until just set.

2 Ceam the butter and sugar until pale and fluffy. Gradually beat in the egg yolks one by one, then stir in the ground almonds and flavouring.

3 Fold in the flour, lemon juice and milk. Whisk one egg white and gently fold into the mixture.

4 Spread the jam over the pastry base. Spoon over the cake mixture, level the surface and sprinkle with flaked almonds.

5 Bake in the oven at 180°C (350°F) mark 4 until golden brown and firm to the touch, about 30 minutes. Cool in the tin. Serve cold.

COOK'S TIP

When rolling out pastry, dust the work surface and the rolling pin, never the pastry, with as little flour as possible. Roll the dough lightly and evenly in one direction only. Always roll away from you, rotating the pastry frequently to keep an even shape. Use light but firm strokes. Over-rolled pastry will shrink dramatically when baked.

STRAWBERRY CUSTARD FLAN

SERVES 6-8

1½ quantity flan pastry (see page 172)	2 eggs, separated
FOR THE FILLING	75 g (3 oz) caster sugar
40 g (1½ oz) cornflour	few drops of vanilla essence
450 ml (¾ pint) milk	350 g (12 oz) strawberries, hulled

1 Roll out the pastry on a floured work surface and use to line a 23 cm (9 inch) flan dish. Chill for 30 minutes. Prick the base of the flan.

2 Bake blind in the oven at 200°C (400°F) mark 6 for 20 minutes or until pale golden and cooked through. Cool in the dish for 30-40 minutes.

3 To make the filling, mix the cornflour to a smooth paste with a little of the milk. Mix the egg yolks with the cornflour paste.

4 Put the rest of the milk in a saucepan with the sugar and vanilla essence. Bring to the boil. Remove from the heat and pour on to the cornflour mixture. Return to the pan, then bring to the boil, stirring, and boil for 2 minutes until thickened. Cover with damp greaseproof paper and leave to cool for 30 minutes.

5 Thinly slice the strawberries into the base of the pastry case, reserving a few for decoration. Whisk the egg whites until stiff, then fold into the cold custard mixture. Smooth the custard mixture evenly over the strawberries. Chill for 1 hour until set.

6 Serve the flan decorated with the reserved strawberry slices, preferably within 2 hours of completion.

SWISS FLAN

SERVES 6-8

1 quantity pâte sucrée (see page 172)	FOR THE MERINGUE
FOR THE FILLING	3 egg whites
225 g (8 oz) granulated sugar	175 g (6 oz) caster sugar
juice of 1 lemon	30 ml (2 tbsp) redcurrant jelly or seedless raspberry jam
900 g (2 lb) dessert apples	

1 Roll out the pastry on a lightly floured work surface to a round 2.5 cm (1 inch) larger than a 23 cm (9 inch) fluted flan tin. Line the tin with the pastry, pressing it well into the flutes. Trim the edge, then prick the pastry well, all over, with a fork. Chill for 30 minutes.

2 Bake blind in the oven at 220°C (425°F) mark 7 for 20- 25 minutes until cooked and lightly browned. Cool. Reduce the temperature to 140°C (275°F) mark 1.

3 To make the filling, put the sugar and lemon juice into a saucepan with the water. Heat gently until the sugar has dissolved, bring to the boil and simmer for 5 minutes.

4 Peel, quarter, core and slice the apples about 5 mm (¼ inch) thick. Add the apples slices, in batches, to the sugar syrup and poach until just tender. Lift out with a slotted spoon and drain on absorbent kitchen paper.

5 Arrange the apple slices neatly inside the flan case.

6 To make the meringue, put the egg whites and sugar into a bowl standing over a pan of simmering water. Whisk until stiff. Remove from the heat and continue whisking until the meringue forms stiff peaks.

7 Put the meringue into a piping bag fitted with a large star nozzle, then pipe stars over the top of the apple flan.

8 Bake in the oven for 1 hour until the meringue is set, but not browned – it must remain as white as possible.

9 Put the redcurrant jelly into a small paper piping bag and cut a small hole in the tip of the bag. Pipe a small bead of jelly on the tip of every meringue star. Serve the flan warm or cold.

HAZELNUT CARTWHEEL

SERVES 8

212 g (7½ oz) packet frozen puff pastry, thawed	75 g (3 oz) hazelnuts, chopped
25 g (1 oz) butter	50 g (2 oz) raisins
25 g (1 oz) light soft brown sugar	finely grated rind of 1 lemon
1 egg, beaten	1 egg, beaten, to glaze
75 g (3 oz) plain cake crumbs	caster sugar, to dredge

1 Roll out the pastry on a lightly floured surface to a rectangle about 40 x 25 cm (16 x 10 inches). Cream the butter and sugar together until pale and fluffy, then beat in the egg and stir in the cake crumbs, hazelnuts, raisins and lemon rind. Spread the mixture over the pastry to within 5 mm (¼ inch) of the edges.
2 Roll up like a Swiss roll starting from the narrow end. Trim the ends, if necessary.
3 Place on a dampened baking sheet and curl round into a circle. Seal the ends together.
4 Snip all round the ring at 4 cm (1½ inch) intervals so the cuts come to within about 2 cm (¾ inch) of the ring's inner edge. Brush with beaten egg to glaze. Bake at 220°C (425°F) mark 7 for 25-30 minutes, until golden brown.
5 Dredge with caster sugar and serve warm.

SPICED PEAR STRUDEL

SERVES 8

75 g (3 oz) fresh white breadcrumbs	450 g (1 lb) pears, peeled, cored and sliced
150 g (5 oz) unsalted butter	4 large sheets of filo pastry
50 g (2 oz) light soft brown sugar	50 g (2 oz) blanched almonds, toasted and chopped
50 g (2 oz) sultanas	15 ml (1 tbsp) redcurrant jelly (optional)
2.5 ml (½ level tsp) ground mixed spice	icing sugar, for dusting
2.5 ml (½ level tsp) ground cinnamon	

1 Fry the breadcrumbs in 50 g (2 oz) of the butter, stirring frequently until crisp and golden. Mix together the brown sugar, sultanas, mixed spice, cinnamon and pear slices.
2 Melt remaining butter. Brush one sheet of filo pastry with a little of the melted butter. Cover with a second sheet of pastry and brush with a little more melted butter.
3 Cover the pastry with half of the fried crumbs, leaving a 5 cm (2 inch) border on all sides. Arrange half the pear mixture over the crumbs and sprinkle with half of the almonds. Dot with half of the redcurrant jelly, if using.
4 Fold the edges over the filling and brush with a little melted butter. Roll up, like a Swiss roll, starting from a long side. Place the strudel on a lightly greased baking sheet (with raised edges) and brush with melted butter.
5 Make a second strudel in the same way using the remaining ingredients.
6 Bake at 190°C (375°F) mark 5 for 35 minutes until crisp and golden, covering with foil during cooking if necessary, to prevent over-browning. Brush halfway through cooking, with butter from the baking sheet.
7 Allow the strudels to cool slightly, then sprinkle liberally with sifted icing sugar. Serve warm or cold, cut into chunky slices, with yogurt or cream.

CARAMELIZED APPLE WAFER

SERVES 6

212 g (7½ oz) packet frozen puff pastry, thawed	75 g (3 oz) butter or margarine, melted
6 small Granny Smith apples, total weight about 450-700 g (1-1½ lb)	60 ml (4 level tbsp) demerara sugar

1 Cut the pastry into two equal pieces. Roll out each half very thinly on a lightly floured work surface to a rectangle measuring about 20 x 10 cm (8 x 4 inches). Trim the edges. Place on a baking sheet.
2 Peel, halve and core the apples. Thinly slice the apple halves but not quite through to the base; the apples should still keep their shape.
3 Evenly space six halves flat side down on each pastry base. Cut each pastry base into three.
4 Brush the apple with the butter and sprinkle over the sugar.
5 Bake in the oven at 230°C (450°F) mark 8 for about 20 minutes or until the pastry is risen and golden. The apples should be quite soft and caramelized. Serve immediately with soured cream, Greek yogurt or crème fraîche.

COOK'S TIP

The richest of all the pastries, puff gives the most even rising, the most flaky effect and the crispest texture, but because of the time it takes, most people make it only occasionally. Bought puff pastry, either chilled or frozen, is very satisfactory, but remember to only roll it out to a maximum thickness of 3 mm (⅛ inch), as it rises very well.
'First rollings' are used where appearance is important. 'Second rollings' (usually the trimmings) can be used where appearance is not so important.

CLEMENTINE BISCUITS WITH APRICOT SAUCE

SERVES 6

75 g (3 oz) plain flour	drop of vanilla essence
pinch of salt	10 ml (2 tsp) brandy
2 egg whites, lightly whisked	30 ml (2 level tbsp) ground almonds
75 g (3 oz) icing sugar, sifted	150 ml (¼ pint) double cream, whipped
57g (2¼ oz) unsalted butter, melted	6-9 clementines peeled, seeded and segmented
icing sugar, for dusting	
FOR THE FILLING	FOR THE APRICOT SAUCE
65 ml (2½ fl oz) milk	50 g (2 oz) sugar
2.5 ml (½ tsp) cornflour	225 g (8 oz) dried apricots, soaked overnight
1 egg yolk	
20-25 g (¾-1 oz) caster sugar	squeeze of lemon juice

1 To make the biscuits, mix flour, salt, egg whites and icing sugar together in a bowl. Stir in the melted butter.
2 Spoon the mixture in 12 equal rounds, spaced a little way apart on lined and greased baking sheets.
3 Bake in the oven at 180°C (350°F) mark 4 for about 10 minutes until light golden. Leave to cool on a wire rack.
4 To make the filling, heat milk to boiling point in a pan. Blend the cornflour with the egg yolk, then stir in the hot milk. Pour into a pan and cook over a low heat, stirring, until the sauce thickens. Remove from the heat and stir in the sugar, vanilla, brandy and ground almonds.
5 Cover and leave to cool. When cold, fold in the cream.
6 To make the sauce, dissolve the sugar in about 60 ml (4 tbsp) water in a pan. Add the drained apricots and lemon juice, then simmer until soft. Purée in a blender or food processor, then leave to cool. Chill.
7 To assemble the dessert, place 6 biscuits on 6 plates. Cover with the filling, then top with clementine segments. Place the remaining biscuits on top and dust with icing sugar. Score with a hot skewer and surround with the apricot sauce to serve.

APPLE AND HAZELNUT LAYER

SERVES 8

75 g (3 oz) hazelnuts, shelled	15 ml (1 tbsp) apricot jam or marmalade
75 g (3 oz) butter	grated rind of 1 lemon
45 ml (3 level tbsp) caster sugar	15 ml (1 level tbsp) candied peel, chopped
115 g (4½ oz) plain flour	30 ml (2 level tbsp) currants
pinch of salt	30 ml (2 level tbsp) sultanas
450 g (1 lb) Cox's apples, peeled, cored and sliced	icing sugar, whipped cream and hazelnuts, to decorate

1 Cut out two 20 cm (8 inch) circles of greaseproof paper. Reserve 8 nuts and finely chop the remainder.

2 Cream the butter and sugar until pale and fluffy. Stir in the flour, salt and chopped nuts, then form into a ball and chill for 30 minutes.

3 Put the apples in a saucepan with the jam and lemon rind and cook over a low heat for 5 minutes, until soft. Add the candied peel and dried fruit and simmer for 5 minutes.

4 Divide the pastry in half, place on the sheets of greaseproof paper and roll out into two circles. Transfer to greased baking sheets.

5 Bake at 190°C (375°F) mark 5 for 7-10 minutes, until light brown. Cut one circle into 8 triangles while warm. Leave to cool.

6 Just before serving, place the complete circle on a serving plate and cover with the apple mixture. Arrange the triangles on top. Dust with icing sugar, pipe cream on top and decorate with hazelnuts.

ECLAIRS

MAKES 12

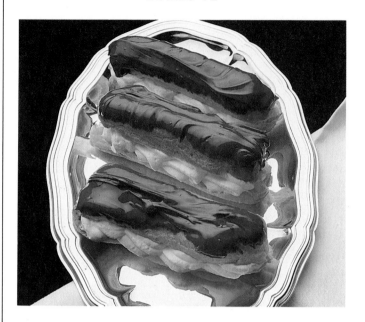

FOR THE CHOUX PASTRY	FOR THE FILLING AND TOPPING
65 g (2½ oz) plain or strong white flour	300 ml (10 fl oz) double cream
50 g (2 oz) butter or block margarine	125 g (4 oz) plain chocolate
150 ml (¼ pint) water	
2 eggs, lightly beaten	

1 Sift the flour on to a plate or piece of paper. Put the fat and water together in a saucepan, heat gently until the fat has melted, then bring to the boil. Remove the pan from the heat. Tip the flour at once into the hot liquid. Beat thoroughly with a wooden spoon.

2 Continue beating the mixture until it is smooth and forms a ball in the centre of the pan (take care not to overbeat or the mixture will become fatty). Leave the mixture to cool for 1-2 minutes.

3 Beat in the eggs a little at a time, adding just enough to give a piping consistency. It is important to beat vigorously at this stage to trap in as much air as possible.

4 Dampen a baking sheet. Put the choux pastry into a piping bag fitted with a medium plain nozzle and pipe 9 cm (3½ inches) lengths on to the baking sheet. Trim with a wet knife.

5 Bake in the oven at 200°C (400°F) mark 6 for about 35 minutes, until crisp and golden.

6 Make a slit down the side of each bun with a sharp, pointed knife to release the steam, then transfer to a wire rack and leave for 20-30 minutes to cool completely.

7 Just before serving, whip the double cream until stiff and use it to fill the éclairs.

8 Break the chocolate into a bowl and place over simmering water. Stir until melted. Pour into a wide shallow bowl. Dip in the tops of the filled éclairs, drawing each one across the surface of the chocolate to coat evenly.

MINCE PIES

MAKES ABOUT 20

1 quantity shortcrust pastry (see page 172)	icing or caster sugar, for dusting
350-450 g (12 oz–1 lb) mincemeat	

1 Roll out the pastry on a floured surface to about 3 mm (⅛ inch) thickness.
2 Cut out about 20 rounds with a 7.5 cm (3 inch) fluted cutter and 20 smaller rounds with a 5.5 cm (2¼ inch) fluted cutter.
3 Line 6 cm (2½ inch) patty tins with the larger rounds and fill with mincemeat. Dampen the edges of the small rounds with water and place firmly on top. Make a small slit in each top.
4 Bake in the oven at 220°C (425°F) mark 7 for 15-20 minutes, until light golden brown. Leave to cool on a wire rack. Serve dusted with sugar.

VARIATION

Puff Pastry Mince Pies

Mince pies can be made using a 368 g (13 oz) packet puff pastry. Roll out the pastry to 3 mm (⅛ inch) thickness. Cut 16 rounds with a 6 cm (2½ inch) cutter. Re-roll trimmings; cut another 16 rounds to use for the bases.
Place the bases on a dampened baking sheet. Put a heaped 5 ml (1 tsp) mincemeat on each and dampen the pastry edges. Cover with the remaining rounds and press the edges lightly together; glaze with beaten egg. Bake in the oven at 230°C (450°F) mark 8 for about 20 minutes.

FRESH FRUIT TARTLETS

MAKES 12

2 x quantity pâte sucrée pastry (see page 172)	125 g (4 oz) green grapes, halved and seeded
300 ml (½ pin) crème pâtissière (see page 172)	2 kiwi fruit, peeled and sliced
125 g (4 oz) strawberries, sliced	FOR THE APRICOT GLAZE
125 g (4 oz) raspberries	225 g (8 oz) apricot conserve
	15 ml (1 tbsp) kirsch
125 g (4 oz) black grapes, halved and seeded	FOR THE REDCURRANT GLAZE
	125 g (4 oz) redcurrant jelly

1 Roll out the pastry on a lightly floured surface and cut out twelve 12 cm (5 inch) circles with a plain cutter. Use to line twelve 10 cm (4 inch) tartlet tins. Trim the edges and prick the base of each tartlet with a fork, then place the lined tins on baking sheets and chill for at least 30 minutes.
2 Bake blind in the oven at 200°C (400°F) mark 6 for 20-25 minutes until very lightly browned. Allow the cases to cool a little in their tins, then carefully transfer to a wire rack to cool.
3 To make the apricot glaze, put the jam and kirsch in a saucepan and heat gently until softened, then simmer for 1 minute. Sieve, then brush evenly over the inside of each pastry case. Reserve the remaining glaze.
4 Divide the crème pâtissière equally between the pastry cases and spread it evenly. Arrange the fruit in the pastry cases.
5 Reheat the remaining apricot glaze until boiling, then carefully brush it over the green grapes and the kiwi fruit to glaze them evenly. Heat the redcurrant jelly until boiling, then carefully brush it over the strawberries, raspberries and black grapes. Serve as soon as possible.

VARIATION

Sprinkle the glazed tartlets with finely chopped nuts or a few toasted almonds.

FRUIT DESSERTS

Make the most of flavourful fresh fruits in season with these delicious recipes. Refreshing fruit salads, tangy fruit jellies and light, creamy mousses are perfect for summer days. Sustaining steamed puddings and crumbles will satisfy winter appetites.

FRUDITES

SERVES 6

2 crisp eating apples	juice of 1 lemon
2 bananas	FOR THE DIP
225 g (8 oz) apricots, stoned	150 ml (¼ pint) double cream
175 g (6 oz) black or green grapes, seeded	150 ml (¼ pint) soured cream
225 g (8 oz) strawberries	30 ml (2 tbsp) icing sugar, sifted

1   To make the dip, whip the two creams and icing sugar together in a bowl until standing in soft peaks. Pipe or spoon into six individual dishes.
2   Quarter and core the apples, but do not peel them. Peel the bananas and cut into 4 cm (1½ inch) chunks.
3   Arrange the fruit on individual serving plates and sprinkle immediately with lemon juice to prevent discoloration.
4   Place the dishes of cream dip next to the fruit and serve immediately. Use fingers or small fondue forks to dunk the fruit into the cream dip.

THREE FRUIT SALAD

SERVES 8

50 g (2 oz) granulated sugar	1 pineapple, weighing about 1.1 kg (2½ lb)
15 ml (1 tbsp) lemon juice	225 g (8 oz) black grapes
15 ml (1 tbsp) kirsch	4 kiwi fruit

1   Put the sugar in a heavy-based saucepan with 150 ml (¼ pint) water. Heat gently until the sugar has dissolved, then bring to the boil and bubble for 2 minutes. Remove from the heat, stir in the lemon juice and kirsch, then set aside to cool.
2   Prepare the pineapple. With a sharp knife, cut off the leafy top and discard. Cut the pineapple into 1 cm (½ inch) pieces. Cut off the skin and dig out the 'eyes' with the tip of the knife. Cut out the core from each slice with an apple corer or small biscuit cutter. Cut the flesh into chunks.
3   Wash and dry the grapes, then halve. Remove the pips by flicking them out with the point of a sharp knife.
4   Peel the kiwi fruit using a potato peeler or sharp knife, then slice the flesh thinly.
5   Stir the prepared fruits into the syrup, cover and chill well in the refrigerator before serving.

GINGER
FRUIT SALAD

SERVES 4

2 apricots	50 g (2 oz) green grapes
2 dessert apples	2 bananas
1 orange	30 ml (2 tbsp) lemon juice
241 ml (8½ fl oz) bottle low-calorie ginger ale	

1   Prepare the fruits to be macerated. Plunge the apricots into a bowl of boiling water for 30 seconds. Drain and peel off the skin with your fingers.
2   Halve the apricots, remove the stones and dice the flesh. Core and dice the apples, but do not peel them. Peel the orange and divide into segments, discarding all white pith.
3   Put the prepared fruits in a serving bowl with the ginger ale. Stir lightly, then cover and leave to macerate for 1 hour.
4   Cut the grapes in half, then remove the seeds by flicking them out with the point of a knife.
5   Peel and slice the bananas and mix them with the lemon juice to prevent discoloration.
6   Add the grapes and bananas to the macerated fruits. Serve in individual glasses, topped with a spoonful of natural yogurt, if desired.

FRAGRANT
FRUIT SALAD

SERVES 8

50 g (2 oz) caster sugar	700 g (1½ lb) lychees
grated rind and juice of 1 lemon	3 ripe mangoes, peeled
2 stem ginger (from a jar of ginger in syrup), finely chopped	450 g (1 lb) fresh or canned pineapple in natural juice
	4 ripe kiwi fruit, peeled
60 ml (4 tbsp) ginger wine	50g (2 oz) Cape gooseberries, to decorate (optional)

1   Put the sugar in a pan with 150 ml (¼ pint) water and the lemon rind and juice. Heat gently until the sugar dissolves. Bring to the boil and simmer for 1 minute. Remove from the heat and stir in the chopped ginger and wine. Leave to cool.
2   Peel the lychees, cut in half and remove the shiny stones. Cut the mango flesh away from the stones. Cut the flesh into cubes.
3   If using fresh pineapple, peel, slice and remove the tough centre from each slice. Cut the pineapple slices into cubes. Thinly slice the kiwi fruit and halve the slices.
4   Mix together the fruit and syrup. Cover and refrigerate for several hours to allow the flavours to develop. If using Cape gooseberries, peel back each calyx to form a 'flower'; clean the orange berry by wiping with a damp cloth. Arrange on top of the fruit salad to serve.

INDIAN FRUIT SALAD

SERVES 6-8

3 ripe peaches	5 ml (1 level tsp) cumin seeds, dry fried
2 ripe guavas	30 ml (2 tbsp) lemon or lime juice
2 ripe bananas	pinch of cayenne
45 ml (3 tbsp) caster sugar	mint sprigs, to decorate

1   To skin the peaches, plunge them into a bowl of boiling water, leave for 30 seconds, then remove the skins.
2   Cut the skinned peaches in half and remove the stones. Slice the peach flesh thinly and place in a serving bowl.
3   Cut the guavas in half, scoop out the seeds and discard them. Peel the halved guavas, then slice them neatly and add to the peaches in the bowl.
4   Peel the bananas, cut into chunks, then mix carefully with the peaches, guavas and remaining ingredients. Serve immediately, decorated with sprigs of mint.

COOK'S TIP

Fresh guavas are available at specialist greengrocers, Indian stores and larger supermarkets. Guavas are a tropical fruit, originally from South America, with a pretty cream-pink skin. The flesh has a delicately scented aroma and a most delicious flavour. The seeds in the centre are not edible and should be removed before serving the fruit.

SPICED DRIED FRUIT COMPOTE

SERVES 4

15 ml (1 level tbsp) jasmine tea	100 g (4 oz) dried prunes, soaked overnight, drained and stoned
2.5 ml (½ level tsp) ground cinnamon	100 g (4 oz) dried apple rings
1.25 ml (¼ level tsp) ground cloves	150 ml (¼ pint) dry white wine
300 ml (½ pint) boiling water	50 g (2 oz) sugar
100 g (4 oz) dried apricots, soaked overnight, drained	toasted flaked almonds, to decorate

1   Put the tea, cinnamon and cloves in a bowl; pour in the boiling water. Leave for 20 minutes.
2   Put the dried fruit in a saucepan, then strain in the tea and spice liquid. Add the wine and sugar; heat gently until the sugar has dissolved.
3   Simmer for 20 minutes until tender, then cover and leave for 1-2 hours until cold.
4   Turn the compote into a serving bowl and chill for at least 2 hours. Sprinkle with almonds just before serving.

AUTUMN COMPOTE

SERVES 6-8

225 g (8 oz) granulated sugar	450 g (1 lb) dessert apples, such as Cox or Russet
juice of 1 lemon	
450 g (1 lb) small ripe, but firm pears	450 g (1 lb) Victoria plums, skinned and stoned

1 To make the sugar syrup, put the sugar, lemon juice and 300 ml (½ pint) cold water in a saucepan. Heat very gently until the sugar has completely dissolved. Bring to the boil and boil the syrup for 1 minute.
2 Thinly peel the pears, cut into half and remove the centre core (if only large pears are available, cut the pears into quarters). Add the pears to the syrup and cook very gently for about 10-15 minutes until barely tender.
3 Meanwhile core the apples. Cut the apples into halves, then cut into slices across the halves. Add the apple slices to the pan and cook for about 5 minutes until the apple slices are just tender. Add the plums and cook for a further 5 minutes.
4 Carefully transfer the fruits and syrup to a serving bowl, taking care not to break up the fruit. Serve hot or cold, with yogurt or cream if desired.

COOK'S TIP

Select very small pears for this compote. Lemon juice added to the syrup prevents the pears and apples discolouring, and adds a tangy flavour.

SUMMER CURRANT COMPOTE

SERVES 6

50-75 g (2-3 oz) granulated sugar	pared rind and juice of 1 medium orange
225 g (8 oz) blackcurrants, stalks removed	30 ml (2 tbsp) honey
450 g (1 lb) redcurrants, stalks removed	350 g (12 oz) strawberries, hulled and sliced

1 Dissolve the sugar in 150 ml (¼ pint) water in a pan. Boil for 1 minute. (Alternatively, microwave on HIGH for 3 minutes, stirring frequently. Continue to microwave on HIGH for 1 minute.)
2 Add the currants and orange rind and simmer until the fruits are just beginning to soften – about 1 minute only. (If cooking in the microwave, microwave on HIGH for 1-2 minutes or until beginning to soften.)
3 Carefully transfer the fruits and syrup to a serving bowl. Stir in the honey and leave to cool.
4 Mix in the orange juice, cover and chill well.
5 Just before serving, stir the sliced strawberries into the compote.

COOK'S TIP

Compotes are mixtures of fruits cooked in sugar syrup, which can be served hot or cold. The syrup may be flavoured with spices or with orange and lemon rind, but the fruits, being quite highly flavoured themselves, require little or no extra flavouring. Hot compotes make perfect desserts for the winter, not only because they are warming, but also because they are full of vitamins. Chilled compotes will keep well for up to a week in the refrigerator.

STRAWBERRIES WITH RASPBERRY SAUCE

SERVES 6

900 g (2 lb) small strawberries	450 g (1 lb) raspberries
	50 g (2 oz) icing sugar

1 Hull the strawberries and place them in individual serving dishes.
2 Purée the raspberries in a blender or food processor until just smooth, then work through a nylon sieve into a bowl to remove the pips.
3 Sift the icing sugar over the bowl of raspberry purée, then whisk in until evenly incorporated. Pour over the strawberries. Chill in the refrigerator for at least 30 minutes before serving.

COOK'S TIP

Freshly picked raspberries freeze successfully (unlike strawberries which tend to lose texture and shape due to their high water content). If you have raspberries which are slightly overripe or misshapen, the best way to freeze them is as a purée; this takes up less space in the freezer and is immensely useful for making quick desserts and sauces at the last minute. For this recipe, for example, you can freeze the purée up to 12 months in advance, then it will only take minutes to assemble the dessert after thawing the purée.

AMARETTI STUFFED PEACHES

SERVES 4

4 yellow peaches, skinned	25 g (1 oz) butter
50 g (2 oz) Amaretti or macaroons	25 g (1 oz) sugar
1 egg yolk	150 ml (¼ pint) dry white wine

1 Lightly grease an ovenproof dish.
2 Cut the peaches in half and carefully ease out the stones. Make the hollows in the peaches a little deeper with a sharp-edged teaspoon and reserve the removed flesh.
3 Crush the macaroons and mix them with the reserved peach flesh, the egg yolk, butter and 15 g (½ oz) of the sugar.
4 Use this mixture to stuff the hollows of the peach halves, mounding the filling slightly. Place the peaches in the prepared ovenproof dish and sprinkle with the rest of the sugar. Pour the white wine over and around the peaches.
5 Bake in the oven at 180°C (350°F) mark 4 for 25-30 minutes or until tender. (Alternatively, arrange around the edge of a large shallow dish, cover and microwave on HIGH for 3-5 minutes or until tender. Leave to stand, covered, for 5 minutes.) Serve hot or cold.

COOK'S TIP

Amaretti are almond macaroons made in Italy. They are available at Italian delicatessens, both in boxes and individually wrapped in tissue paper. Amaretti are delicious served with coffee and liqueurs at the end of a meal. If you cannot find them, use shop bought or home-made macaroons instead.

WHISKY MARINATED GRAPES

SERVES 6

350 g (12 oz) black grapes	45 ml (3 tbsp) clear honey
350 g (12 oz) green grapes	5 ml (1 tsp) lemon juice
30 ml (2 tbsp) whisky	

1 Wash the grapes, drain well and dry with absorbent kitchen paper.
2 Cut the grapes carefully in half lengthways, then ease out the pips with the point of a knife.
3 In a large mixing bowl, stir together the whisky, honey and lemon juice. Add the grapes and stir well. Cover and leave in a cool place (not the refrigerator) to marinate for at least 4 hours, preferably overnight.
4 Spoon into a serving dish and chill in the refrigerator for 30 minutes before serving. Serve with yogurt or cream.

COOK'S TIP

When choosing grapes for eating, avoid fruit which is shiny; fresh grapes should have a powdery whitish bloom on their skin. For this recipe, try to buy the seedless green grapes, which will save you time on preparation.

RØDGRØD

SERVES 4-6

450 g (1 lb) redcurrants or blackcurrants, stalks removed	100-175 g (4-6 oz) caster sugar
450 g (1 lb) raspberries or strawberries, hulled, or cherries, stoned	TO DECORATE whipped cream mint sprigs
30 ml (2 tbsp) arrowroot	

1 Place the currants and 60 ml (4 tbsp) water in a saucepan. Cover and simmer gently for about 20 minutes or until really soft. Leave to cool.
2 Meanwhile, purée half of the berries in a blender or food processor until smooth, then press through a nylon sieve.
3 Blend a little of the purée with the arrowroot. Put the rest into a pan and bring slowly to the boil. Stir into the blended mixture, then return it all to the pan. Bring to the boil again, cook for 4-5 minutes and sweeten to taste. Leave to cool for 10 minutes. Stir in the cooked currants and the remaining raspberries, strawberries or cherries.
4 Pour the Rødgrød into individual glasses and chill for 30 minutes. Top with whipped cream and mint sprigs just before serving.

COOK'S TIP

Rødgrød is a Danish dessert which essentially is a thick fruit soup. It is always made with fresh soft summer fruit, depending on what is available. An important point to remember is to mix at least two fruits together to provide good flavour and colour. In Russia, it is known as Kisel.

BOOZY BANANA

15 g (½ oz) butter or margarine	30 ml (2 tbsp) sherry
15 ml (1 tbsp) soft brown sugar	1.25 ml (¼ level tsp) ground cinnamon
30 ml (2 tbsp) freshly squeezed orange juice	1 banana
	orange twist, to decorate (optional)

1 Melt the butter in a heavy-based frying pan. Add the remaining ingredients, except the banana. Heat gently, stirring, until the sugar has dissolved.

2 Peel the banana, then cut in half lengthways. Place in the pan and cook over gentle heat for about 10 minutes until tender. Baste the banana frequently with the sauce and turn the pieces over once during cooking. Serve hot, decorated with an orange twist, if liked.

SERVING SUGGESTION

Serve with chilled cream or vanilla ice cream. Alternatively, if you prefer the combination of sweet and tart flavours, serve with Greek yogurt, Quark or fromage frais.

PLUM CROUTE

1 large slice of white bread	25 g (1 oz) demerara sugar
15 g (½ oz) butter or margarine, melted	1.25 ml (½ level tsp) ground cinnamon
2 ripe red plums, eg Victoria	

1 Cut the crusts off the slice of bread and discard. Brush both sides of the bread with the melted butter, making sure the bread is coated right to the edges.

2 Place the bread in an individual Yorkshire pudding tin, pressing it down well, but leaving the corners protruding over the edge.

3 Bake the croûte in the oven at 200°C (400°F) mark 6 for 15-20 minutes until crisp and golden brown.

4 Meanwhile, halve and stone the plums, then place in a pan with the sugar and cinnamon. Sprinkle in 5-10 ml (1-2 tsp) water, then cook gently for about 5 minutes until the plums are tender and juicy but still retaining their shape.

5 When the croûte is cooked, transfer to a serving plate. Spoon the plums in the centre and serve immediately, with chilled cream or thick Greek yogurt.

BRANDIED STUFFED APRICOTS

SERVES 4

16 small apricots	150 g (5 oz) cottage cheese
120 ml (8 tbsp) apricot brandy	50 g (2 oz) full fat soft cheese
30 ml (2 tbsp) caster sugar	15 ml (1 tbsp) icing sugar, sifted
finely grated rind and juice of 1 lemon	chopped toasted hazelnuts, to decorate

1 Place the apricots, brandy, caster sugar, 15 ml (1 tbsp) lemon juice and 150 ml (¼ pint) water in a saucepan. Poach gently for about 15 minutes until just tender. Remove the apricots and leave to cool for 30 minutes.
2 Boil the poaching liquid for 2-3 minutes until well reduced and syrupy. Leave to cool for 20 minutes.
3 Using a sharp knife, skin the apricots. Slice almost in half and remove the kernel.
4 Sieve the cottage cheese into a bowl, add the full fat soft cheese, icing sugar and grated lemon rind, then beat together until well mixed.
5 Sandwich the apricots together with a little of the cheese mixture. Divide the apricots between four individual glass dishes.
6 Spoon a little of the cooled syrup over the apricots. Chill for 2-3 hours, then decorate with chopped nuts before serving.

VARIATION

Smaller and more unusual than its relations the nectarine and peach, the apricot is highly prized for its unique flavour and aroma. Fresh apricots do not keep well and their season is short. If fresh apricots are not available, this recipe can be made with small peaches or nectarines, but as these are larger than apricots you will only need half the quantity.

PEARS IN HONEY AND CINNAMON

SERVES 4-6

60 ml (4 tbsp) white wine, vermouth or sherry	100 g (4 oz) wholewheat breadcrumbs (made from a day-old loaf)
60 ml (4 tbsp) clear honey	50 g (2 oz) demerara sugar
5 ml (1 level tsp) ground cinnamon	4 ripe dessert pears
50 g (2 oz) margarine or butter	

1 In a jug, mix together the wine, honey and half of the cinnamon. Set aside.
2 Melt the margarine in a small pan, add the breadcrumbs, sugar and remaining cinnamon and stir together until evenly mixed. Set aside.
3 Peel and halve the pears. Remove the cores. Arrange the pear halves, cut side down, in a greased ovenproof dish and pour over the white wine mixture.
4 Sprinkle the pears evenly with the breadcrumb mixture and bake in the oven at 190°C (375°F) mark 5 for 40 minutes. Serve hot.

COOK'S TIP

Accompany with yogurt flavoured with grated orange rind.

PEARS
IN RED WINE

SERVES 4

4 large firm Comice pears	50 g (2 oz) caster sugar
25 g (1 oz) blanched almonds, split in half	300 ml (½ pint) red wine
	2 cloves

1 Peel the pears, leaving the stalks on. Spike the pears with the almond halves.

2 Put the sugar, wine and cloves in a saucepan just large enough to hold the pears and heat gently until the sugar has dissolved. Add the pears, standing them upright in the pan. Cover and simmer gently for about 15 minutes until the pears are just tender. Baste them from time to time with the liquid. (Alternatively, put the sugar, wine and cloves in a bowl and microwave on HIGH for 3-4 minutes until boiling, stirring occasionally. Add the pears, cover and microwave on HIGH for 8-10 minutes until the pears are tender.)

3 Using a slotted spoon, transfer the pears to a serving dish. Boil the syrup in the pan until the liquid is reduced by half. (If cooking in the microwave, uncover and cook on HIGH for 10 minutes or until reduced by half.)

4 Pour the wine syrup over the pears. Serve hot or cold with thick natural yogurt or clotted cream.

VARIATION

Use medium dry cider in place of the red wine.

POIRES
BELLE HELENE

SERVES 6

100 g (4 oz) sugar	225 g (8 oz) plain chocolate, broken into pieces
900 ml (1½ pints) water	60 ml (4 tbsp) orange-flavoured liqueur
thinly pared rind and juice of 2 oranges	orange slices, to decorate
6 cooking pears (preferably Conference)	

1 Put the sugar, water and half the orange rind in a large heavy-based saucepan and heat gently, without stirring, until the sugar has dissolved.

2 Meanwhile, peel the pears quickly (to prevent discoloration), leaving the stalks on. Cut out the cores from the bottom and level them so that the pears will stand upright.

3 Stand the pears in the syrup, cover the pan and simmer gently for 20 minutes or until tender. Remove from the heat and leave to cool, covered tightly. Spoon the syrup over the pears occasionally during cooling.

4 Meanwhile, make the decoration. Cut the remaining orange rind into thin matchstick julienne strips. Blanch in boiling water for 2 minutes, then drain and immediately refresh under cold running water. Leave to drain on absorbent kitchen paper.

5 Make the chocolate sauce. Put the chocolate and liqueur in a heatproof bowl standing over a pan of gently simmering water Heat gently until the chocolate melts.

6 Remove the pears from the syrup, stand on a large serving dish, or 6 individual dishes and chill for 2 hours. Discard the orange rind from the syrup. Stir the melted chocolate into 150 ml (¼ pint) of the syrup with the orange juice, then slowly bring to the boil, stirring constantly. Simmer, stirring, until the sauce is thick and syrupy.

7 To serve, pour the hot chocolate sauce over the cold pears and sprinkle with the orange julienne. Decorate with orange slices and serve immediately.

ORANGES IN CARAMEL

SERVES 6

8 medium juicy oranges	30 ml (2 tbsp) Grand Marnier or other orange-flavoured liqueur
225 g (8 oz) caster sugar	

1 Thinly pare the rind from half the oranges and cut into very thin julienne strips. Place in a small saucepan and cover with water. Cover the pan and cook for 5 minutes until tender. Drain and rinse under cold water.

2 Cut away the pith from the oranges and both rind and pith from the four remaining oranges.

3 Slice the orange flesh into rounds, reserving any juice and discarding pips; arrange in a serving dish. (If liked, the orange rounds can be reassembled in the shape of oranges and secured with wooden cocktail sticks.)

4 Place the sugar and 300 ml (½ pint) water in a saucepan and heat gently until the sugar has dissolved. Bring to the boil and boil until the syrup is caramel coloured.

5 Remove the pan from the heat, carefully add 45 ml (3 tbsp) water and return it to a low heat to dissolve the caramel. Add the reserved orange juice and the liqueur.

6 Leave the caramel syrup to cool for 10 minutes, then pour over the oranges. Top with the julienne strips. Chill in the refrigerator for 2-3 hours, turning the oranges occasionally.

STUFFED FIGS

SERVES 8

225 g (8 oz) ricotta cheese, at room temperature	16 ripe fresh figs
150 ml (¼ pint) double or whipping cream	fig or vine leaves and rose petals, to serve (optional)
few drops of almond extract or rose water	

1 Beat the ricotta cheese in a bowl until softened. Whip the cream in another bowl until just standing in soft peaks, then fold into the ricotta, with almond extract or rose water according to taste.

2 With a sharp knife, cut a cross in each fig at the top (stem end). Continue cutting down almost to the base of the fig, but keeping the fruit whole. With your fingers, gently prise the four 'petals' of each fig apart, to allow room for the filling.

3 Spoon the ricotta mixture into a piping bag fitted with a large rosette nozzle and pipe into the centre of each fig. Chill in the refrigerator until serving time.

4 To serve, place the figs on individual serving plates. Alternatively arrange fig or vine leaves decoratively over a flat serving platter, place the stuffed figs on top and scatter rose petals around. Serve chilled.

COOK'S TIP

Ricotta, a soft Italian cheese, can be bought in tubs or loose by the kg (lb) at large supermarkets and Italian delicatessens. Made from the whey of sheep's or cow's milk, depending on the region where it is produced, it is mild in flavour, yet delightfully rich and creamy. If you are unable to obtain it, curd cheese is the best alternative.

MOCK FRUIT BRULEES

SERVES 6

6 large ripe peaches	30 ml (2 tbsp) almond-flavoured liqueur or a few drops of almond essence
30 ml (2 tbsp) lemon juice	
150 ml (¼ pint) double cream	150 ml (¼ pint) soured cream
30 ml (2 tbsp) icing sugar	90-120 ml (6-8 tbsp) demerara sugar

1 To skin the peaches, dip them in a bowl of boiling water for 30 seconds, then drain and plunge immediately into a bowl of cold water. Carefully peel off the skins.
2 Cut the peaches in half. Twist them to separate and remove the stones. Thinly slice the flesh. Toss in lemon juice.
3 Whip the double cream with the icing sugar until it just holds its shape. Gradually whisk in the liqueur or almond essence. Fold in the soured cream and peach slices.
4 Divide the mixture equally between six 150 ml (¼ pint) ramekin dishes. Cover and chill in the refrigerator overnight.
5 Sprinkle the demerara sugar evenly on top of each ramekin, to completely cover the peaches and cream mixture. Place under a preheated hot grill for 3-4 minutes until the sugar becomes caramelised. Chill thoroughly in the refrigerator for at least 1 hour before serving.

PINEAPPLE AND BANANA FLAMBE

SERVES 6-8

1 medium pineapple	125 g (4 oz) demerara sugar
900 g (2 lb) firm bananas	45 ml (3 tbsp) lemon juice
125 g (4 oz) dried figs	2.5 ml (½ level tsp) ground mixed spice
50 g (2 oz) butter or margarine	60 ml (4 tbsp) dark rum

1 Slice the pineapple into 1 cm (½ inch) pieces. Snip off the skin and cut the flesh into chunks, discarding the core.
2 Peel and thickly slice the bananas into the bottom of a shallow ovenproof dish; spoon the pineapple on top.
3 Cut the figs into coarse shreds and scatter over the fruit. Then put the butter, sugar, strained lemon juice and spice together in a saucepan and heat until well blended; pour over the prepared fruit.
4 Cover tightly and bake in the oven at 200°C (400°F) mark 6 for 25 minutes until the fruit is tender.
5 Heat the rum gently in a small saucepan, remove from the heat and ignite with a match. Pour immediately over the fruit and bring the dish to the table while still flaming.

SERVING SUGGESTION

For a special occasion, you can serve this dessert in the pineapple shells. Any mixture which will not fit into the pineapple shells can be served separately in a fruit bowl.
To make two pineapple shells from one pineapple: with a large sharp knife, slice the pineapple in half lengthways, cutting right through the crown and base. Insert the blade of a long, serrated knife into the flesh of one pineapple half, about 5 mm (¼ inch) in from the edge of the shell, and cut all around the inside. Cut through the flesh in parallel lines, first lengthways and then crossways to produce squares of flesh (take care not to cut through the skin at the base). Scoop out the flesh with a sharp-edged teaspoon. Repeat with the second pineapple half, then turn both shells upside-down and leave to drain before filling.

BRANDIED CHERRIES

SERVES 8

450 g (1 lb) cherries, washed	1 cinnamon stick
225 g (8 oz) sugar	about 150 ml (¼ pint) brandy

1 Prick the cherries all over with a fine skewer or darning needle.
2 Make a light syrup by dissolving 100 g (4 oz) of the sugar in 300 ml (½ pint) water. Add the cherries and cinnamon stick and poach gently for 4-5 minutes.
3 Remove the pan from the heat and drain the cherries, reserving the syrup but removing the cinnamon stick. Cool, then arrange the fruit in small sterilized jars.
4 Add the remaining sugar to the reserved syrup and dissolve it slowly. Bring to the boil and boil to 110°C (230°F), then allow to cool.
5 Measure the syrup and add an equal quantity of brandy. Pour over the cherries. Cover and store in a cool, dry place for 2-3 weeks before eating.
6 Serve with thick yogurt or cream.

SPICED FRUIT WAFERS

SERVES 8

FOR THE WAFERS	pared rind and juice of 1 orange
75 g (3 oz) butter, softened	
75 g (3 oz) caster sugar	6 fresh peaches, stoned and sliced
few drops of vanilla flavouring	225 g (8 oz) redcurrants
pinch of grated nutmeg	225 g (8 oz) strawberries
2 egg whites	300 ml (½ pint) double cream, whipped
75 g (3 oz) plain flour	150 ml (5 fl oz) Greek-style yogurt
FOR THE FILLING	
175 g (6 oz) caster sugar	icing sugar for dusting
1 cinnamon stick	

1 To make the wafers, cream together the butter and sugar until very soft and light. Add the vanilla flavouring and nutmeg. Gradually beat in the lightly whisked egg whites. Fold in the flour.
2 Drop heaped teaspoons of the mixture onto greased baking sheets allowing space to spread. Bake at 200°C (400°F) mark 6 for 6-7 minutes or until set and pale golden around the edges. Remove from the baking sheet and cool on a wire rack.
3 To make the filling, place the caster sugar, cinnamon and orange rind in a saucepan with 300 ml (½ pint) water over a low heat until the sugar has dissolved. Bring to the boil, bubble for 2 minutes then add the peaches and redcurrants. Simmer for 2-3 minutes or until just tender. With a slotted spoon, transfer the fruit to a bowl and add the strawberries.
4 Return the liquid to the heat, bring to the boil and bubble for 4-5 minutes or until reduced and syrupy. Add the strained orange juice and cool.
5 Mix the cream with the yogurt. Layer up the wafers with the cream and spiced fruits. Dust the top with icing sugar to serve.

WILD STRAWBERRY AND CHAMPAGNE JELLY

SERVES 6

100 g (4 oz) caster sugar	450 ml (¾ pint) pink champagne
pared rind and juice of 1 lemon	175 g (6 oz) Alpine strawberries or frais du bois
20 ml (4 level tsp) powdered gelatine	edible flowers or mint sprigs, to decorate

1 Put the sugar, lemon rind and 300 ml (½ pint) water in a saucepan. Heat gently until the sugar has dissolved. (Alternatively, microwave on HIGH for 3 minutes or until dissolved, stirring occasionally.) Leave to cool.
2 Sprinkle the gelatine over the lemon juice in a small bowl and leave to soak for 2-3 minutes. Place the bowl over a pan of simmering water and stir until dissolved. (Alternatively, microwave on HIGH for 30 seconds or until dissolved.)
3 Mix the sugar syrup with the dissolved gelatine and the champagne. Divide most of the strawberries between six champagne flutes. Carefully pour over a little of the jelly and chill until set. When the jelly has set, pour over the remaining jelly. Chill until set.
4 Decorate with the reserved strawberries and edible flowers or mint sprigs.

COOK'S TIP

The Alpine strawberry is a version of the rare wild strawberry, that is now cultivated in France. Also known as frais du bois, these deliciously flavoured baby strawberries do not need to be hulled before they are eaten.

LAYERED FRUIT TERRINE

SERVES 6

FOR THE JELLY	200 g (7 oz) small green seedless grapes
30 ml (6 level tsp) powdered gelatine	FOR THE SAUCE
450 ml (¾ pint) clear grape or apple juice	225 g (8 oz) fresh raspberries, hulled, or frozen, thawed
275 g (10 oz) small even-sized strawberries, hulled	icing sugar, to taste
200 g (7 oz) small black seedless grapes	lemon juice
4 large oranges, peeled, segmented and well drained	dash of kirsch (optional)
	TO DECORATE
	few strawberries
	mint sprigs

1 To make the jelly, sprinkle the gelatine over 150 ml (¼ pint) of the grape juice in a small bowl and leave to soak for 2-3 minutes. Place the bowl over a pan of simmering water and stir until dissolved. (Alternatively, microwave on HIGH for 30 seconds or until dissolved.) Stir the dissolved gelatine into the remaining juice and mix well.
2 Pour a 5 mm (¼ inch) layer of jelly into the base of a 750 ml (1¼ pint) non-stick (or non-corrosive) loaf tin or mould. Chill until set.
3 Arrange the whole strawberries in a tightly packed layer over the set jelly. Arrange the black grapes in a thick layer over the strawberries, followed by the oranges, then the green grapes. Slowly pour the fruit jelly over the fruit until it just covers the final layer. Tap the mould very lightly on the work surface to remove any air bubbles. Chill for at least 4 hours or until completely set.
4 To make the sauce, purée the raspberries in a blender or food processor until smooth. Press through a sieve if liked, and add sugar and lemon juice to taste. Stir in the liqueur, if using. Cover and chill.
5 To serve, dip the tin or mould in a bowl of lukewarm water for 10 seconds and invert on to a flat plate. Decorate with strawberries and mint. Serve with the sauce.

RHUBARB
AND ORANGE FOOL

SERVES 6

450 g (1 lb) rhubarb	300 ml (½ pint) whipping cream
grated rind and juice of 1 orange	5 ml (1 tsp) orange flower water
pinch of ground cinnamon	
25-50 g (1-2 oz) sugar	shredded orange rind, to decorate

1 Chop the rhubarb into 2.5 cm (1 inch) pieces, discarding the leaves and the white ends of the stalks.
2 Put the rhubarb, orange rind, juice, cinnamon and sugar into a pan. Cover and cook gently for about 15 minutes.
3 Uncover and boil rapidly for 10 minutes, stirring frequently, until the mixture becomes a thick purée. Leave to cool for 1 hour.
4 When cool, whip the cream until stiff. Fold into the mixture with the orange flower water to taste.
5 Spoon the fool into glasses and chill for 1-2 hours until required. Decorate with orange rind and serve with sponge fingers.

COOK'S TIP

Serve this fool well chilled with sponge fingers or crisp biscuits. Follow the basic recipe to make other fruit fools of your choice.

GOOSEBERRY
MACAROON CRUNCH

SERVES 6

450 g (1 lb) gooseberries, topped and tailed	100 g (4 oz) French almond macaroons (ratafias), crumbled
30 ml (2 tbsp) water	
100 g (4 oz) caster sugar	150 ml (¼ pint) whipping cream
30 ml (2 tbsp) kirsch	3 macaroons or 6 ratafias, to decorate

1 Cook the gooseberries with the water and sugar for 10-15 minutes until the fruit is soft and well reduced, then sieve it. Stir in the kirsch. Chill for 30 minutes.
2 Arrange the macaroon crumbs and gooseberry purée in alternate layers in 6 tall glasses. Chill in the refrigerator for several hours for the flavours to mellow.
3 Whip the cream until it barely holds its shape. Spoon some of the soft cream over each portion and top each with a halved macaroon or whole ratafias. Serve immediately.

VARIATIONS

According to seasonal availability, you can use different fruit from the gooseberries and an alternative liqueur to the kirsch. For example, cherries and kirsch would go well together; strawberries or raspberries and an orange-flavoured liqueur (in which case you can use the fruit raw); stewed apples and calvados or brandy; banana with rum; peaches or apricots go well with the Italian almond-flavoured liqueur Amaretto, which would also complement the flavour of the almond macaroons. For a less rich (and less fattening) dessert, natural yogurt can be used instead of the whipping cream.

PRUNE AND PORT FOOL

SERVES 4

100 g (4 oz) stoned prunes, soaked overnight	150 ml (¼ pint) thick custard, cooled
50 g (2 oz) caster sugar	150 ml (¼ pint) double cream
60 ml (4 tbsp) port	orange twists, to decorate
finely grated rind and juice of 1 orange	

1 Drain the prunes, then put in a saucepan with the sugar, port, orange rind and juice. Simmer for about 15 minutes until soft. (Alternatively, microwave, covered, on HIGH for 8 minutes or until soft.)

2 Leave to cool slightly, then purée in a blender or food processor. Leave to cool completely.

3 Fold the cooled custard into the puréed prunes. Whip the cream until standing in soft peaks, then fold into the prune custard until evenly blended.

4 Divide the mixture between four individual glasses. Chill for about 2 hours until firm. Decorate with orange twists and serve chilled, with sweet biscuits.

COOK'S TIP

Because the flavours in this fool are so strong you can get away with using canned custard instead of home-made.

BANANA WHIPS

SERVES 4

2 egg whites	60 ml (4 level tbsp) soft brown sugar
300 ml (½ pint) natural set yogurt	2 medium bananas
finely grated rind and juice of ½ orange	50 g (2 oz) crunchy breakfast cereal

1 Whisk the egg whites until standing in stiff peaks. Put the yogurt in a bowl and stir until smooth. Fold in the egg whites until evenly incorporated.

2 In a separate bowl, mix together the orange rind and juice and the sugar. Peel the bananas and slice thinly into the juice mixture. Fold gently to mix.

3 Put a layer of the yogurt mixture in the bottom of 4 individual glasses. Cover with a layer of cereal, then with a layer of the banana mixture. Repeat these 3 layers once more. Serve immediately..

COOK'S TIP

A quickly made dessert that appeals particularly to children of all ages.

CREAM CROWDIE

SERVES 4

50 g (2 oz) medium oatmeal	45 ml (3 tbsp) whisky
300 ml (½ pint) double cream	350 g (12 oz) raspberries, hulled
60 ml (4 tbsp) clear honey	

1 Place the oatmeal in a grill pan (without the rack) and toast until golden brown, stirring occasionally with a spoon. Leave for 15 minutes until cool.

2 Whip the cream until just standing in soft peaks. Stir in the honey, whisky and cooled toasted oatmeal.

3 Reserve a few raspberries for decoration, then layer up the remaining raspberries and cream mixture in 4 tall glasses. Cover and chill for at least 1 hour.

4 Allow to come to room temperature for 30 minutes before serving. Decorate each glass with the reserved raspberries.

COOK'S TIP

In Scotland, crowdie can mean a cream cheese or a kind of porridge. This recipe for cream crowdie is so called because it contains oatmeal, which the Scots use for making porridge.

PASKHA

SERVES 8-10

175 g (6 oz) unsalted butter	100 g (4 oz) raisins, chopped
finely grated rind of 1 lemon	50 g (2 oz) blanched almonds, chopped
finely grated rind of 1 orange	50 g (2 oz) glacé cherries, chopped
175 g (6 oz) caster sugar	50 g (2 oz) glacé pineapple, chopped
2 eggs	
5 ml (1 tsp) vanilla essence	TO DECORATE
900 g (2 lb) curd cheese	citron peel, glacé cherries, glacé pineapple and flaked almonds
150 ml (¼ pint) double cream	
25 g (1 oz) each candied citron, lemon and orange peel, chopped	

1 Beat the butter with the lemon and orange rind and sugar in a bowl until very light and fluffy. Beat in the eggs, one at a time, beating well after each addition. Add the vanilla essence and curd cheese and beat until smooth.

2 Beat in the cream, then mix in the candied peels, raisins, nuts, cherries and pineapple. Set aside.

3 Line a 12 cm (5 inch) deep, 16 cm (6½ inch) wide clay flower pot smoothly with a large square of muslin.

4 Fill the flower pot with the paskha mixture, then bring the overhanging muslin up and over the mixture to enclose it completely. Place a small flat plate on top of the paskha, then weight down, to compress the mixture. Stand the flower pot on a plate, then refrigerate overnight.

5 To unmould the paskha, open out the muslin on the top, then place a flat serving plate on top of the paskha. Invert the plate and the flower pot together. Remove the flower pot, then very carefully peel away the muslin.

6 Decorate the paskha attractively with strips of citron peel, cherries, pineapple and almonds. Keep the paskha refrigerated until ready to serve.

DANISH PEASANT GIRL IN-A-VEIL

SERVES 4

50 g (2 oz) butter or margarine	juice of ½ lemon
175 g (6 oz) fresh rye or brown breadcrumbs	sugar, to taste
	150 ml (¼ pint) double or whipping cream
75 g (3 oz) light soft brown sugar	50 g (2 oz) grated chocolate, to decorate
700 g (1½ lb) cooking apples	

1 Melt the butter in a frying pan. Mix the breadcrumbs and sugar together. Add to the pan and fry until crisp, stirring frequently with a wooden spoon to prevent the crumbs from catching and burning.

2 Peel, core and slice the apples. Put them in a saucepan with 30 ml (2 tbsp) water, the lemon juice and sugar to taste. Cover and cook gently for 10-15 minutes until they form a purée. (Alternatively, put the apples, lemon juice and sugar in a bowl. Cover and microwave on HIGH for 7-10 minutes until they form a pulp, stirring frequently.) Leave to cool, then taste for sweetness and add more sugar if required.

3 Put alternate layers of the fried crumb mixture and apple purée into a glass serving dish, finishing with a layer of crumbs. Chill for 2-3 hours.

4 Whip the cream until stiff. Pipe around the top of the crumb mixture and decorate with grated chocolate. Serve chilled.

COOK'S TIP

This simple but delicious pudding of stewed apples layered with fried breadcrumbs and sugar is very similar to an apple charlotte. In Denmark, where it is called *bondepige med slør*, it takes its name from the fact that the apple and crumbs are 'veiled' or covered with cream.

MANGO MOUSSE

SERVES 6

2 ripe mangoes, about 350 g (12 oz) each	15 ml (1 level tbsp) powdered gelatine
finely grated rind and juice of 1 orange	300 ml (10 fl oz) double cream
3 whole eggs, plus 1 egg yolk	shredded orange rind, to decorate (optional)
40 g (1½ oz) caster sugar	

1 Stand the mangoes on a board on their long rounded edges. Cut a thick slice down either side of the mango keeping the knife as close to the stone as possible.

2 Scrape the mango flesh out of the skin. Purée in a blender or food processor. Rub through a nylon sieve. Add the orange rind.

3 Place the whole eggs and egg yolk in a large bowl, add the caster sugar and whisk until the mixture is very pale, thick and creamy.

4 Whisk the mango purée, a little at a time, into the mixture, whisking well after each addition.

5 Sprinkle the gelatine over the orange juice in a small bowl and leave to soak. Place the bowl over a pan of simmering water and stir until dissolved.

6 Meanwhile, pour half the cream into a bowl and lightly whip, then, using a metal spoon, lightly fold the cream into the mango mixture. Pour the gelatine in a thin stream into the mango mixture, stirring gently.

7 Pour the mixture into a 2 litre (3½ pint) shallow serving dish. Chill in the refrigerator for about 1 hour until beginning to set, then cover and chill for several hours, or overnight, until set.

8 Lightly whisk the remaining cream until it just holds its shape. Spoon the cream into a piping bag fitted with a star nozzle and pipe small rosettes around the edge of the mousse. Decorate with shredded orange rind if desired.

STRAWBERRY AND ORANGE MOUSSE

SERVES 6

700 g (1½ lb) strawberries, hulled	125 g (4 oz) caster sugar
finely grated rind and juice of 1 large orange	15 ml (1 level tbsp) powdered gelatine
45 ml (3 level tbsp) icing sugar	300 ml (10 fl oz) double cream
3 egg yolks and 2 egg whites	150 ml (5 fl oz) single cream

1 Thinly slice enough strawberries to form a ring around the side of a 2.3 litre (4 pint) shallow glass dish.
2 Purée half the remainder in a blender or food processor with the orange rind, 75 ml (5 tbsp) juice and the icing sugar. Pass through a nylon sieve to give a very smooth texture. Reserve the remaining strawberries for decoration.
3 Whisk the egg yolks and caster sugar until thick and light. Then gradually whisk in the strawberry purée.
4 Sprinkle the gelatine in 45 ml (3 tbsp) water in a small bowl and leave to soak. Place the bowl over a saucepan of simmering water and stir until dissolved. Leave to cool, then stir into the mousse mixture.
5 Lightly whip the creams together. Fold one third into the mousse and keep the rest covered in the refrigerator. Whisk the two egg whites until stiff and fold into the mixture. Pour into the strawberry-lined dish, and chill in the refrigerator for 2-3 hours, until set.
6 Decorate with piped cream and strawberries.

STRAWBERRY YOGURT MOULD

SERVES 6

3 eggs	20 ml (4 level tsp) powdered gelatine
50 g (2 oz) caster sugar	150 ml (5 fl oz) natural yogurt
finely grated rind and juice of 1 lemon	150 ml (5 fl oz) strawberry yogurt
450 g (1 lb) strawberries	

1 Put the eggs, sugar and lemon rind in a large bowl. Using an electric mixer, whisk together until the mixture is pale, thick and creamy and leaves a trail when the whisk is lifted from the bowl.
2 Hull half of the strawberries and place in a blender or food processor with half of the lemon juice. Purée until smooth.
3 Gradually whisk the purée into the mousse mixture, whisking well to keep the bulk.
4 Sprinkle the gelatine over the remaining lemon juice in a small bowl and leave to soak for 5 minutes. Place the bowl over a saucepan of simmering water and stir until dissolved. Leave until lukewarm, then gradually add to the mousse mixture with the natural and strawberry yogurts. Stir carefully but thoroughly to mix. Pour into a greased 1.7 litre (3 pint) ring mould and chill for 4-5 hours or until set.
5 To serve, dip the mould briefly in hot water, then invert on to a serving plate. Hull most of the remaining strawberries, but leave a few of the green hulls on for decoration. Fill the centre of the ring with the fruit. Serve with extra natural yogurt, if liked.

MANDARIN AND LYCHEE MOUSSE

SERVES 6

3 eggs, separated	310 g (11 oz) can lychees in syrup
2 egg yolks	
75 g (3 oz) caster sugar	15 ml (1 level tbsp) powdered gelatine
298 g (10½ oz) can mandarin oranges in natural juice	150 ml (¼ pint) double cream

1 Whisk the five egg yolks and sugar in a large bowl standing over a saucepan of gently simmering water until the mixture is thick and holds a ribbon trail. Remove the bowl from the pan. Leave to cool for 30 minutes, whisking occasionally.

2 Reserve 60 ml (4 tbsp) of the mandarin juice. Purée half the oranges and the remaining juice in a blender or food processor with the lychees and half the syrup.

3 Sprinkle the gelatine over the reserved mandarin syrup in a small bowl and leave to soak for 2-3 minutes. Place the bowl over a saucepan of simmering water and stir until dissolved. (Alternatively, microwave on HIGH for 30 seconds or until dissolved.) Cool slightly.

4 Stir the mandarin purée into the cooled egg yolk mixture, then stir in the dissolved gelatine until evenly mixed.

5 Whip the cream until standing in soft peaks. Whisk the egg whites until stiff. Fold first the cream, then the egg whites into the mousse until evenly blended. Turn into a glass serving bowl and chill for at least 2 hours until set.

6 When the mousse is set, serve decorated with the reserved mandarin oranges and extra whipped cream.

BANANA CHARTREUSE

SERVES 4-6

135 g (4¾ oz) packet lemon jelly, broken into squares	15 ml (1 level tbsp) powdered gelatine
3 bananas	60 ml (4 tbsp) dark rum
juice of ½ lemon	150 ml (¼ pint) double cream
about 6 shelled pistachio nuts	50 g (2 oz) icing sugar, sifted

1 Chill an 18 cm (6 inch) charlotte mould.

2 Make up the jelly according to the packet instructions, using only 300 ml (½ pint) boiling water. Leave to cool for 30 minutes.

3 Pour about one third of the jelly into the prepared mould. Chill for 30 minutes until set.

4 Peel 1 banana, slice thinly, then sprinkle with a little lemon juice to prevent browning.

5 Arrange the banana slices on top of the set jelly in an attractive pattern. Cut the pistachios in half lengthways and carefully place between or around the banana slices.

6 Slowly spoon over the remaining cool jelly, taking care not to dislodge the pattern of bananas and pistachios. Chill for 30 minutes until set.

7 Sprinkle the gelatine over the rum and remaining lemon juice in a small bowl. Place the bowl over a saucepan of simmering water and stir until dissolved. (Alternatively, microwave on HIGH for 30 seconds or until dissolved.) Leave to cool for 5 minutes.

8 Whip the cream with the icing sugar. Peel and mash the remaining bananas, then combine with the cream and dissolved gelatine liquid. Spoon on top of the set jelly. Chill for about 2 hours until set.

9 To serve, dip the base of the mould briefly in hot water, then invert the banana chartreuse on to a serving plate. Serve chilled.

SUMMER PUDDING

SERVES 4-6

700 g (1½ lb) mixed summer fruit, such as redcurrants, blackcurrants, raspberries, prepared	8-10 thin slices of day-old bread, crusts removed
about 25 g (1 oz) light soft brown sugar	fruit and mint sprigs, to decorate

1   Stew the fruit gently with 60-90 ml (4-6 tbsp) water and the sugar until soft but still retaining their shape. The exact amounts of water and sugar depend on the ripeness and sweetness of the fruit.

2   Meanwhile, cut a round from one slice of bread to neatly fit the bottom of a 1.1 litre (2 pint) pudding basin and cut 6-8 slices of the bread into fingers about 5 cm (2 inches) wide. Put the round at the bottom of the basin and arrange the fingers around the sides, overlapping them so there are no spaces.

3   When the fruit is cooked, and still hot, pour it gently into the basin, being careful not to disturb the bread framework. Reserve about 45 ml (3 tbsp) of the juice. When the basin is full, cut the remaining bread and use to cover the fruit so a lid is formed.

4   Cover with a plate or saucer which fits just inside the bowl and put a weight on top. Leave the pudding until cold, then put into the refrigerator and chill overnight.

5   To serve, run a knife carefully round the edge to loosen, then invert the pudding on to a serving dish. Pour the reserved juice over the top. Decorate with fruit and mint sprigs. Serve cold with cream.

VARIATION

Autumn Pudding

Replace the summer fruits with a selection of autumn fruits, such as apples or pears, blackberries and plums.

CABINET PUDDING

SERVES 4

425 ml (15 fl oz) milk	25 g (1 oz) caster sugar
1 vanilla pod	2 trifle sponge cakes, diced
25 g (1 oz) glacé cherries, halved	40 g (1½ oz) ratafias, crushed
25 g (1 oz) angelica, chopped	25 g (1 oz) large raisins, chopped, or sultanas
3 eggs	

1   Put the milk and the vanilla pod in a saucepan and bring slowly to the boil. Remove from the heat, cover and leave for 15 minutes.

2   Arrange some of the cherries and angelica in a buttered 750 ml (1¼ pint) charlotte mould or other plain mould.

3   Lightly whisk the eggs and sugar together. Remove the vanilla pod from the milk then stir the milk into the eggs.

4   Mix the sponge cakes, ratafias, raisins or sultanas and remaining cherries and angelica together and spoon into the mould. Strain in the egg and milk and leave to soak for 15 minutes.

5   Place the mould in a deep baking tin, surround with boiling water and cover with greaseproof paper. Bake in the oven at 170°C (325°F) mark 3 for about 1 hour until just set.

6   Remove the mould from the tin and leave to stand for 2-3 minutes before unmoulding.

COOK'S TIP

This type of custard-based pudding was very popular in the eighteenth century. Richer versions use single, even double, cream instead of milk, a higher proportion of ratafias, and sometimes brandy is added as well.

EVE'S PUDDING

SERVES 4

450 g (1 lb) cooking apples, peeled and cored	75 g (3 oz) caster sugar
	1 egg, beaten
75 g (3 oz) demerara sugar	150 g (5 oz) self-raising flour
grated rind of 1 lemon	a little milk, to mix
75 g (3 oz) butter or block margarine	

1 Grease a 900 ml (1½ pint) ovenproof dish. Slice the apples and place in the dish. Sprinkle over the sugar and lemon rind.
2 Cream the fat and caster sugar together until pale and fluffy. Add the egg, a little at a time, beating well after each addition.
3 Fold in the flour with enough milk to give a smooth dropping consistency and spread the mixture over the apples.
4 Bake in the oven at 180°C (350°F) mark 4 for 40-45 minutes, until the apples are tender and the sponge mixture golden brown.

VARIATION

Add 25 g (1 oz) ground almonds with the flour and sprinkle 25 g (1 oz) flaked almonds over the top of the pudding.

BLACKBERRY AND PEAR COBBLER

SERVES 4

FOR THE FILLING	FOR THE TOPPING
450 g (1 lb) blackberries	225 g (8 oz) self-raising flour
450 g (1 lb) ripe cooking pears, such as Conference	pinch of salt
finely grated rind and juice of 1 lemon	50 g (2 oz) butter or margarine
2.5 ml (½ level tsp) ground cinnamon	25 g (1 oz) caster sugar
	about 150 ml (¼ pint) milk, plus extra to glaze

1 To make the filling, pick over the blackberries and wash them. Peel and core the pears, slice thickly.
2 Put the blackberries and pears into a saucepan with the lemon rind and juice and the cinnamon. Poach for 15-20 minutes until the fruit is tender. Cool.
3 To make the topping, place the flour and salt in a bowl. Rub in the butter until the mixture resembles fine breadcrumbs, then stir in the sugar. Gradually add the milk to mix to a fairly soft dough.
4 Roll out the dough on a floured work surface until 1 cm (½ inch) thick. Cut out rounds using a fluted 5 cm (2 inch) pastry cutter.
5 Put the fruit in a pie dish and top with overlapping pastry rounds, leaving a gap in the centre.
6 Brush the top of the pastry rounds with milk. Bake in the oven at 220°C (425°F) mark 7 for 10-15 minutes until the pastry is golden brown. Serve hot.

COOK'S TIP

Recipes with the strange-sounding title of 'cobbler' are invariably American in origin, although very little is known for certain about the meaning behind the word in culinary terms. Cobblers always have a scone dough topping which is stamped into small rounds.

CRANBERRY UPSIDE DOWN CAKE

SERVES 8

FOR THE TOPPING	large pinch of salt
25 g (1 oz) butter, melted	1 egg
350 g (12 oz) cranberries	finely grated rind and juice of 1 large orange
75 g (3 oz) caster sugar	50 ml (2 fl oz) milk
60 ml (4 tbsp) cranberry sauce	100 g (4 oz) butter or margarine, softened
FOR THE CAKE	100 g (4 oz) caster sugar
225 g (8 oz) self-raising flour	
5 ml (1 level tsp) baking powder	

1 Grease a 23 cm (9 inch) round spring-release cake tin.
2 To make the topping, pour the melted butter into the prepared cake tin. Mix the cranberries, sugar and cranberry sauce together. Spoon the cranberry mixture evenly over the base of the cake tin.
3 To make the cake, put all the ingredients into a large bowl and beat until smooth and glossy. Carefully pour over the cranberries and level the surface.
4 Bake in the oven at 180°C (350°F) mark 4 for about 1 hour or until well risen and firm to the touch. Cover the top with a double sheet of greaseproof paper after 40 minutes to prevent overbrowning.
5 Leave to cool in the tin for 5 minutes, then turn the cake out on to a serving plate. Serve warm with ice cream or whipped cream.

BLUEBERRY OAT CRUMBLE

SERVES 6-8

FOR THE FILLING	FOR THE CRUMBLE TOPPING
900 g (2 lb) blueberries	100 g (4 oz) butter
45 ml (3 level tbsp) light soft brown sugar	100 g (4 oz) plain flour
30 ml (2 level tbsp) plain flour	100 g (4 oz) light soft brown sugar
15 ml (1 tbsp) lemon juice	75 g (3 oz) rolled oats
	50 g (2 oz) pecan or walnut halves, chopped and toasted
	grated nutmeg (optional)

1 To make the filling, mix the blueberries with the sugar, flour and lemon juice in a 1.4 litre (2½ pint) pie dish.
2 To make the crumble topping, rub the butter into the flour in a bowl. Stir in the sugar, oats and nuts. Flavour with grated nutmeg, if liked. Spoon the crumble mixture on top of the berries and lightly press down.
3 Bake in the oven at 190°C (375°F) mark 5 for about 30-35 minutes or until golden brown. Serve warm or cold with custard or cream.

RHUBARB BROWN BETTY

SERVES 6

450 g (1 lb) rhubarb	2.5 ml (½ level tsp) ground ginger
225 g (8 oz) fresh wholewheat breadcrumbs	50 ml (2 fl oz) fresh orange juice
50 g (2 oz) muscovado sugar	

1 Trim the rhubarb and cut the stalks into short lengths. Put in a greased 900 ml (1½ pint) ovenproof dish.

2 Mix the breadcrumbs, sugar and ground ginger together and sprinkle over the fruit. Spoon the orange juice over the crumbs.

3 Bake in the oven at 170°C (325°F) mark 3 for 40 minutes or until the fruit is soft and the topping browned. Serve hot or cold, with natural yogurt.

COOK'S TIP

Rhubarb Brown Betty is equally good served hot or cold, with natural yogurt. Any leftover will also reheat well.

SPICED APPLE AND PLUM CRUMBLE

SERVES 6

450 g (1 lb) plums	7.5 ml (1½ level tsp) ground mixed spice
700 g (1½ lb) cooking apples	175 g (6 oz) plain wholemeal flour
100 g (4 oz) butter or margarine	50 g (2 oz) blanched hazelnuts, toasted and chopped
100 g (4 oz) sugar	

1 Using a sharp knife, cut the plums in half, then carefully remove the stones.

2 Peel, quarter, core and slice the apples. Place the apples in a medium saucepan with 25 g (1 oz) of the butter, 50 g (2 oz) of the sugar and about 5 ml (1 tsp) of the mixed spice. Cover and cook gently for 15 minutes until the apples begin to soften.

3 Stir in the plums. Transfer the fruit mixture to a 1.1 litre (2 pint) shallow ovenproof dish. Leave to cool for about 30 minutes.

4 Stir the flour and remaining mixed spice well together. Rub in the remaining butter until the mixture resembles fine breadcrumbs. Stir in the rest of the sugar with the hazelnuts. Spoon the crumble over the fruit.

5 Bake in the oven at 180°C (350°F) mark 4 for about 40 minutes or until the top is golden, crisp and crumbly.

COOK'S TIP

All plums can be cooked, but dessert varieties tend to be more expensive, so it makes good sense to look for cooking plums. Whether you cook with red or yellow plums is entirely a matter of personal choice but cooking plums worth looking for are Czars, small red cherry plums, Pershore Yellow Egg, Purple Pershore and Belle de Loutain. Greengages and damsons come from the plum family and can be used in any recipe for plums, although extra sugar may be required.

WALNUT AND ORANGE PUDDING

SERVES 6

125 g (4 oz) soft tub margarine	5 ml (1 tsp) vanilla essence
50 g (2 oz) walnut pieces, chopped	75 g (3 oz) self-raising flour
75 g (3 oz) caster sugar	5 ml (1 level tsp) baking powder
15 ml (1 level tbsp) golden syrup	grated rind of 1 orange
2 eggs	60 ml (4 tbsp) fresh orange juice

1 Grease six ovenproof ramekins.
2 Place all the ingredients together in a large bowl and beat thoroughly until smooth.
3 Two-thirds fill the ramekins with the mixture. Place on a baking tray and bake in the oven at 180°C (350°F) mark 4 for 20-25 minutes or until firm to the touch.
4 Turn out or leave in the ramekins if preferred, and serve warm with custard.

BLACKBERRY UPSIDE DOWN PUDDING

SERVES 8

FOR THE TOPPING	5 ml (1 level tsp) baking powder
90 ml (6 tbsp) raspberry jam	large pinch of salt
350 g (12 oz) blackberries	1 egg
1 large eating apple, peeled, cored and roughly chopped	finely grated rind and juice of 1 large orange
FOR THE CAKE	30 ml (2 tbsp) milk
75 g (3 oz) self-raising flour	75 g (3 oz) butter or soft tub margarine
75 g (3 oz) self-raising wholemeal flour	75 g (3 oz) caster sugar

1 Grease a 23 cm (9 inch) round spring-release cake tin.
2 To make the topping, gently heat the jam in a small saucepan and pour into the prepared cake tin. Arrange the blackberries and apple evenly over the base of the cake tin.
3 To make the cake, put all the ingredients into a large bowl and beat until smooth and glossy. Carefully spread over the fruit and level the surface.
4 Bake in the oven at 190°C (375°F) mark 5 for about 1 hour or until well risen and firm to the touch. Cover the top with a double sheet of greaseproof paper after 40 minutes to prevent overbrowning.
5 Leave the pudding to cool in the tin for 5 minutes, then turn out and serve.

BAKED APPLE AND COCONUT PUDDING

SERVES 6

finely grated rind and juice of 1 lemon	100 g (4 oz) plain wholemeal flour
100 g (4 oz) soft light brown sugar, plus 30 ml (2 tbsp)	7.5 ml (1½ tsp) baking powder
6 medium eating apples, each weighing about 100 g (4 oz), peeled, cored and sliced	25 g (1 oz) desiccated coconut
100 g (4 oz) butter	about 60 ml (4 tbsp) apricot jam, warmed
2 eggs, separated	shredded coconut, toasted, to decorate

1   Pour the lemon juice into a large bowl; stir in the 30 ml (2 tbsp) sugar and add the apples, making sure they are well coated.

2   Gradually beat the 100 g (4 oz) sugar into the butter until well blended. Add the lemon rind, then beat in the egg yolks one at a time. Stir in the flour, baking powder and desiccated coconut.

3   Whisk the egg whites until stiff but not dry, then fold into the creamed ingredients. Spoon into a lightly greased 24-25 cm (9½-10 inch) fluted flan dish. Press the apples into the mixture, spooning any juices over them.

3   Stand the dish on a baking sheet and bake in the oven at 170°C (325°F) mark 3 for 1-1¼ hours or until well browned and firm to the touch, covering lightly with greaseproof paper if necessary.

4   Cool for about 15 minutes, then brush with the apricot jam and scatter over the toasted shredded coconut. Serve while still warm with custard.

DAMSON AND APPLE TANSY

SERVES 4

2 large Cox's apples, peeled, cored and thinly sliced	40 g (1½ oz) sugar
225 g (8 oz) damsons, halved, stoned and quartered	pinch of ground cloves
	pinch of ground cinnamon
15 g (½ oz) butter	4 eggs, separated
	45 ml (3 tbsp) soured cream

1   Put the apples, damsons, butter and half of the sugar in a large frying pan. Cook over a gentle heat until the fruit is softened, stirring continuously. Stir in the cloves and cinnamon, then remove from the heat.

2   Beat the egg yolks and cream together and stir into the fruit. Whisk the egg whites until stiff, then fold in.

3   Cook over a low heat until the mixture has set. Sprinkle the top with the remaining sugar, then brown under a hot grill. Serve immediately, straight from the pan, with soured cream.

COOK'S TIP

Tansies originally always included the bitter-sweet herb called tansy, which still lends its name to many custard and omelette-type puddings. This sweet/tart combination with Cox's apples traditionally used the Witherslack damsons which grow south of Lake Windermere.

STEAMED FRUIT PUDDING

SERVES 4

450 g (1 lb) fresh fruit, prepared and stewed, or drained canned fruit	2 eggs, beaten
	few drops of vanilla essence
100 g (4 oz) butter or margarine	175 g (6 oz) self-raising flour
	little milk, to mix
100 g (4 oz) caster sugar	

1 Half-fill a steamer or large saucepan with water and put it on to boil. Grease a 900 ml (1½ pint) pudding basin and spoon the fruit into the bottom.
2 Cream the butter and sugar together in a bowl until pale and fluffy. Add the eggs and vanilla essence, a little at a time, beating well after each addition.
3 Using a metal spoon, fold in half the flour, then fold in the rest, with enough milk to give a smooth dropping consistency.
4 Pour the mixture into the prepared pudding basin. Cover with greased greaseproof paper and foil and secure with string. Steam for 1½ hours. Serve with custard.

VARIATIONS

Syrup or Jam Pudding
Put 30 ml (2 tbsp) golden syrup or jam into the bottom of the basin instead of the fruit.

Individual Dried Fruit Puddings
Add 75g (3 oz) dried mixed fruit to the basic mixture. Omit the stewed fruit. Spoon into greased individual pudding moulds filling them two-thirds full. Cover each mould with greased foil and secure with string. Steam for 30-45 minutes depending on size. (Illustrated above.)

RICH CHRISTMAS PUDDING

SERVES 8

100 g (4 oz) prunes	75 g (3 oz) fresh breadcrumbs
175 g (6 oz) currants	
175 g (6 oz) seedless raisins	100 g (4 oz) shredded suet
175 g (6 oz) sultanas	100 g (4 oz) dark soft brown sugar
100 g (4 oz) plain flour	
1.25 ml (¼ level tsp) grated nutmeg	25 g (1 oz) blanched almonds, chopped
	finely grated rind of ½ lemon
1.25 ml (¼ level tsp) ground cinnamon	150 ml (¼ pint) brown ale
2.5 ml (½ level tsp) salt	2 eggs, beaten

1 Snip the prunes into small pieces, discarding the stones.
2 Half-fill a steamer or large saucepan with water and put it on to boil. Grease a 1.3 litre (2½ pint) pudding basin.
3 Place the prunes in a large mixing bowl and stir in the remaining ingredients. Stir well until evenly mixed.
4 Put the mixture into the prepared basin, pushing down well. Cover with greased, pleated greaseproof paper and foil. To cook, steam for about 8 hours.
5 Leave the greaseproof paper in position, allow to cool, then cover with a clean dry cloth or foil and store in a cool place for at least 2 weeks before serving.
6 To reheat, steam for 2½ hours. Turn out on to a warmed serving plate and serve with brandy butter.

INDIVIDUAL PLUM PUDDINGS

SERVES 4

8 prunes, stoned and chopped	2.5 ml (½ level tsp) ground mixed spice
45 ml (3 tbsp) seedless raisins	pinch of salt
45 ml (3 tbsp) currants	30 ml (2 tbsp) fresh breadcrumbs
45 ml (3 tbsp) sultanas	30 ml (2 tbsp) shredded suet
12 whole blanched almonds, chopped	30 ml (2 tbsp) soft brown sugar
finely grated rind and juice of 1 tangerine	1 egg, size 4, beaten
30 ml (2 level tbsp) plain flour	30 ml (2 tbsp) brown ale
	30 ml (2 tbsp) brandy

1 Place the dried fruits in a bowl with the nuts and tangerine rind and juice. Mix well.

2 In a separate bowl, sift together the flour, mixed spice and salt. Add the breadcrumbs, suet and sugar and mix well together.

3 Pour in the beaten egg and brown ale, beat well, then stir in the dried fruit mixture. Cover and leave in a cool place for 24 hours.

4 The next day, add the brandy, stirring well. Butter 4 dariole moulds or ramekins and pack in the pudding mixture tightly.

5 Cover the moulds with pleated greaseproof paper and foil and secure tightly with string.

6 Place the moulds in a large saucepan, then pour in enough boiling water to come halfway up the sides of the moulds. Steam the puddings for about 1 hour, topping up with boiling water when necessary.

7 Remove the puddings from the pan and allow to cool.

8 Uncover the puddings, then re-cover in fresh greaseproof paper and foil. Store in a cool, dry place for at least 1 month before serving.

9 To serve, steam in the same way for 1 hour. Turn out on to warmed individual plates. Serve with custard.

SPOTTED DICK

SERVES 4

100 g (4 oz) fresh breadcrumbs	175 g (6 oz) currants
75 g (3 oz) self-raising flour	finely grated rind of 1 lemon
75 g (3 oz) shredded suet	75 ml (5 tbsp) milk
50 g (2 oz) caster sugar	lemon slices, to decorate

1 Half-fill a preserving pan or large saucepan with water and put on to boil.

2 Place the breadcrumbs, flour, suet, sugar, currants and lemon rind in a bowl and stir well until thoroughly mixed.

3 Pour in the milk and stir until well blended. Using one hand, bring the ingredients together to form a soft, slightly sticky dough.

4 Turn the dough on to a floured surface and knead gently until just smooth. Shape into a neat roll about 15 cm (6 inches) in length.

5 Make a 5 cm (2 inch) pleat across a clean tea towel or pudding cloth. Or pleat together sheets of greased greaseproof paper and strong foil. Encase the roll in the cloth or foil, pleating the open edges tightly together.

6 Tie the ends securely with string to form a cracker shape. Make a string handle across the top. Lower the suet roll into the pan of boiling water and boil for about 2 hours.

7 Lift the spotted dick out of the water using the string handle. Place on a wire rack standing over a plate and allow excess moisture to drain off.

8 Snip the string and gently roll the pudding out of the cloth or foil on to a warmed serving plate. Cut into slices and decorate with lemon slices. Serve with custard.

SOUFFLES & MERINGUES

Impress your guests with a sensational soufflé or an elaborate meringue gâteau. Choose a cold soufflé or meringue concoction for a prepare-ahead dessert; a hot soufflé must be served immediately for maximum effect. Meringues have the added advantage that they can be made well in advance and stored in an airtight container.

ORANGE SEMOLINA SOUFFLES

SERVES 6

5 large juicy oranges	3 eggs, separated
25 g (1 oz) granulated sugar	icing sugar, for dusting
25 g (1 oz) semolina	orange slices, to decorate

1 Finely grate the rind and squeeze the juice from 2 of the oranges into a measuring jug. You will need 300 ml (½ pint) juice. Make up with juice from one of the remaining oranges if there is not enough.

2 Halve the remaining oranges. Scoop out any loose flesh still attached to the skins and eat separately or use in another recipe. You need six clean orange halves to serve the soufflés in. Cut a thin slice from the bottom of each so that they stand flat.

3 Place the orange juice and rind, sugar and semolina in a pan and simmer until thickened, stirring all the time.

4 Cool slightly, then stir in the egg yolks. Whisk the egg whites until stiff and fold into the mixture. Spoon into the reserved orange shells and stand on a baking sheet.

5 Bake in the oven at 200°C (400°F) mark 6 for 15-20 minutes or until risen and golden brown. Dust with icing sugar and serve immediately, surrounded by orange slices.

HOT APRICOT SOUFFLE

SERVES 4

450 g (1 lb) fresh apricots, halved and stoned	150 ml (¼ pint) milk
40 g (1½ oz) butter or margarine	50 g (2 oz) caster sugar
	4 eggs, size 2, separated
60 ml (4 level tbsp) plain flour	15 ml (1 tbsp) apricot brandy
	icing sugar, for dusting

1 Grease a 2 litre (3½ pint) soufflé dish. Put the apricots in a saucepan with 30 ml (2 tbsp) water and cook until soft. Purée the fruit in a blender or food processor; seive to remove the skins.

2 Melt the butter in a saucepan, stir in the flour and cook for 1 minute, stirring. Remove from the heat and gradually stir in the milk and apricot purée. Bring to the boil, and cook, stirring, until the sauce thickens. Remove from the heat.

3 Stir in the sugar, egg yolks and brandy. Whisk the egg whites until stiff, then fold into the mixture.

4 Pour into the soufflé dish and bake in the oven at 180°C (350°F) mark 4 for 45 minutes, until well risen. Dust with icing sugar and serve immediately.

HOT CHOCOLATE CINNAMON SOUFFLE

SERVES 4

50 g (2 oz) butter or margarine, plus extra for greasing	40 g (1½ oz) plain flour
	2.5 ml (½ level tsp) ground cinnamon
75 g (3 oz) plain chocolate	5 eggs, separated
300 ml (½ pint) plus 15 ml (1 tbsp) milk	25 g (1 oz) caster sugar
	icing sugar, for dusting

1   Tie a double strip of greaseproof paper around a 1.4 litre (2½ pint) soufflé dish to make a 7.5 cm (3 inch) collar. Brush the inside of the dish and the paper with melted butter.

2   Break the chocolate into small pieces. Place in a heatproof bowl with the 15 ml (1 tbsp) milk. Stand the bowl over a pan of simmering water and heat gently until the chocolate melts. Remove from the heat.

3   Melt the butter in a large heavy-based saucepan. Add the flour and cook for 1 minute, then blend in the remaining milk and the cinnamon. Bring to the boil, stirring all the time, and cook for about 1 minute.

4   Cool slightly, then beat in the egg yolks, sugar and chocolate.

5   Whisk the egg whites until stiff but not dry. Beat one spoonful into the sauce mixture to lighten it, then carefully fold in the remaining egg whites.

6   Gently pour the soufflé mixture into the prepared dish. Level the top with a palette knife and make a few cuts through the outer edges of the mixture – this helps it to rise evenly. Stand the dish on a baking sheet.

7   Bake in the oven at 190°C (375°F) mark 5 for about 35-40 minutes or until well risen, just set and well browned. Remove the paper and dust lightly with icing sugar. Serve straight away.

INDIVIDUAL CHOCOLATE SOUFFLES

SERVES 6

75 g (3 oz) plain chocolate or chocolate dots	knob of butter or margarine
150 ml (¼ pint) milk	3 egg yolks
50 g (2 oz) caster sugar	4 egg whites
60 ml (4 level tbsp) flour	icing sugar for dusting

1   Lightly grease six 150 ml (¼ pint) ramekin dishes. Dust them out with icing sugar.

2   Put the chocolate in a bowl with 30 ml (2 tbsp) water and melt over a pan of simmering water.

3   Heat the milk, reserving a little, with the sugar, then pour on to the melted chocolate.

4   Blend the flour to a smooth paste with the remaining milk, and stir in the chocolate mixture. Return to the pan, bring to the boil, stirring, then cook for 2 minutes, stirring occasionally. Add the butter, in small pieces, then leave until lukewarm.

5   Stir in the egg yolks. Whisk the egg whites until stiff and fold into the mixture. Divide between the prepared ramekin dishes so that each is three-quarters full.

6   Bake in the oven at 180°C (350°F) mark 4 for about 30 minutes or until just set and golden brown. Dust quickly with icing sugar. Serve straight away with single cream.

COOK'S TIP

Make sure that the temperature in the oven remains constant and that there are no draughts while the soufflé is baking – which means no peeking! A hot soufflé is cooked when it is risen and golden, and just firm to the touch. Test it in the oven, in case it needs more time. The creamy middle should be a little gooey – if it is dry it tastes like overcooked scrambled egg.

INDIVIDUAL APPLE SOUFFLES

SERVES 6

icing sugar, for dusting	30 ml (2 level tbsp) plain flour
350 g (12 oz) cooking apples	
50 g (2 oz) butter or margarine	150 ml (¼ pint) milk
	3 eggs, separated
25 g (1 oz) caster sugar	30 ml (2 tbsp) apple brandy

1 Lightly grease six 150 ml (¼ pint) ramekin dishes. Dust them out with icing sugar.

2 Peel, quarter, core and roughly chop the apples. Place in a small saucepan with 25 g (1 oz) of the butter and the sugar. Cover tightly and cook gently until the apples are very soft. Uncover and cook over a moderate heat, stirring frequently until all excess moisture evaporates. (Alternatively, cover and microwave on high for 5 minutes, or until really soft, stirring.) Mash or beat until smooth; cool slightly.

3 Melt the remaining butter in a pan, add the flour and cook for 2 minutes. Remove from the heat and stir in the milk. Cook, stirring, for 2-3 minutes. (Alternatively, put everything in a bowl and microwave on HIGH for 3-4 minutes or until boiling and thickened, whisking.)

4 Remove from the heat, cool slightly, then stir in the apple purée and egg yolks. Gently mix in the apple brandy. Whisk the egg whites until stiff but not dry. Stir one large spoonful into the apple mixture, then gently fold in the remaining egg whites. Divide between the prepared ramekin dishes so that each is three-quarters full.

5 Bake in the oven at 180°C (350°F) mark 4 for about 30 minutes or until just set and golden brown. Dust quickly with icing sugar. Serve straight away with cream.

CHILLED CHOCOLATE MINT CHIP SOUFFLE

SERVES 4

450 ml (¾ pint) milk	75 g (3 oz) caster sugar
50 g (2 oz) plain chocolate	15 ml (3 level tsp) powdered gelatine
113 g (4 oz) packet chocolate mint sticks, roughly chopped	
	300 ml (10 fl oz) whipping cream
3 eggs, separated, plus 1 egg white	

1 Prepare a 900 ml (1½ pint) soufflé dish with a paper collar (as for Citrus Soufflé, page 118).

2 Heat the milk, chocolate and 25 g (1 oz) chocolate mint sticks until melted, then bring to the boil, whisking. Remove from the heat.

3 Beat the egg yolks with the sugar until light. Pour on the flavoured milk, return to the pan and cook over a gentle heat, without boiling, until the custard coats the back of a spoon. Pour into a bowl; cool.

4 Soak the gelatine in 45 ml (3 tbsp) water in a small bowl. Dissolve by standing the bowl over a pan of gently simmering water. Stir into the custard and chill.

5 Whip the cream until softly stiff. Stir half into the custard when it is on the point of setting. Stir 50 g (2 oz) chocolate mint sticks into the custard.

6 Whisk the four egg whites until stiff then fold into the mixture. Spoon into a soufflé dish; refrigerate to set.

7 Remove the paper. Decorate soufflé with remaining cream and chocolate mint sticks.

COOK'S TIP

Cold soufflés are very light mixtures set high above a soufflé dish, as imitations of hot soufflés. They are not true soufflés but mousses set with gelatine. The preparation of the dish is all important. Do not tie the paper collar so tightly as to flute the paper and spoil the final appearance of the soufflé. To remove the paper from the cold soufflé once it has set, rinse a round bladed knife in hot water and slip it, upright between the paper and the soufflé, peeling away the paper.

CITRUS SOUFFLE

SERVES 6-8

finely grated rind and juice of 1 lemon	4 eggs, separated
finely grated rind and juice of 1 orange	100 g (4 oz) caster sugar
juice of 1 grapefruit	300 ml (10 fl oz) double cream
15 ml (3 level tsp) powdered gelatine	crushed sweet biscuits and crystallised oranges and lemons, to decorate

1 Prepare an 18 cm (6 inch) soufflé dish. Cut a double thickness of greaseproof paper long enough to go around the outside of the dish and 5-7.5 cm (2-3 inches) deeper. Secure around the outside with paper clips and string.
2 Pour the fruit juices into a heatproof bowl and sprinkle in the gelatine. Stand the bowl over a saucepan of hot water and heat gently until dissolved. Remove the bowl from the water and set aside to cool slightly.
3 Put the fruit rinds, egg yolks and sugar in a large heatproof bowl and stand over the pan of gently simmering water. Whisk until the mixture is thick and holds a ribbon trail.
4 Remove the bowl from the pan and whisk in the gelatine liquid. Leave until beginning to set, whisking occasionally.
5 Whip the cream until it will stand in soft peaks. Whisk the egg whites until stiff. Fold the cream into the soufflé, then the egg whites, until evenly blended.
6 Pour the mixture into the prepared soufflé dish and level the surface. Chill in the refrigerator for at least 4 hours until set.
7 Carefully remove the paper from the edge of the soufflé. Press the crushed biscuits around the edge, then decorate the top with crystallised fruit. Serve chilled.

CHILLED APRICOT SOUFFLE

SERVES 6-8

225 g (8 oz) dried apricots, soaked overnight	4 eggs, separated
175 g (6 oz) caster sugar	300 ml (10 fl oz) double cream
30 ml (2 tbsp) almond-flavoured liqueur	ratafia biscuits and whipped cream, to decorate
15 ml (3 level tsp) powdered gelatine	

1 Prepare a 15 cm (6 inch) soufflé dish. Cut a double thickness of greaseproof paper long enough to go around the outside of the dish and 5-7.5 cm (2-3 inches) deeper. Secure around the outside with paper clips and string.
2 Drain the apricots, then put them in a saucepan with 120 ml (8 tbsp) water and 50 g (2 oz) of the sugar. Heat gently until the sugar has dissolved, then cover and simmer for about 30 minutes until tender. Leave to cool slightly, then rub through a sieve or purée in a blender. Stir in the liqueur and leave to cool for about 30 minutes.
3 Meanwhile, place 60 ml (4 tbsp) water in a small heatproof bowl and sprinkle in the gelatine. Stand the bowl over a saucepan of hot water and heat gently until dissolved. Remove and cool slightly.
4 Put the egg yolks and remaining sugar in a large heatproof bowl and stand over the pan of gently simmering water. Whisk until the mixture is thick and holds a ribbon trail, then remove and cool, whisking occasionally.
5 Whip the cream until it will stand in soft peaks. Whisk the egg whites until stiff.
6 Stir the gelatine liquid into the apricot purée, then fold into the egg yolk mixture until evenly blended. Fold in the whipped cream, then the egg whites.
7 Put the mixture into the prepared soufflé dish. Level the surface, then chill for at least 4 hours until set.
8 Carefully remove the paper from the edge of the soufflé. Press the crushed ratafias around the exposed edge. Decorate top with apricots and whipped cream.

CHOCOLATE ORANGE SOUFFLE

SERVES 6-8

450 ml (¾ pint) milk	grated rind and juice of 1 orange
150 g (5 oz) plain chocolate	300 ml (10 fl oz) whipping cream
3 eggs, separated, plus 1 egg white	15 ml (1 tbsp) crème de cacao or other chocolate-flavoured liqueur
75 g (3 oz) sugar	
15 ml (1 level tbsp) powdered gelatine	chocolate caraque or grated chocolate, to decorate

1 Prepare a 900 ml (1½ pint) soufflé dish with a paper collar (as for Citrus Soufflé, page 118).
2 Put the milk in a saucepan and break the chocolate into it. Heat gently until the chocolate melts, then cook over a high heat until almost boiling.
3 Whisk the egg yolks and sugar together until pale and thick. Gradually pour on the chocolate milk, stirring. Return to the saucepan and cook, stirring continuously, until it coats the back of a wooden spoon; this takes about 20 minutes. Do not boil.
4 Sprinkle the gelatine in 45 ml (3 tbsp) water in a small bowl and leave to soak. Place the bowl over a saucepan of simmering water and stir until dissolved. Stir into the custard with the orange rind and juice. Cool.
5 Whip the cream until it just holds its shape, then fold most of the cream into the cold mixture. Whisk the egg whites until stiff and fold into the mixture.
6 Pour the mixture into the prepared dish and leave to set. Remove the paper collar.
7 Stir the liqueur into the remaining cream and pipe on top of the soufflé. Decorate with caraque or grated chocolate to serve.

APPLE MINT MERINGUES

SERVES 8

FOR THE MERINGUE	15 ml (1 tbsp) granulated artificial sweetener
2 egg whites	
125 g (4 oz) caster sugar	4 mint sprigs
FOR THE FILLING	150 g (5 oz) Greek-style yogurt, or fromage frais
450 g (1 lb) sweet eating apples, peeled, cored and thinly sliced	15 ml (1 level tbsp) icing sugar
	mint sprigs and apples slices, to decorate

1 Whisk the egg whites until stiff but not dry. Add half of the sugar and whisk until stiff and shiny. Fold in the remaining sugar.
2 Mark sixteen 7.5 cm (3 inch) rounds on a sheet of non-stick baking parchment. Place on a baking sheet, pencil side down. Divide the meringue mixture between the rounds and spread with a round bladed knife to fill. Alternatively, using a 5 mm (¼ inch) plain nozzle, pipe the mixture into the rounds. Bake at 140°C (275°F) mark 1 for about 1 hour or until completely dried out and crisp. Leave to cool on a wire rack.
3 Place the apple in a saucepan with the sweetener, mint and 30 ml (2 tbsp) water. Cover and cook very gently for about 10 minutes or until the apple has softened. Cool, cover and chill for at least 1 hour.
4 To serve, spoon a little apple onto 8 meringue rounds. Top with the yogurt and the remaining meringues. Dust lightly with icing sugar and decorate with the sprigs of fresh mint and apple slices to serve.

COOK'S TIP

The egg whites must be whisked until they are very stiff and will hold an unwavering peak on the end of the whisk. The sugar can be added in two halves or whisked in a little at a time. This type of meringue is known as meringue Suisse.

CREAM MERINGUES

SERVES 8-10

FOR THE MERINGUE	FOR THE FILLING
3 egg whites, size 2	150 ml (¼ pint) double cream
75 g (3 oz) granulated sugar and 75 g (3 oz) caster sugar, or 175 g (6 oz) caster sugar	

1 Line two baking sheets with non-stick baking parchment.
2 Whisk egg whites until stiff. Gradually whisk in half the sugar, whisking after each addition until thoroughly incorporated, then fold in the remaining sugar very lightly with a metal spoon.
3 Spoon the meringue into a piping bag fitted with a large star nozzle and pipe small rounds on to the prepared baking sheets. Alternatively, spoon the mixture into fingers.
4 Bake in the oven at 110°C (225°F) mark ¼ for about 2½-3 hours, until firm and crisp, but still white. If they begin to brown, prop the oven door open a little. Transfer to a wire rack to cool.
5 To serve, whip the cream until thick. Sandwich the meringues together in pairs with cream.

COOK'S TIP

The secret of these delicious melt-in-the-mouth meringues, sandwiched lavishly with fresh cream, is to let them 'dry out' rather than bake, in a very slow oven.

Historians of cookery say that meringues were invented in 1720 by a Swiss pastry-cook called Gasparini. They have been a popular sweet for royalty for centuries and legend has it that Marie-Antoinette, the doomed Queen of France, used to make them herself.

MERINGUE BASKET

SERVES 6-8

FOR THE MERINGUE	FOR THE FILLING
4 egg whites	300 ml (½ pint) whipping cream
225 g (8 oz) icing sugar	about 450 g (1 lb) prepared fruit, eg strawberries, raspberries, bananas

1 Line three baking sheets with non-stick baking parchment and draw a 19 cm (7½ inch) circle on each. Turn the paper over.
2 To make the meringue, place three of the egg whites in a large bowl standing over a pan of simmering water. Sift in 175 g (6 oz) of the icing sugar. Whisk the egg whites and sugar until the mixture stands in very stiff peaks. Do not allow the bowl to get too hot.
3 Spoon one third of the meringue mixture into a piping bag fitted with a large star nozzle. Pipe rings of meringue, about 1 cm (½ inch) thick, inside two of the circles on the paper. Fill the bag with the remaining meringue and, starting from the centre, pipe a continuous coil of meringue on the third sheet of paper to make the base of the basket.
4 Bake all in the oven at 110°C (225°F) mark ¼ for 2½-3 hours until dry. Swap the positions of the meringues during this time so that they cook evenly.
5 Use the remaining egg white and sugar to make meringue as before and put into the piping bag. Remove the cooked meringue rings from the paper and layer up on the base, piping a ring of fresh meringue between each. Return to the oven for a further 1½-2 hours.
6 Leave to cool, then slide on to a wire rack and peel off the base paper. Just before serving, stand the meringue shell on a flat serving plate.
7 To make the filling, lightly whip the cream and spoon half into the base of the meringue basket; top with fruit. Cover with the remaining cream and top with fruit.

MERINGUE MEDLEY

MAKES 44 SMALL MERINGUES

FOR THE MERINGUE	15 ml (1 tbsp) orange-flavoured liqueur
6 egg whites	
350 g (12 oz) caster sugar	25 g (1 oz) pecans, walnuts or hazelnuts, finely chopped
15 ml (1 tbsp) finely chopped pistachio nuts	
FOR THE FILLING	15 ml (1 tbsp) raspberry purée
300 ml (¼ pint) double cream	75 g (3 oz) plain chocolate, melted

1 Line several baking sheets with non-stick baking parchment.

2 To make the meringue, whisk the egg whites and sugar together in a large bowl standing over a large pan of simmering water until very stiff and shiny. Remove from the heat and continue whisking until the meringue will hold unwavering peaks; do not let the meringue become too hot.

3 Fill a large piping bag fitted with a large star nozzle with meringue. Pipe into 7.5 cm (3 inch) plain and wavy lengths and into small whirls on the prepared baking sheets. Sprinkle the plain fingers with chopped pistachios.

4 Bake in the oven at 140°C (275°F) mark 1 for 2-2½ hours until dry. Change the sheets around in the oven during cooking to ensure that they all dry evenly. Allow the meringues to cool, then remove from the paper.

5 Whisk 150 ml (¼ pint) of the double cream with the liqueur until it will hold soft peaks, then fold in the chopped nuts. Sandwich the meringue whirls together, in pairs, with the nut cream.

6 Whisk the remaining cream until thick, then fold in the raspberry purée. Put the cream into a piping bag fitted with a large star nozzle. Sandwich the wavy meringue fingers together, in pairs, with the raspberry cream.

7 Dip the base of each pistachio meringue in the melted chocolate to coat evenly. Place on a sheet of greaseproof paper and leave until set.

BROWN SUGAR AND HAZELNUT MERINGUES

MAKES ABOUT 20

FOR THE MERINGUE	FOR THE FILLING
25 g (1 oz) hazelnuts	ice cream or whipped cream
3 egg whites	
175 g (6 oz) light brown soft sugar	

1 Line two large baking sheets with non-stick baking parchment.

2 Toast the hazelnuts under the grill until golden brown. Tip on to a clean tea towel and rub off the loose skins. Chop roughly.

3 Whisk the egg whites in a bowl until stiff. Whisk in the sugar, 15 ml (1 tbsp) at a time. Spoon the meringue mixture into a piping bag fitted with a large star nozzle and pipe about 40 small swirls on to the prepared baking sheets. Sprinkle with the hazelnuts.

4 Bake in the oven at 110°C (225°F) mark ¼ for about 2-3 hours or until dry. If the baking sheets are on different shelves, swap them halfway through cooking to ensure even browning. Leave to cool.

5 Sandwich the meringues together in pairs with a little ice cream or whipped cream to serve.

ROSE PETAL MERINGUES

SERVES 8

FOR THE MERINGUE	FOR THE FILLING
3 egg whites	300 ml (½ pint) double or whipping cream, whipped
175 g (6 oz) caster sugar	few drops of rose water (optional)
	crystallised rose petals (see below)

1 Mark eight 6 cm (2½ inch) circles on a sheet of non-stick baking parchment. Place on a baking sheet pencil side down.
2 Whisk the egg whites until stiff but not dry. Add half of the sugar and whisk until thick and glossy. Fold in the remaining sugar.
3 Transfer the meringue to a piping bag fitted with a 1 cm (½ inch) plain or star-shaped nozzle. Starting at the centre of each circle pipe the meringue in a spiral out to the edge of the marked circles. Pipe another ring around the edge of each round to form small nest shapes.
4 Bake at 140°C (275°F) mark 1 (or at your ovens lowest setting) for about 1-1½ hours or until firm and dried out. Leave to cool on the baking sheet.
5 Flavour the cream with a few drops of rose water, if wished and use to fill the meringues. Sprinkle with crystallised rose petals.

COOK'S TIP

To crystallise rose petals, carefully break off the petals, brush with egg white and dip in caster sugar. Arrange on a sheet of greaseproof paper and leave to set.
Unfilled meringue nests keep well in an airtight container for several weeks. To prevent meringues softening, serve the cream separately and allow guests to help themselves. Once filled, meringues should be eaten right away.

ALMOND RUM MERINGUE

SERVES 8

75 g (3 oz) ground almonds	16 flaked almonds
4 eggs, separated	15 ml (1 tbsp) dark rum
250 g (9 oz) caster sugar	50 g (2 oz) unsalted butter
10 ml (2 level tsp) cornflour	150 ml (5 fl oz) double cream
10 ml (2 tsp) white vinegar	225 g (8 oz) raspberries

1 Spread the ground almonds out on a baking sheet and brown in the oven at 200°C (400°F) mark 6 for 5-10 minutes. Remove from the oven and leave for about 15 minutes to cool.
2 Line a large baking sheet with non-stick baking parchment. Lower the oven temperature to 150°C (300°F) mark 2.
3 Whisk the egg whites until stiff. Add 100 g (4 oz) sugar, the cornflour and vinegar. Whisk again until very stiff and shiny. Fold in a further 100 g (4 oz) sugar and the ground almonds.
4 With a palette knife, spread one third of the meringue in a 20 cm (8 inch) square on the non-stick paper.
5 Spoon the remaining meringue into a piping bag fitted with a large star nozzle. Pipe lines to make a square at each corner of the meringue and then pipe a square in the centre to form nine boxes. Decorate with flaked almonds.
6 Put into the oven and immediately lower it to 140°C (275°F) mark 1. Bake for about 1½ hours or until well dried out. Slide on to a wire rack and cool.
7 Put the egg yolks, rum and remaining sugar into a bowl. Melt the butter gently in a small pan and pour over the egg yolks, whisking constantly until thick.
8 Lightly whip the double cream until it just holds its shape and fold into the egg mixture. When the meringue is cold, carefully peel off the paper and place on a flat plate.
9 Spoon the cream into the meringue boxes and decorate with the raspberries. Refrigerate for 20 minutes before serving.

PAVLOVA

SERVES 8

FOR THE MERINGUE	FOR THE FILLING
3 egg whites	2 passion fruit
175 g (6 oz) caster sugar	2 kiwi fruit
5 ml (1 tsp) cornflour	225 g (8 oz) strawberries
5 ml (1 tsp) vinegar	225 g (8 oz) fresh pineapple
2.5 ml (½ tsp) vanilla essence	450 ml (¾ pint) double cream
	walnuts, pecans or almonds, to decorate

1 Line a baking sheet with greased foil or non-stick baking parchment.

2 To make the meringue, whisk the egg whites in a large bowl until very stiff. Add 50 g (2 oz) of the sugar and whisk until very stiff. Add another 50 g (2 oz) sugar and whisk once more until the mixture returns to its stiff texture. Spoon in the remaining sugar and whisk again until shiny and standing in stiff peaks.

3 Fold in the cornflour, vinegar and vanilla essence.

4 Pile or pipe the meringue in a 23 cm (9 inch) round or oval on to the prepared baking sheet, making sure there is a substantial dip or hollow in the centre to hold the filling.

5 Bake in the oven at 130°C (250°F) mark ½ for 1¼-1½ hours or until pale brown and dry but a little soft in the centre. Press lightly with a finger to test if the meringue is cooked. Leave to cool slightly, then peel off the foil or paper and place on a serving dish to cool completely. At this stage the meringue will probably crack and sink a little – this is to be expected with a Pavlova.

6 To make the filling, halve the passion fruit and scoop out the pulp. Peel and slice the kiwi fruit. Halve the strawberries. Slice the pineapple, discard skin and core, and roughly chop the flesh. Whip the cream until it just holds its shape. Either fold the fruit into the cream and spoon into the Pavlova or fill the centre with cream. Scatter with nuts and serve immediately.

HAZELNUT MERINGUE GATEAU

SERVES 6-8

FOR THE MERINGUE	FOR THE FILLING
3 egg whites	300 ml (½ pint) double cream
175 g (6 oz) caster sugar	350 g (12 oz) raspberries, hulled
50 g (2 oz) hazelnuts, skinned, toasted and finely chopped	icing sugar, for dusting
	finely chopped pistachio nuts, to decorate

1 Line two baking sheets with non-stick baking parchment, then draw a 20 cm (8 inch) circle on each one. Invert the paper.

2 To make the meringue, whisk the egg whites in a bowl until very stiff, but not dry. Gradually add the caster sugar, a little at a time, whisking well between each addition until stiff and very shiny. Carefully fold in the chopped hazelnuts.

3 Divide the meringue equally between the prepared baking sheets, then spread neatly into rounds. With a palette knife, mark the top of one of the rounds into swirls – this will be the top meringue.

4 Bake in the oven at 140°C (275°F) mark 1 for about 1½ hours until dry. Change the positions of the baking sheets during cooking so that the meringues dry out evenly. Turn the oven off, and allow the meringues to cool in the oven.

5 To make the filling, whip the cream until it will hold soft peaks. Carefully remove the meringues from the paper. Place the smooth meringue round on a large flat serving plate, then spread with the cream. Arrange the raspberries on top of the cream, then place the second meringue on top. Sift icing sugar over the top of the gâteau, then sprinkle with the nuts. Serve the gâteau as soon as possible.

RASPBERRY AND LAVENDER PAVLOVA

SERVES 8

3 egg whites	300 ml (½ pint) Greek-style yogurt
190 g (6½ oz) lavender sugar (see below)	450 g (1 lb) fresh raspberries
5 ml (1 level tsp) cornflour	150 ml (¼ pint) double cream
5 ml (1 tsp) raspberry vinegar	a few lavender flowers, to decorate

1 Draw a 23 cm (9 inch) oval on a piece of non-stick baking parchment and place on a baking sheet.
2 To make the meringue, whisk the egg whites in a large bowl until very stiff. Add 50 g (2 oz) of the sugar and whisk until stiff. Add another 50 g (2 oz) sugar and whisk again. Add a further 50 g (2 oz) sugar and continue whisking until the meringue forms soft peaks. Fold in the cornflour and vinegar.
3 Pile or pipe the meringue into the oval marked on the baking sheet. Make a dip in the middle to hold the filling.
4 Bake in the oven at 180°C (350°F) mark 4 for 5 minutes, then at 130°C (250°F) mark ½ for a further 45-50 minutes or until set but still soft in the middle.
5 Leave to cool slightly, then carefully peel off the paper. Don't worry if the meringue cracks at this stage.
6 When completely cold, whip the cream with the remaining sugar until it just holds its shape, then fold in the yogurt. Roughly crush half of the raspberries and fold into the cream mixture. Pile on top of the Pavlova.
7 Push the remaining raspberries through a sieve to make a raspberry sauce. Drizzle the sauce over the Pavlova. Decorate with lavender flowers.

COOK'S TIP

To make the lavender sugar, put a few sprigs of fresh or dried lavender in a screw topped jar filled with caster sugar. Leave for at least two weeks. Shake well then discard the lavender and use as required.

STRAWBERRY MERINGUE

SERVES 4

FOR THE MERIGUE	FOR THE FILLING
3 egg whites	300 ml (10 fl oz) double cream
pinch of salt	350 g (12 oz) strawberries, sliced
250 g (9 oz) caster sugar	
5 ml (1 tsp) vanilla flavouring	
5 ml (1 tsp) vinegar	

1 Draw a 23 cm (9 inch) circle on a piece of non-stick baking parchment and place on a baking sheet.
2 Whisk the egg whites with the salt until very stiff, then gradually whisk in the sugar. Beat until it forms stiff peaks again. Fold in the vanilla flavouring and vinegar.
3 Spread the meringue mixture over the circle and bake in the oven at 140°C (275°F) mark 1 for about 1 hour until firm.
4 Leave to cool. Then carefully remove the paper and place the meringue on a plate. Whip the cream until stiff then pile on to the meringue and decorate with the fruit.

COOK'S TIP

The light, crisp texture of meringues is the perfect foil to creamy fillings and slices of soft fruit. To make the meringue filling lower in calories, use a mixture of half natural yogurt and half cream or fromage frais.

BAKED ALASKA

SERVES 6-8

225 g (8 oz) plus 10 ml (2 level tsp) caster sugar	225 g (8 oz) fresh or frozen raspberries
50 g (2 oz) plus 5 ml (1 level tsp) plain flour	30 ml (2 tbsp) orange-flavoured liqueur
2 eggs, size 2	4 egg whites, at room temperature
finely grated rind of 1 orange	450 ml (15 fl oz) vanilla ice cream

1 Grease a 20 cm (8 inch) non-stick flan tin. Sprinkle over 10 ml (2 level tsp) caster sugar and tilt the tin to give an even coating of sugar. Add 5 ml (1 level tsp) plain flour and coat similarly.

2 Place the eggs and 50 g (2 oz) caster sugar in a bowl and whisk until the mixture is very thick. Fold in the orange rind and sifted flour.

3 Pour the mixture into the tin and level the surface. Bake in the oven at 180°C (350°F) mark 4 for 20-25 minutes, until golden. Turn out on to a wire rack to cool.

4 Place the raspberries in a shallow dish and sprinkle over the liqueur. Cover and leave in a cool place for 2 hours turning occasionally.

5 Place the cold sponge flan on a large ovenproof serving dish and spoon the raspberries with the juice into the centre of the flan.

6 Stiffly whisk the egg whites. Whisk in half the remaining sugar, then carefully fold in the rest.

7 Fit a piping bag with a large star nozzle and fill with the meringue mixture. Place the ice cream on top of the raspberries. Pipe the meringue on top; start from the base and pipe the meringue around and over the ice cream to cover completely.

8 Immediately bake in the oven at 230°C (450°F) mark 8 for 3-4 minutes, until the meringue is tinged with brown; do not allow to burn. Serve immediately.

FLOATING SPICE ISLANDS

SERVES 6-8

FOR THE SAUCE	FOR THE MERINGUE
350 g (12 oz) blackcurrants, stalks removed	2 egg whites
75 g (3 oz) granulated sugar	50 g (2 oz) caster sugar
30 ml (2 tbsp) blackcurrant-flavoured liqueur	grated nutmeg
	pinch of salt

1 To make the sauce, place the blackcurrants, granulated sugar and 60 ml (4 tbsp) water in a small saucepan. Cover tightly and cook gently until the fruit softens. Rub through a nylon sieve, then leave to cool. Stir in the liqueur. Cover and chill.

2 Meanwhile to make the meringue, whisk the egg whites in a bowl until stiff, but not dry. Gradually whisk in the caster sugar, keeping the mixture stiff. Fold in 1.25 ml (¼ tsp) grated nutmeg.

3 Pour 2 cm (¾ inch) water into a large frying pan and bring to a gentle simmer. Add the salt.

4 Shape the meringue into small egg shapes, using two spoons as moulds. Slide about six or eight at a time into the liquid and poach gently for 2-3 minutes. The meringue will pull up then shrink back a little. When cooked, it will be firm if lightly touched. Remove with a fish slice and drain on absorbent kitchen paper. Poach the remaining mixture. Store in a cool place for not more than 2 hours.

5 To serve, spoon a little blackcurrant sauce on to individual serving dishes. Float a few 'islands' on top and sprinkle with nutmeg.

LIGHT BATTERS & OMELETTES

Quick and easy fruit-filled pancakes, classic French flambéed crêpes, crisp light fritters and soufflé omelettes are included in this chapter. For a special occasion, try one of the desserts based on a yeast batter – savarin, strawberry babas or blueberry blinis.

PANCAKES

MAKES 8 PANCAKES OR CRÊPES

100 g (4 oz) plain flour	300 ml (½ pint) milk
pinch of salt	oil for frying
1 egg	

1 Sift the flour and salt into a bowl and make a well in the centre. Break in the egg and beat well with a wooden spoon. Gradually beat in the milk, drawing in the flour from the sides to make a smooth batter.
2 Heat a little oil in an 18 cm (7 inch) heavy-based frying pan, running it around the base and sides of the pan, until hot. Pour off any surplus.
3 Pour in just enough batter to thinly coat the base of the pan. Cook for 1-2 minutes until golden brown. Turn or toss and cook the second side until golden.
4 Transfer the pancake to a plate and keep hot. Repeat with the remaining batter to make eight pancakes. Pile the cooked pancakes on top of each other with greaseproof paper in between each one and keep warm in the oven while cooking the remainder.
5 Serve as soon as they are all cooked, sprinkled with sugar and lemon juice.

CHERRY AND ALMOND PANCAKES

SERVES 4

425 g (15 oz) can cherry pie filling	8 pancakes (see left)
225 g (8 oz) can Morello cherries pitted	50 g (2 oz) flaked almonds, toasted
15 ml (1 tbsp) kirsch or cherry brandy	150 ml (¼ pint) double cream

1 Heat the pie filling and cherries with the kirsch or cherry brandy.
2 Spread the mixture evenly over four pancakes, place on a large ovenproof plate or dish, cover with the four remaining pancakes and sprinkle the tops with flaked almonds.
3 Cover lightly with foil and bake in the oven at 180°C (350°F) mark 4 for 25-30 minutes. Serve with the cream.

COOK'S TIP

An essential for pancake and omelette making is a good heavy-based frying pan. Ideally it should be kept solely for this purpose and should never be scrubbed, just wiped out with absorbent kitchen paper after use. Choose a pan with a base area of about 20-23 cm (8-9 inches), with or without a non-stick coating.

PANCAKES CREOLE

SERVES 4

8 pancakes (see page 126)	60 ml (4 tbsp) dark rum
finely grated rind and juice of 1 lime	2.5 ml (½ level tsp) ground cinnamon
50 g (2 oz) butter or margarine	3-4 bananas
50 g (2 oz) demerara sugar	orange and lime, to decorate

1   As they are cooked, slide each pancake out of the pan on to a warm plate and stack with greaseproof paper in between.

2   Put the lime rind and juice in a saucepan with the fat, sugar, rum and cinnamon. Heat gently until the fat has melted and the sugar dissolved, stirring occasionally.

3   Peel the bananas and slice thinly into the sauce. Cook gently for 5 minutes until tender.

4   Remove the banana slices from the sauce with a slotted spoon. Place a few slices in the centre of each pancake, then fold the pancakes into 'envelopes' around the cooked bananas.

5   Place in a warmed serving dish and pour over the hot sauce. Decorate with orange and lime twists and serve with cream, if liked.

CLAFOUTIS

SERVES 6

45 ml (3 tbsp) kirsch	pinch of salt
450 g (1 lb) black cherries, stoned	25 g (1 oz) butter, melted
FOR THE BATTER	300 ml (½ pint) creamy milk
75 g (3 oz) plain flour	3 eggs, beaten
50 g (2 oz) icing sugar	icing sugar, for dusting

1   Generously grease a shallow ovenproof dish or tin.

2   Pour the kirsch over the cherries and leave to macerate for at least 30 minutes.

3   To make the batter, mix the flour, icing sugar and salt together in a bowl, then make a well in the centre. Pour in the butter, milk and eggs. Beat together to make a smooth batter. Pour a very thin layer of batter into the prepared dish.

4   Bake in the oven at 220°C (425°F) mark 7 for 5-10 minutes or until just set.

5   Drain the cherries, reserving the liquid, and arrange in a layer over the batter. Stir the reserved liquid into the remaining batter, pour evenly over the cherries. Return to the oven and bake for a further 40-45 minutes or until risen and golden brown.

6   Leave to cool for 5 minutes, then dust generously with icing sugar and serve while still warm with single cream.

COOK'S TIP

A Clafoutis is a baked batter pudding popular throughout France. It is usually made with black cherries. Traditionalists insist that the cherries must not be stoned; we found that with stoned cherries it was much easier and daintier to eat! The choice is yours.

CREPES SUZETTE

MAKES 8

50 g (2 oz) butter or margarine	30 ml (2 tbsp) Grand Marnier or other orange-flavoured liqueur
25 g (1 oz) caster sugar	45 ml (3 tbsp) brandy or rum
finely pared rind and juice of 1 large orange	8 freshly cooked pancakes (see page 126)

1 Melt the butter in a large frying pan. Remove from the heat and add the sugar, shredded orange rind and juice, and the liqueur. Heat gently to dissolve the sugar.
2 Fold each pancake in half and then in half again to form a fan shape. Place the pancakes in the frying pan in overlapping lines.
3 Warm the brandy, pour it over the pancakes and set alight. Shake gently, then serve at once with cream.

CREPES ANNETTE

SERVES 6

FOR THE CREPES	
250 g (9 oz) plain flour	25 g (1 oz) butter, melted
5 ml (1 level tsp) baking powder	2 eggs, beaten
2.5 ml (½ level tsp) bicarbonate of soda	oil for frying
	FOR THE FILLING
pinch of salt	425 g (15 oz) can black cherries
135 ml (9 tbsp) kirsch	175 g (6 oz) full fat soft cheese
600 ml (1 pint) milk	50 g (2 oz) caster sugar

1 To make the crêpes, sift the flour, baking powder, bicarbonate of soda and salt into a bowl. Add 90 ml (6 tbsp) of the kirsch, the milk, butter and eggs, then beat until smooth.
2 Heat a little oil in a heavy-based frying pan. Pour in 30 ml (2 tbsp) batter. Swirl around the pan and cook until golden underneath. Turn over and cook on the other side. Make 12 crêpes.
3 Stack the crêpes with greaseproof paper in between and keep warm in the oven.
4 To make the filling, drain the cherries; reserve the juice and a few cherries. Stone the cherries, if necessary. Beat the soft cheese and sugar together until soft and fluffy. Chop the remaining cherries roughly and fold them into the cheese mixture.
5 Spread a little filling on each crêpe and fold into triangles; or put the filling in the centre and roll up the crêpes. Arrange in a serving dish and keep warm.
6 Heat the reserved cherries and syrup in a pan. Gently warm the remaining kirsch. Drizzle the cherries and syrup over the crêpes, then add the kirsch and set alight. Serve immediately.

ORANGE AND NECTARINE CREPES

SERVES 4-6

8 pancakes (see page 126)	4 large ripe nectarines
finely grated rind and juice of 2 oranges	30 ml (2 tbsp) orange-flavoured liqueur
50 g (2 oz) caster sugar	45 ml (3 tbsp) brandy

1   Grease an ovenproof dish.

2   Stack the crêpes with greaseproof paper in between and keep warm in the oven.

3   Make the orange juice up to 150 ml (¼ pint) with water. Place the rind and juice in a saucepan with the sugar. Warm gently until the sugar dissolves, then boil for 1 minute.

4   Meanwhile, quarter each nectarine, skin and roughly chop the flesh. Place the flesh in the syrup and simmer gently for 3-4 minutes.

5   Remove from the heat and stir in the liqueur. Strain off the syrup and reserve.

6   Fill the pancakes with the nectarines, then fold each pancake into a fan shape. Place, slightly overlapping, in the prepared ovenproof dish. Pour over the syrup and cover tightly with greased foil.

7   Bake in the oven at 190°C (375°F) mark 5 for about 25 minutes or until thoroughly hot.

8   Place the brandy in a small saucepan. Warm slightly, then set alight with a match and immediately pour over the crêpes. Serve straight away, with cream or yogurt.

VARIATION

Use peaches instead of nectarines for the crêpe filling.

BEIGNETS DE FRUITS

SERVES 8

225 g (8 oz) plain flour	2 large eating apples, peeled, cored and cut into rings
large pinch of salt	2 firm nectarines, stoned and cut into quarters
15 ml (1 tbsp) icing sugar	
300 ml (½ pint) beer	2 bananas, peeled and cut into chunks
2 eggs, separated	
15 ml (1 tbsp) oil	caster sugar, for sprinkling
oil for deep-frying	

1   To make the batter, mix the flour, salt and icing sugar together in a bowl, then make a well in the centre. Add the beer and egg yolks. Beat together to make a smooth batter. Add the oil. Whisk the egg whites until stiff, then fold into the batter.

2   Heat the oil in a deep-fryer to 190°C (375°F). Dip the prepared fruits in the batter and deep-fry in batches. The apple will take about 4 minutes and the nectarine and banana about 3 minutes.

3   Drain on absorbent kitchen paper and keep warm while frying the remainder. Serve hot, sprinkled with caster sugar.

COOK'S TIP

Most fruits make delicious beignets. Remember that soft fruits like apricots or peaches will require a much shorter cooking time than fruits such as apples and pears.

APPLE AND BANANA FRITTERS

SERVES 4-6

100 g (4 oz) plain flour	1 large cooking apple
pinch of salt	2 bananas
90 ml (6 tbsp) lukewarm water	juice of ½ a lemon
20 ml (4 tsp) vegetable oil	oil for deep-frying
2 egg whites	caster sugar, to serve

1 Place the flour and salt into a bowl. Make a well in the centre. Add the water and oil and beat to form a smooth batter.
2 Beat the egg whites in a clean dry bowl until they are stiff; then set aside.
3 Peel, quarter and core the apple. Peel the bananas. Slice the fruit thickly and sprinkle at once with the lemon juice to prevent discoloration.
4 Fold the beaten egg whites into the batter, then immediately dip in the slices of fruit.
5 Deep-fry the fritters a few at a time in hot oil until puffed and light golden. Remove with a slotted spoon and pile on to a serving dish lined with absorbent kitchen paper. Serve immediately, sprinkled with caster sugar.

GULAB JAMUN

SERVES 4-6

225 g (8 oz) granulated sugar	50 g (2 oz) self-raising flour
6 green cardamom pods, lightly crushed	15 ml (1 level tbsp) semolina
175 g (6 oz) dried skimmed milk with vegetable fat	about 150 ml (¼ pint) milk
	oil for deep-frying
10 ml (2 level tsp) baking powder	rose water, for sprinkling

1 Put the sugar and 450 ml (¾ pint) water in a saucepan. Bring slowly to the boil, stirring until the sugar has dissolved. Add the crushed cardamoms and boil rapidly for 4 minutes. Remove from the heat and cover.
2 Mix the dried milk, baking powder, flour, semolina and enough milk together in a bowl to mix to a stiff dough, rather like shortcrust pastry.
3 Knead the dough on a work surface until smooth. Divide into 24 pieces. Keep covered to prevent the dough drying out. Roll each piece into a completely smooth ball.
4 Heat the oil in a deep-fat fryer to 170°C (325°F). Deep fry the dough pieces in batches for 2-3 minutes until golden brown on all sides, turning them with a slotted spoon to ensure even browning. They must not fry too quickly as they have to cook all the way through before becoming too brown on the outside. Remove with a slotted spoon, drain on absorbent kitchen paper and keep warm while frying the remainder.
5 While the Gulab Jamuns are still hot, transfer them to a warmed serving dish. Pour over the warm syrup and sprinkle with rose water. Serve warm or cold.

COOK'S TIP

Gulab Jamun are popular in India; they are very sweet and syrupy, with a wonderfully exotic aroma of rose water, which is worth adding at the end for an authentic Gulab Jamun. Rose water is available in bottles at chemists, delicatessens and herbalists.

FRUIT AND RUM SAVARIN

SERVES 6

15 g (½ oz) fresh yeast	225 g (8 oz) granulated sugar
45 ml (3 tbsp) tepid milk	120 ml (8 tbsp) dark rum
100 g (4 oz) strong plain flour, sifted with a pinch of salt	2 bananas, peeled and sliced
30 ml (2 tbsp) caster sugar	450 g (1 lb) black grapes, halved and seeded
2 eggs, beaten	2 kiwi fruit, peeled and sliced
50 g (2 oz) unsalted butter	2 small oranges, skinned and segmented

1 Grease and flour a 1.1 litre (2 pint) savarin mould.

2 Cream the yeast in a small bowl with the milk. Add 25 g (1 oz) of the flour and beat well with a fork. Leave in a warm place for 10-15 minutes until frothy.

3 Put remaining flour in a warmed large bowl with 5 ml (1 tsp) of the caster sugar and the eggs. Add the frothy yeast mixture, then beat until an elastic dough is formed. Cover and leave in a warm place until doubled in size.

4 Beat the softened butter into the dough a little at a time until evenly incorporated.

5 Put the dough in the prepared mould. Cover with a floured tea towel and leave to prove in a warm place until it has risen to the top of the mould. Uncover the mould.

6 Bake in the oven at 200°C (400°F) mark 6 for 25-30 minutes until risen and golden brown.

7 Meanwhile, make the rum syrup. Put the granulated sugar and 200 ml (7 fl oz) water in a heavy-based saucepan and heat gently until the sugar has dissolved. Bring to the boil and boil steadily for 5 minutes until syrupy. Remove from the heat and stir in 90 ml (6 tbsp) of the rum.

8 Turn the savarin out on to a wire rack placed over a large plate. Prick all over with a fine skewer, then slowly spoon over the warm syrup. Leave until cold.

9 Toss the fruits together with the remaining caster sugar and rum. Place the savarin on a serving plate and pile the fruits in the centre. Serve immediately, with cream.

STRAWBERRY BABAS

SERVES 6

15 g (½ oz) fresh yeast or 7.5 ml (1½ tsp) dried	25 g (1 oz) desiccated coconut
45 ml (3 tbsp) tepid milk	90 ml (6 tbsp) redcurrant jelly or sieved strawberry jam
2 eggs, lightly beaten	
50 g (2 oz) butter, melted and cooled	75 ml (5 tbsp) lemon juice
100 g (4 oz) plain flour	450 g (1 lb) strawberries, hulled
15 ml (1 tbsp) caster sugar	

1 Lightly oil six 9 cm (3½ inch) individual ring moulds and turn upside down on absorbent kitchen paper to drain off the excess oil.

2 Blend the fresh yeast with the milk. If using dried yeast, sprinkle it on to the milk and leave in a warm place for 15 minutes or until frothy. Gradually beat the eggs and butter into the yeast liquid.

3 Mix the flour, sugar and coconut together in a bowl. With a wooden spoon, gradually stir in the yeast mixture to form a thick smooth batter. Beat together.

4 Turn the batter into the prepared moulds, cover and leave in a warm place for about 30 minutes or until the moulds are nearly two-thirds full.

5 Bake in the oven at 190°C (375°F) mark 5 for 15-20 minutes until golden. Turn out on to a wire rack placed over a large plate.

6 Put the jelly and lemon juice into a small pan over a low heat. (Alternatively, microwave on HIGH for 1-2 minutes.) When the jelly has melted, spoon over the warm babas until well glazed, allowing any excess to collect on the plate under the wire rack. Transfer to individual serving plates.

7 Return the excess jelly mixture to the pan and add the strawberries; stir to coat. Remove from heat and cool for 15-20 minutes or until almost set. Spoon into the centre of the babas. Serve warm or cold, with cream.

BLUEBERRY AND BUTTERMILK BLINIS

SERVES 8

125 g (4 oz) plain flour	450 ml (¾ pint) buttermilk
125 g (4 oz) buckwheat flour	1 egg, separated
30 ml (2 tbsp) caster sugar	vegetable oil for frying
2.5 ml (½ level tsp) salt	225 g (8 oz) blueberries
2.5 ml (½ level tsp) fast action dried yeast	raspberry sauce and soured cream or maple syrup, to serve

1   Put the flours, sugar, salt and yeast into a bowl and mix well. Gradually beat in the buttermilk to make a smooth batter. Cover and leave in a warm place for about 40 minutes or until doubled in size.

2   Beat in the egg yolk. Whisk the egg white until stiff, then fold into the batter with the blueberries.

3   Heat a griddle or large flat, heavy-based frying pan. Brush generously with oil and heat until the oil is hot.

4   Using a measuring jug or a ladle, drop three or four small 'pools' of batter onto the hot griddle.

5   Cook over medium heat for 2-3 minutes until bubbles rise to the surface and burst, then turn the blinis over with a palette knife. Continue cooking for a further 2-3 minutes until golden brown on the other side.

6   Keep the blinis warm, wrapped in a clean tea towel in a low oven while you cook the remainder. Re-grease the griddle or frying pan in between cooking each batch. Serve warm with raspberry sauce and soured cream or maple syrup.

RUM SOUFFLE OMELETTE

SERVES 1

2 eggs, separated	15 g (½ oz) butter
5 ml (1 tsp) caster sugar	5 ml (1 tbsp) apricot jam, warmed
15 ml (1 tbsp) dark rum	30 ml (2 tbsp) icing sugar

1   Mix the egg yolks, caster sugar and rum together in a bowl.

2   Whisk the egg whites until stiff and standing in peaks.

3   Melt the butter in a heavy-based omelette pan until foaming. Fold the egg whites quickly into the egg yolk mixture, then pour into the foaming butter.

4   Cook over moderate heat for 2-3 minutes until the underside of the omelette is golden brown. Place the pan under a preheated hot grill and cook for a few minutes more until the top is golden brown.

5   Slide the omelette on to a sheet of foil placed on a warmed serving plate. Spread with the warmed jam, then tip the foil to fold over the omelette.

6   Sift the icing sugar thickly over the top of the omelette, then mark in a criss-cross pattern with hot metal skewers, if liked. Carefully remove the foil and serve immediately.

VARIATIONS

Fruit Soufflé Omelette
Replace the apricot jam with sliced fresh fruit or berries, such as raspberries or strawberries.

Chocolate Soufflé Omelette
Omit the jam and drizzle the omelette with 40 g (1½ oz) melted chocolate (in step 5). Add a few chopped nuts. Sprinkle the soufflé omelette with a mixture of icing sugar and ground cinnamon.

CUSTARDS & CREAM DESSERTS

From fragrant custards and syllabubs – delicately flavoured with vanilla, subtle spices and herbs – to sophisticated bavarois and classic Italian tiramisu, here you will find smooth, creamy desserts to tempt every palate. Childhood favourites such as blancmange and junket are included too.

CREME CARAMEL

SERVES 4

125 g (4 oz) sugar plus 15 ml (1 level tbsp)	600 ml (1 pint) milk
4 eggs	1.25 ml (¼ tsp) vanilla flavouring

1 Place the 125 g (4 oz) sugar in a small saucepan and carefully pour in 150 ml (¼ pint) water. Heat gently until all the sugar has dissolved, stirring occasionally.
2 Bring the syrup to a fast boil and cook rapidly until the caramel is a golden brown. Remove from the heat and leave for a few seconds to darken. Pour into a 15 cm (6 inch) soufflé dish and cool.
3 Whisk the eggs and remaining sugar in a bowl. Warm the milk and pour on to the egg mixture. Whisk in the vanilla, then strain the custard on to the cool caramel.
4 Stand the dish in a roasting tin containing enough hot water to come halfway up the sides of the dish. Bake in the oven at 170°C (325°F) mark 3 for about 1 hour. The custard should be just set and firm to the touch.
5 When cold, cover the dish and leave in the refrigerator for several hours, preferably overnight. Take out of the refrigerator 30 minutes before serving. Carefully invert on to plates, allowing the caramel to run down the sides.

CREME BRULEE

SERVES 6

600 ml (1 pint) double cream	4 egg yolks
1 vanilla pod	125 g (4 oz) caster sugar

1 Pour the cream into the top of a double boiler or into a mixing bowl placed over a pan of simmering water. Add the vanilla pod and warm gently until almost boiling, then remove from the heat. Remove the vanilla pod.
2 Beat together the egg yolks and 50 g (2 oz) of the caster sugar until light in colour. Gradually pour on the cream, stirring until evenly mixed.
3 Stand 6 individual ramekin dishes in a roasting tin containing enough hot water to come halfway up the sides of the dishes. Pour the custard mixture slowly into the ramekins, dividing it equally between them.
4 Bake in the oven at 150°C (300°F) mark 2 for about 1 hour until set. Do not allow the skin to colour. Remove from the tin and leave to cool, then refrigerate overnight.
5 Sprinkle the remaining sugar evenly over the top of each and put under a preheated hot grill for 2-3 minutes until the sugar turns to a caramel. Leave to cool, then chill before serving.

TANGERINE BRULEES

SERVES 2

150 ml (¼ pint) double cream	45 ml (3 tbsp) caster sugar
few drops of vanilla flavouring	1 tangerine, peeled and segmented
2 egg yolks, size 6	20 ml (4 tsp) orange-flavoured liqueur

1 Pour the cream into a small saucepan and heat until almost boiling, then remove from the heat. Add the vanilla flavouring.

2 In a medium bowl, beat together the egg yolks and 15 ml (1 tbsp) of the caster sugar until light in colour.

3 Pour the cream gradually on to the egg yolk and sugar mixture, stirring well.

4 Strain the mixture into the saucepan and cook, stirring over a gentle heat for about 10 minutes, or until the mixture coats the back of a spoon. Cover with greaseproof paper and allow to cool for 20 minutes.

5 Lay the segments of tangerine in the bottom of two 150 ml (¼ pint) ramekins and add 10 ml (2 tsp) liqueur to each one. Spoon the cooled custard mixture evenly into the ramekins, dividing it equally between them.

6 Cover and chill in the refrigerator for at least 3 hours or overnight.

7 Sprinkle the remaining sugar evenly over the top of each ramekin and put under a preheated hot grill for 2-3 minutes until the sugar turns to a caramel. Leave to cool for 15 minutes, then chill for at least 2 hours before serving.

MINTED STRAWBERRY CUSTARDS

SERVES 6

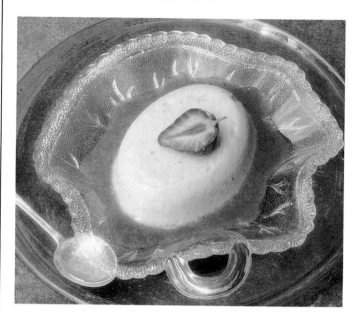

450 ml (¾ pint) milk	20 ml (4 level tsp) powdered gelatine
4 large sprigs mint	700 g (1½ lb) strawberries, hulled
1 egg	
2 egg yolks	15 ml (1 tbsp) icing sugar
45 ml (3 tbsp) caster sugar	strawberries, to decorate

1 Oil six 150 ml (¼ pint) ramekin dishes.

2 Place the milk and mint sprigs in a saucepan. Bring slowly to the boil, cover and leave to infuse for about 30 minutes.

3 Whisk the egg and yolks with the caster sugar in a bowl. Strain over the milk. Return to the pan and cook gently, stirring, until the custard just coats the back of the spoon; do not boil. Leave to cool.

4 Sprinkle the gelatine over 45 ml (3 tbsp) water in a small bowl and leave to soak for 2-3 minutes. Place the bowl over a pan of simmering water and stir until dissolved. (Alternatively, microwave on HIGH for 30 seconds or until dissolved.) Stir the gelatine into the custard.

5 Purée and sieve the strawberries. Whisk about two thirds into the cold, but not set, custard. Pour the custard into the dishes and chill to set – about 3 hours.

6 Meanwhile, whisk the icing sugar into the remaining strawberry purée. Chill.

7 To serve, turn out the custards. Surround with strawberry sauce, then decorate with strawberries.

VARIATION

Replace the mint sprigs with a few lemon geranium leaves.

COEURS A LA CREME

SERVES 4-6

225 g (8 oz) curd or ricotta cheese	few drops of vanilla essence
300 ml (½ pint) crème fraîche	25 g (1 oz) caster sugar
	2 egg whites

1 Line four small heart-shaped perforated moulds with muslin.
2 Press the cheese through a nylon sieve into a bowl. Lightly whip the cream, vanilla essence and sugar together. Mix into the cheese.
3 Whisk the egg whites until stiff, then fold into the cheese mixture.
4 Turn the mixture into the prepared moulds. Leave to drain overnight in the refrigerator. Turn out and serve with strawberries and single cream.

COOK'S TIP

Light, delicate and refreshing, this may be eaten with cream, or with soft summer fruit, ideally, tiny wild strawberries. This dessert takes its name from the small heart-shaped white porcelain colanders in which it is made.

COCONUT CUSTARDS WITH TROPICAL FRUITS

SERVES 8

225 g (8 oz) granulated sugar	60 ml (4 tbsp) shredded or desiccated coconut
3 eggs	2 mangoes, peeled
2 egg yolks	1 large pawpaw, peeled
30 ml (2 tbsp) caster sugar	juice of 1-2 limes
600 ml (1 pint) thin coconut milk	2 passion fruit
300 ml (½ pint) evaporated milk	

1 Have ready eight warmed 150 ml (¼ pint) ramekins. Put the granulated sugar in a heavy saucepan, pour in 150 ml (¼ pint) cold water and heat gently, until dissolved. Increase the heat and boil, without stirring, until dark caramel in colour. Immediately pour into the ramekins, swirling the caramel around the sides quickly.
2 Put the eggs, egg yolks and caster sugar in a bowl and beat to mix. Pour the coconut and evaporated milks into a saucepan and heat to scalding point. Pour over the egg mixture, stirring all the time.
3 Strain the custard into the ramekins. Place the ramekins in a roasting pan and pour in enough hot water to come halfway up the sides. Cover with lightly oiled foil, then bake in the oven at 170°C (325°F) mark 3 for 50 minutes or until set, but still wobbly around the edges. Remove from the oven and leave to cool in the pan of hot water. Chill in the refrigerator overnight.
4 Meanwhile, dry fry the coconut in a wok or heavy frying pan over low heat for 5-6 minutes, stirring, until golden. Slice the mangoes and pawpaw lengthways.
5 To serve, run a knife around the edge of each custard, then carefully invert onto dessert plates, allowing the caramel to run down the sides. Arrange a few slices of mango and pawpaw to the side of each custard, then sprinkle with lime juice and squeeze the passion fruit pulp over the top. Sprinkle toasted coconut on top.

CAPPUCCINO CREAMS

SERVES 8

550 g (1¼ lb) fromage frais	175 g (6 oz) dark or bitter chocolate
15-30 ml (1-2 tbsp) finely ground espresso coffee	chocolate curls, to decorate
15-30 ml (1-2 tbsp) icing sugar (optional)	

1 Mix the fromage frais with the coffee and icing sugar, if liked.
2 Pulverise the chocolate in an electric blender or liquidiser until very fine. Alternatively grate finely.
3 Spoon half the fromage frais into eight individual ramekins or glass dishes. Sprinkle over most of the chocolate mixture. Top with the remaining fromage frais and sprinkle with the remaining chocolate mixture. Decorate with chocolate curls.

COOK'S TIP

These little desserts are light but creamy and can be made with low-fat fromage frais if preferred. Use a good dark chocolate – the flavour is so much better.

ALMOND CUSTARD TARTS

SERVES 10

1 quantity shortcrust pastry (see page 172)	50 g (2 oz) caster sugar
FOR THE FILLING	1.25 ml (¼ tsp) almond flavouring
200 ml (7 fl oz) milk	flaked almonds, toasted
2 eggs	icing sugar, for dusting

1 Grease ten 75 cm (3 inch) fluted brioche tins and place on a baking sheet.
2 Roll out the pastry thinly on a floured work surface and use to line the tins. Chill for 20 minutes.
3 Bake blind in the oven at 200°C (400°F) mark 6 for 15 minutes.
4 To make the filling, whisk the milk, eggs, caster sugar and almond flavouring together. Pour into the pastry cases. Scatter toasted almonds on top.
5 Reduce the oven temperature to 180°C (350°F) mark 4 and bake for a further 15-20 minutes until just set. Leave the tarts to cool before serving. Dust with icing sugar.

VANILLA BAVARIAN RING

SERVES 6

15 ml (1 level tbsp) powdered gelatine	300 ml (½ pint) single cream
6 egg yolks	5 ml (1 tsp) vanilla essence
50 g (2 oz) caster sugar	300 ml (½ pint) double cream

1 Sprinkle the gelatine over 45 ml (3 tbsp) water in a small bowl and leave to soak for 2-3 minutes. Place the bowl over a pan of simmering water and stir until dissolved. (Alternatively, microwave on HIGH for 30 seconds or until dissolved.)
2 Lightly whisk the egg yolks and sugar together in a bowl. Bring the single cream and the vanilla essence almost to the boil, then whisk into the egg yolks. Place the bowl over a pan of simmering water and cook the custard, stirring, until it thickens enough to coat the back of the spoon. (Alternatively, microwave on HIGH for 2-2½ minutes, stirring every 30 seconds with a wire whisk.)
3 Strain the custard through a nylon sieve into a clean bowl and add the dissolved gelatine, stirring. Leave the custard to cool, stirring frequently to prevent a skin forming.
4 Whip the cream until it just holds soft peaks, then fold into the custard. Pour into a 1.1 litre (2 pint) ring mould. Chill until set.
5 To unmould the bavarois, dip the mould briefly, right up to the rim, into hot water. Place a serving plate on top, then invert the mould.

STRAWBERRY BAVAROIS

SERVES 6-8

	FOR THE STRAWBERRY SAUCE
350 g (12 oz) strawberries	225 g (8 oz) strawberries
22.5 ml (1½ level tbsp) powdered gelatine	50 g (2 oz) caster sugar
6 egg yolks	15 ml (1 tbsp) framboise (optional)
50 g (2 oz) caster sugar	TO DECORATE
300 ml (½ pint) milk	150 ml (¼ pint) double cream, whipped
300 ml (½ pint) double cream	sliced strawberries

1 Press the strawberries through a very fine nylon sieve to make a purée, about 300 ml (½ pint).
2 Sprinkle the gelatine over 60 ml (4 tbsp) water in a small bowl and leave to soften while making the custard.
3 Lightly whisk the egg yolks and sugar together. Bring the milk almost to the boil, then whisk into the egg yolks. Set the bowl over a saucepan of hot water and cook the custard, stirring, until it thickens enough to coat the back of the spoon.
4 Strain through a nylon sieve into a clean bowl and add the gelatine, stirring until dissolved. Set aside until cold, but not set, stirring to prevent a skin forming.
5 Whip cream until it will just hold soft peaks. Stir the strawberry purée into the custard, then fold in the cream. Pour into a 1.4 litre (2½ pint) mould. Chill until set.
6 Meanwhile, make the sauce, slice the strawberries and put them into a bowl. Sprinkle with the sugar and the liqueur, if using, cover and leave to stand for about 1 hour, then press through a nylon sieve to form a purée; chill.
7 To unmould the bavarois, quickly dip the mould, right up to the rim, into hot water. Place a serving plate on top, then invert the mould and the plate together, giving the mould a sharp shake to free the bavarois. Decorate with whipped cream and strawberries. Serve the bavarois with the chilled strawberry sauce.

COFFEE BAVAROIS

SERVES 6

125 g (4 oz) well roasted coffee beans	20 ml (4 level tsp) powdered gelatine
900 ml (1½ pints) milk	300 ml (10 fl oz) double cream
6 egg yolks	
75 g (3 oz) caster sugar	grated chocolate and sugar coffee beans, to decorate

1 Put the coffee beans in a saucepan and place over a low heat; warm very gently for 2-3 minutes, shaking the pan frequently. Remove from the heat, pour the milk into the pan, return to the heat and bring to the boil. Remove from the heat, cover and leave to infuse for 30 minutes.

2 Place the egg yolks and caster sugar in a deep mixing bowl and beat until thick and light in colour. Strain the coffee infusion on to the egg yolks, stirring well.

3 Return the custard mixture to the rinsed-out saucepan and cook very gently, stirring, until the custard thickens slightly. Do not boil. Strain into a large bowl and cool.

4 In a small bowl, sprinkle the gelatine over 60 ml (4 tbsp) water. Place over a pan of hot water and stir until dissolved. Stir the gelatine into the cooled custard. Stand the custard in a roasting tin half-filled with water and surround with ice cubes. Stir the custard frequently while it cools to setting point.

5 Meanwhile, lightly whip half the cream and grease a 1.4 litre (2 pint) soufflé dish or mould.

6 When the custard is well chilled and beginning to thicken, fold in the whipped cream. Pour the setting custard into the dish and refrigerate until completely set.

7 With a dampened finger, gently ease the edges of the bavarois away from the dish. Moisten a flat plate and place over the dish. Invert the plate and shake gently. Ease off the dish and slide the bavarois on to the plate.

8 Whisk the remaining cream until it holds its shape. Decorate the bavarois with piped cream, grated chocolate and coffee beans.

CALEDONIAN CREAMS

SERVES 6

90 ml (6 level tbsp) thin shred marmalade	juice of 1 lemon
25 g (1 oz) caster sugar	300 ml (10 fl oz) double or whipping cream
60 ml (4 tbsp) whisky liqueur	

1 Mix together the marmalade, sugar, liqueur and lemon juice.

2 Whip the cream until softly stiff. Gently whisk in the marmalade mixture until the cream stands in soft peaks; take care not to overwhip. Serve in small glasses.

COOK'S TIP

Properly whipped cream is essential when a smooth, airy texture is required. Choose double or whipping cream for whipping. To achieve more volume, add 15 ml (1 tbsp) milk to each 150 ml (¼ pint) cream before starting. Chill the cream and all the utensils thoroughly beforehand. Whip quickly at first, using a balloon whisk or hand-held electric whisk, until the cream begins to look matt on the surface. Continue whipping, a little more slowly until it stands in soft peaks and does not fall off the upturned whisk. Extra care is needed if using an electric whisk.

If overwhipped, the cream will look granular and the flavour will be affected. It is impossible to rescue if this happens. Overwhipped cream will not fold smoothly into mousses, bavarois and other creamy desserts.

DAMASK CREAM

SERVES 4

600 ml (1 pint) single cream	15 ml (1 tbsp) brandy
45 ml (3 tbsp) caster sugar	60 ml (4 tbsp) clotted or double cream
10 ml (2 tsp) rennet essence	
large pinch of grated nutmeg	5 ml (1 tsp) rose water
	rose petals, to decorate (optional)

1 Put the cream and 30 ml (2 tbsp) of the sugar in a saucepan. Heat gently until tepid, stirring until the sugar dissolves. (When the mixture is tepid it will register 36.9°C (98.4°F) on a sugar thermometer, or not feel hot or cold if you put your finger in it.)

2 Stir in the rennet, nutmeg and brandy, then pour into a serving dish. Leave for 2-3 hours until set. It is important not to disturb the junket during this time or it will not set.

3 When the junket is set, mix the remaining sugar, the cream and rose water together and spoon carefully over the top. Decorate with rose petals, if liked.

COOK'S TIP

This subtly flavoured dish, also known as Devonshire junket, is a far cry from a junket that comes from a packet. Do not serve it until you are ready to eat, as once it is cut the shape will disintegrate. Rose petals make a pretty decoration.

TEA CREAM

SERVES 4

300 ml (½ pint) milk	30 ml (2 tbsp) caster sugar
15 g (½ oz) Earl Grey tea leaves	15 ml (1 level tbsp) powdered gelatine
2 eggs, separated	150 ml (¼ pint) double cream

1 Put the milk into a saucepan, add the tea and bring to the boil. Remove from the heat and leave to infuse for 10-15 minutes or until the milk is well coloured with the tea.

2 Beat the egg yolks and sugar together, then strain on the milk and mix well. Return to the pan and cook gently for 10 minutes, stirring all the time, until the custard thickens slightly and just coats the back of the spoon.

3 Sprinkle the gelatine over 45 ml (3 tbsp) water in a small bowl and leave to soak for 2-3 minutes. Place the bowl over a pan of simmering water and stir until dissolved. (Alternatively, microwave on HIGH for 30 seconds or until dissolved.)

4 Mix the dissolved gelatine into the tea mixture. Leave for about 2 hours until beginning to set. Stir the mixture occasionally.

5 Whip the cream until thick but not stiff, then fold into the custard. Finally, whisk the egg whites until stiff, then fold into the mixture.

6 Pour the cream mixture into a dampened 600 ml (1 pint) mould. Chill for about 2-3 hours until set. Turn out on to a chilled dish and decorate with grapes and crisp biscuits, if liked.

SERVING SUGGESTION

Smooth puddings such as fools, bavarois, syllabubs and creams are best served with crisp biscuits to give a contrast in texture.

ZABAGLIONE

4 egg yolks	100 ml (4 fl oz) Marsala
65 g (2½ oz) caster sugar	

1   Beat the egg yolks and sugar together in a large bowl. Add the Marsala and beat until mixed.
2   Place the bowl over a saucepan of simmering water and heat gently, whisking the mixture until it is very thick and creamy.
3   To serve, pour the zabaglione into six glasses and serve immediately, with sponge fingers.

COOK'S TIP

A classic, rich Italian dessert to serve after a light main course. It should be served as soon as it is made so that it remains light, fluffy and slightly warm. Serve with sponge fingers or crisp dessert biscuits.

LEMON BALM SYLLABUB

30 ml (2 tbsp) finely chopped lemon balm leaves	5 ml (1 tsp) caster sugar, or to taste
600 ml (1 pint) double cream	TO DECORATE
150 ml (¼ pint) sweet white wine	nutmeg, lemon shreds and sprigs of lemon balm
grated rind and juice of 2 lemons	

1   Whisk together all the ingredients until the mixture is the consistency of custard.
2   Leave in the refrigerator for 2-3 hours to chill. To serve, spoon the syllabub into tall glasses, grate a little nutmeg on the top and garnish with lemon shreds and sprigs of lemon balm.

OLD ENGLISH SYLLABUB

SERVES 4

1 clove	finely grated rind and juice of 1 lemon
1 allspice	
2.5 cm (1 inch) cinnamon stick	90 ml (6 tbsp) pale cream sherry
little grated nutmeg	300 ml (½ pint) double cream
50 g (2 oz) caster sugar	24 ratafia biscuits

1 Very finely grind the clove, allspice and cinnamon stick with a pestle and mortar, then sift through a fine sieve.
2 Put the ground spices, nutmeg, sugar, lemon rind, lemon juice and sherry into a bowl. Stir well until the sugar dissolves, then cover and leave to stand for 1 hour.
3 Strain the sherry mixture through a fine nylon sieve into a clean bowl. Pour in the cream in a continuous stream, whisking all the time. Whip the cream mixture until it is just thick enough to hold a trail when the whisk is lifted.
4 Place four ratafias in each of four serving glasses, then fill each glass with the spicy syllabub. Chill for about 1 hour. Decorate with the remaining ratafias.

COOK'S TIP

Bring out the full fragrance of the spices by grinding them just before use. Decorate the syllabub with fresh edible flower petals such as nasturtium, geranium and rose, or with borage flowers.

WINE JELLY CREAM

SERVES 4

300 ml (½ pint) white wine	15 ml (1 tbsp) cornflour
45 ml (3 tbsp) sugar	2. 5 ml (½ tsp) vanilla flavouring
15 g (½ oz) powdered gelatine	
450 ml (¾ pint) milk	150 ml (5 fl oz) whipping cream
2 egg yolks	strawberries, to decorate

1 Heat half the wine, 30 ml (2 tbsp) of the sugar and the gelatine in a small saucepan. Dissolve over a gentle heat, then mix with remaining wine and set aside to cool.
2 Pour into 4 wine glasses. Place in the refrigerator to set at a 45° angle.
3 Pour the milk into a medium saucepan and heat almost to boiling point. In a medium bowl, blend together the egg yolks, cornflour, remaining sugar and vanilla flavouring until pale, then pour on the hot milk, stirring continuously.
4 Strain the mixture into a medium heavy-based or double saucepan and stir over a gentle heat until the custard thickens enough to coat the back of a wooden spoon; this takes about 20 minutes. Cool. Whip the cream until stiff, then fold into the cooled custard.
5 When the wine jelly is set, stand the glasses upright and pour in the custard. Return to the refrigerator to chill. Decorate with strawberries and serve with dessert biscuits.

HONEY MOUSSE

SERVES 6

3 eggs, separated	300 ml (10 fl oz) whipping cream
100 g (4 oz) caster sugar	30 ml (2 tbsp) clear honey
finely grated rind of 2 lemons	pistachio nuts or coarsely grated chocolate, to decorate
90 ml (6 tbsp) lemon juice	
10 ml (2 level tsp) powdered gelatine	

1 Whisk together the egg yolks, sugar and lemon rind until thick. Add 45 ml (3 tbsp) lemon juice and place over a pan of simmering water until thick and mousse-like. Remove from the heat and whisk occasionally until cold.
2 Soak the gelatine in the remaining lemon juice in a small bowl. Place the bowl over a pan of hot water and stir until dissolved.
3 Whip the cream until softly stiff. Whisk the egg whites until stiff. Fold half the cream into the mousse with the gelatine, honey and whisked egg whites. Turn into a 1.1 litre (2 pint) glass bowl.
4 Decorate with the remaining whipped cream and chopped pistachio nuts.

GOOSEBERRY CHARLOTTE

SERVES 6

450 g (1 lb) gooseberries, topped and tailed	2 egg yolks
75 g (3 oz) caster sugar	300 ml (½ pint) milk
10 ml (2 level tsp) powdered gelatine	300 ml (½ pint) double cream
	20 langue de chat biscuits, trimmed to size

1 Oil a 15 cm (6 inch) soufflé dish and line the base with greaseproof paper.
2 Place the gooseberries in a small saucepan with 60 ml (4 tbsp) water. Cover and simmer for about 10 minutes until the fruit softens to a pulpy consistency.
3 Purée the gooseberries in a blender or food processor, then sieve to remove pips. Stir in 50 g (2 oz) of the sugar.
4 Sprinkle the gelatine over 30 ml (2 tbsp) water in a small bowl and leave to soak for 2-3 minutes. Place the bowl over a pan of simmering water and stir until dissolved. (Alternatively, microwave on HIGH for 30 seconds or until dissolved.)
5 Meanwhile, make the custard. Beat the egg yolks and remaining sugar together in a bowl until light in colour. In a small saucepan, warm the milk, and pour over the eggs and sugar, stirring until blended.
6 Return to the pan and cook over a low heat, stirring all the time, until the custard thickens sufficiently to lightly coat the back of the spoon – do not boil.
7 Remove from the heat and add the dissolved gelatine. Pour the custard out into a large bowl and mix in the gooseberry purée. Leave to cool for 45 minutes.
8 Lightly whip the cream. When the gooseberry mixture is cold, but not set, stir in half the cream until evenly blended. Pour the gooseberry mixture into the prepared dish. Chill for 1-2 hours to set. When firm, turn out on to a flat serving plate.
9 Spread a thin covering of the remaining cream around the side of the charlotte and press on the biscuits. Decorate with the remaining cream.

BOODLE'S ORANGE FOOL

SERVES 6

4-6 trifle sponge cakes, cut into 1 cm (½ inch) thick slices	25-50 g (1-2 oz) sugar
grated rind and juice of 2 oranges	300 ml (10 fl oz) double cream
grated rind and juice of 1 lemon	orange slices or segments, to decorate

1 Use the sponge cake slices to line the bottom and halfway up the sides of a deep dish or individual bowls.
2 Mix the orange and lemon rinds and juice with the sugar and stir until the sugar has completely dissolved.
3 In another bowl, whip the cream until it just starts to thicken, then slowly add the sweetened fruit juice, continuing to whip until the cream is light and thickened and the juice all absorbed.
4 Pour the mixture over the sponge cakes and refrigerate for at least 2 hours. Decorate with orange slices, or segments to serve.

CHILLED BLACKBERRY SNOW

SERVES 6

450 g (1 lb) blackberries, fresh or frozen, thawed	300 ml (10 fl oz) double cream
2 egg whites	few blackberries, to decorate
50 g (2 oz) caster sugar	

1 Rub the blackberries through a nylon sieve. Pour the purée into a rigid container and freeze for about 2 hours or until mushy.
2 Whisk the egg whites until stiff, then add the sugar gradually, whisking until the mixture stands in soft peaks. Whip the cream until it just holds its shape.
3 Remove the frozen blackberry purée from the freezer and mash to break down the large ice crystals, being careful not to break it down completely.
4 Fold the cream and egg white mixture together, then quickly fold in the semi-frozen blackberry purée to form a 'swirled' effect. Spoon into tall glasses and decorate with blackberries. Serve immediately, with crisp wafers.

COOK'S TIP

The swirled layers of iced fruit purée and creamy egg white are very effective in this recipe but do finish it off just before it is needed and serve immediately. If really necessary, it can be kept refrigerated for a couple of hours, but it will start to lose some volume.

BLANCMANGE

SERVES 4

60 ml (4 level tbsp) cornflour	strip of lemon rind
600 ml (1 pint) milk	45 ml (3 level tbsp) sugar

1 Blend the cornflour to a smooth paste with 30 ml (2 tbsp) of the milk.
2 Put the remaining milk in a saucepan with the lemon rind, bring to the boil, then strain it on to the blended mixture, stirring well.
3 Return the mixture to the pan and bring to the boil, stirring until the mixture thickens; cook for a further 3 minutes. Add sugar to taste.
4 Pour into a 600 ml (1 pint) dampened jelly mould and leave for several hours until set. Turn out to serve.

VARIATIONS

Omit the lemon rind and add 50 g (2 oz) melted chocolate or 15-30 ml (1-2 tbsp) coffee essence to the cooked mixture.

ZUPPA INGLESE

SERVES 6-8

600 ml (1 pint) milk	150 ml (¼ pint) water
1 vanilla pod	16 trifle sponge cakes
4 eggs	300 ml (10 fl oz) double cream
50 g (2 oz) caster sugar	
225 ml (8 fl oz) Marsala	glacé cherries and angelica, to decorate

1 To make the custard, bring the milk to the boil with the vanilla pod added and immediately remove from the heat. Leave to infuse for 20 minutes, then strain.
2 Put the eggs and sugar in a heatproof bowl and lightly whisk together. Slowly pour in the milk, whisking all the time.
3 Stand the bowl over a pan of gently simmering water and stir until thick enough to coat the back of a spoon. (Be patient – this can take as long as 20 minutes.)
4 Remove the bowl from the 4 heat, cover the surface of the custard closely with greaseproof paper and leave until cold.
5 Mix the Marsala and water together in a shallow dish. Dip a few of the trifle sponges in the liquid, then use them to line the bottom of a glass serving bowl.
6 Pour one third of the cold custard over the sponges. Dip a few more trifle sponges in the liquid and place on top of the custard. Cover with another third of the custard.
7 In a separate bowl, whip the cream until thick, then spread half over the custard.
8 Finish with a layer each of the remaining sponges and liquid, the custard and cream. Chill in the refrigerator for at least 4 hours, preferably overnight. Decorate with glacé cherries and angelica just before serving.

OLDE ENGLISH TRIFLE

SERVES 6-8

4 trifle sponges	450 ml (¾ pint) milk
60 ml (4 tbsp) cherry jam	3 eggs
15 ratafia biscuits	50 g (2 oz) caster sugar
60 ml (4 tbsp) sherry	150 ml (5 fl oz) double cream
2 bananas, peeled and sliced	few cherries, to decorate
grated rind and juice of ½ lemon	25 g (1 oz) chopped nuts, toasted, to decorate
225 g (8 oz) cherries, stoned	

1 Cut the trifle sponges in half and spread with jam, then sandwich together. Arrange in the base of a glass serving dish.

2 Cover with ratafias and sprinkle with sherry. Coat the bananas in lemon juice. Arrange the bananas and cherries on top of the ratafias.

3 Heat the milk in a medium saucepan until almost boiling. In a large bowl, whisk together the eggs, lemon rind and sugar until pale, then pour on the hot milk, stirring continuously.

4 Return to the saucepan and heat gently, stirring continuously, until the custard thickens enough to coat the back of a wooden spoon; do not allow to boil. This takes about 20 minutes. Set aside to cool.

5 Pour the custard over the trifle and leave until cold.

6 Whip the cream until softly stiff and spread on the top of the trifle. Decorate with cherries and nuts.

TIRAMISU

SERVES 8

four 250 g (9 oz) cartons mascarpone cheese	425 ml (14 fl oz) very strong cold black coffee
40 g (1½ oz) caster sugar	about 30 savoiardi (Italian sponge fingers)
3 eggs, separated	cocoa powder, for sprinkling
250 ml (8 fl oz) kahlua or other coffee-flavoured liqueur	

1 Put the mascarpone cheese, sugar and egg yolks in a bowl and beat with an electric mixer until evenly blended and creamy.

2 Whisk the egg whites until standing in stiff peaks. Fold into the mascarpone mixture until evenly incorporated. Spoon a quarter of the mixture into the base of a glass serving bowl.

3 Mix the liqueur and coffee together in a shallow dish. One at a time, dip one third of the savoiardi in this mixture for 10-15 seconds, turning once so they become soaked through but do not lose their shape. After each one has been dipped, place it on top of the mascarpone in the bowl, making a single layer of savoiardi that covers the mascarpone completely.

4 Cover the savoiardi with one third of the remaining mascarpone, then dip another third of the savoiardi in the liqueur and coffee mixture and layer them in the bowl as before.

5 Repeat with another layer of mascarpone and savoiardi, then spread the remaining mascarpone over the top and swirl with a palette knife. Sift cocoa powder liberally all over the top. Cover the bowl and chill in the refrigerator for 24 hours. Serve chilled.

RUM AND COFFEE JUNKET

SERVES 4

600 ml (1 pint) plus 60 ml (4 tbsp) milk	150 ml (¼ pint) soured cream
30 ml (2 tbsp) caster sugar	10 ml (2 tsp) coffee and chicory essence
10 ml (2 tsp) rennet essence	chocolate curls, to decorate
10 ml (2 tsp) rum	

1 Put the 600 ml (1 pint) milk in a saucepan and heat until just warm to the finger.

2 Add the sugar, rennet and rum, then stir until the sugar has dissolved.

3 Immediately, pour the mixture into four individual dishes or a 900 ml (1½ pint) shallow serving dish. Leave in a warm place, undisturbed, for 4 hours to set.

4 Lightly whisk the soured cream. Gradually add the 60 ml (4 tbsp) milk and the coffee essence, whisking until smooth.

5 Carefully flood the top of the junket with the coffee cream, taking care not to disturb the junket. Decorate with chocolate curls. Chill for 1 hour.

COOK'S TIP

A sophisticated version of the nursery pudding. Do not use UHT, long-life or sterilized milk – or the junket will not set.

CREMA FRITTA

SERVES 4-6

3 eggs	finely grated rind of ½ lemon
50 g (2 oz) caster sugar	100 g (4 oz) dry white breadcrumbs
50 g (2 oz) plain flour	
225 ml (8 fl oz) milk	oil for shallow frying
300 ml (½ pint) single cream	caster sugar, for sprinkling

1 Grease a shallow 18 cm (7 inch) square cake tin.

2 Beat two of the eggs and the sugar together in a large bowl until the mixture is pale.

3 Add the flour, beating all the time. Very slowly, beat in the milk and cream. Add the lemon rind. Pour the mixture into the prepared tin.

4 Bake in the oven at 180°C (350°F) mark 4 for about 1 hour until a skewer inserted in the centre comes out clean. Leave to cool for 2-3 hours, preferably overnight.

5 When completely cold, cut into 16 cubes and remove from the cake tin.

6 Beat the remaining egg in a bowl. Dip the cubes in the egg, then in the breadcrumbs until well coated.

7 Heat the oil in a frying pan and, when hot, slide in the cubes. Fry for 2-3 minutes until golden brown and a crust is formed. Turn and fry the second side. Drain well on absorbent kitchen paper. Serve immediately, sprinkled with caster sugar.

COOK'S NOTE

Literally translated, this simple dessert means 'fried cream', which is in fact exactly what it is. In Italy, it is traditional to celebrate Carnevale – the day before Lent – by eating crema fritta. Children and young people invite friends home and everyone eats crema fritta in the way that people in other countries eat pancakes.

KHEER

SERVES 4-6

seeds of 4 green cardamoms	100 g (4 oz) caster sugar
4 whole cloves	1.25 ml (¼ tsp) orange flower water
2.5 cm (1 inch) stick cinnamon	split pistachio nuts or almonds, to decorate
1.2 litres (2 pints) milk	
75 g (3 oz) short grain pudding rice	

1 Grind the cardamom seeds, whole cloves and cinnamon stick in a small electric mill or with a pestle and mortar to a coarse powder.
2 Pour the milk into a heavy-based saucepan, add the rice, sugar and crushed spices and bring slowly to the boil, stirring.
3 Lower the heat and simmer very gently, uncovered, for 1 hour or until the rice is tender. Stir frequently during this time to prevent the rice sticking to the bottom of the pan.
4 Remove the pan from the heat and pour the Kheer into a bowl. Add the orange flower water and stir well to mix.
5 Cover the bowl with cling film. Leave until cold, then chill for at least 2 hours before serving.
6 To serve, pour the Kheer into 4-6 individual glasses or glass dishes and decorate with pistachios or almonds. Serve well chilled.

BAKED SAFFRON YOGURT

SERVES 8

300 ml (½ pint) milk	383 g (13.5 oz) can condensed milk
pinch of saffron threads	300 ml (½ pint) natural yogurt
6 green cardamoms	1 large ripe mango, to decorate
2 eggs	
2 egg yolks	

1 Pour the milk into a heavy-based sausepan, add the saffron and cardamoms and bring slowly to the boil. Remove from the heat, cover and infuse for 10-15 minutes.
2 Put the eggs, egg yolks, condensed milk and yogurt in a bowl and beat together.
3 Strain in the milk, stirring gently to mix. Divide between 8 ramekin dishes.
4 Place the ramekins in a roasting tin. Add hot water to come halfway up the sides. Bake in the oven at 180°C (350°F) mark 4 until firm to the touch.
5 Cool the baked yogurt desserts completely, then chill for at least 2 hours before serving.
6 To serve, run a blunt-edged knife around the edge of each yogurt, then turn out on to individual dishes.
7 Peel the mango and slice thinly on either side of the central stone. Serve with the saffron yogurts.

SERVING SUGGESTION

These individual, golden-tinted yogurts make an attractive finale to an Indian meal. They are also excellent for children at tea-time, served with fresh fruit.

QUEEN
OF PUDDINGS

SERVES 4

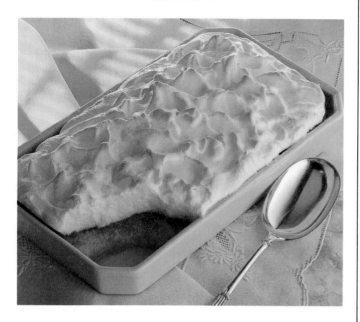

4 eggs	45-60 ml (3-4 level tbsp) raspberry jam
600 ml (1 pint) milk	75 g (3 oz) caster sugar
100 g (4 oz) fresh breadcrumbs	

1 Separate 3 eggs and beat together the 3 egg yolks and 1 whole egg. Add to the milk and mix well. Stir in the breadcrumbs.
2 Spread the jam on the bottom of a pie dish. Pour over the milk mixture and leave for 30 minutes.
3 Bake in the oven at 150°C (300°F) mark 2 for 1 hour, until set.
4 Whisk the egg whites until stiff, then fold in the sugar. Pile on top of the custard and return to the oven for a further 15-20 minutes until the meringue is set.

OSBORNE
PUDDING

SERVES 4

4 thin slices day-old wholemeal bread	2 eggs
butter for spreading	15 ml (1 tbsp) brandy or rum (optional)
orange marmalade for spreading	finely grated rind of 1 orange
50 g (2 oz) currants or sultanas	15 ml (1 tbsp) light soft brown sugar
450 ml (¾ pint) milk	grated nutmeg

1 Spread the bread with butter and marmalade, then cut into triangles. Arrange, buttered side up, in a buttered ovenproof serving dish, sprinkling the layers with the fruit.
2 Heat the milk, but do not boil. Beat the eggs with the brandy, if using, and the orange rind, then gradually pour on the warm milk, stirring continuously. Pour over the bread and leave to stand for at least 15 minutes to allow the bread to absorb the milk.
3 Sprinkle the sugar and nutmeg on top of the pudding and bake at 180°C (350°F) mark 4 for 30-40 minutes, until set and lightly browned. Serve hot with custard or cream.

CHOCOLATE DESSERTS

These unashamedly rich desserts are guaranteed to satisfy all chocolate addicts. Choose from smooth creamy mousses, rich gooey puddings and a mouth-watering selection of luxurious chocolate gâteaux. Elaborate concoctions for special occasions include a sensational truffle cake, chocolate chestnut vacherin and an irresistible roulade.

CHOCOLATE LACE BASKETS

SERVES 6

150 g (5 oz) plain chocolate-flavoured cake covering	¼ fresh pineapple
1 small mango	12 strawberries
	1 passion fruit

1 Break the cake covering into small pieces. Place in a heatproof bowl standing over a pan of simmering water and heat gently until it melts.

2 Invert six 8.5 cm (3½ inch) ring moulds and stretch cling film over the rounded bases to cover completely.

3 Spoon half the melted chocolate cake covering into a greaseproof paper piping bag and snip off the point. Pipe three of the ring moulds with a lacy pattern of cake covering.

4 Fill a second bag with melted cake covering and pipe the remaining three moulds. Chill until set.

5 Meanwhile, peel the mango and chop the flesh. Cut the pineapple flesh into pieces. Hull the strawberries. Halve the passion fruit and scoop out the pulp.

6 Carefully lift the chocolate baskets with the cling film, then remove the cling film from the shells. Fill the baskets with the fruit. Serve with whipped cream.

PROFITEROLES

SERVES 4

1 quantity choux pastry (see page 86)	15 g (½ oz) butter or margarine
FOR THE CHOCOLATE SAUCE AND FILLING	30 ml (2 tbsp) golden syrup
	2-3 drops of vanilla essence
100 g (4 oz) plain chocolate	150 ml (¼ pint) double cream

1 Put the choux pastry in a piping bag fitted with a 1 cm (½ inch) plain nozzle. Pipe about 20 small bun shapes on two dampened baking sheets.

2 Bake in the oven at 220°C (425°F) mark 7 for about 20-25 minutes until well risen and golden brown. Reduce the oven temperature to 180°C (350°F) mark 4. Remove the choux buns from the oven and make a hole in the side of each bun with a knife. Return to the oven for 5 minutes to dry out completely. Leave to cool on a wire rack.

3 For the chocolate sauce, melt the chocolate, butter, 30 ml (2 tbsp) water, the golden syrup and vanilla essence in a small saucepan over a very low heat. Stir until smooth.

4 Whip the cream until it just holds its shape. Spoon into a piping bag, fitted with a medium plain nozzle and use to fill the choux buns through the hole in the sides.

5 Serve with the chocolate sauce spooned over.

CHOCOLATE MOUSSE CUPS

SERVES 6

3 large sheets filo pastry, about 25 x 50 cm (10 x 20 inches)	2 eggs, separated
25 g (1 oz) butter	150 ml (¼ pint) double cream, lightly whipped
100 g (4 oz) plain chocolate	toasted flaked almonds, to decorate
30 ml (2 tbsp) brandy	icing sugar, for dusting
15 ml (1 level tbsp) instant coffee powder	

1 Cut each filo pastry sheet into 12 squares. Line 12 deep bun tins with three overlapping squares, brushing with melted butter between each layer.

2 Bake blind in the oven at 200°C (400°F) mark 6 for 10-12 minutes or until the pastry is crisp, golden brown and cooked through. Turn out on to a wire rack to cool.

3 Break the chocolate into small pieces. Place in a heatproof bowl with the brandy, coffee powder and 15 ml (1 tbsp) water. Stand the bowl over a pan of simmering water and heat gently until the chocolate melts. Stir the mixture until smooth. (Alternatively, microwave on LOW for 4-6 minutes or until melted, stirring occasionally.)

4 Stir in the egg yolks, cool slightly, then mix in the cream. Whisk the egg whites until stiff but not dry, then fold into the chocolate mixture. Leave to set until the consistency of thick cream. Spoon the mousse into the pastry cups and chill for 1 hour.

5 Sprinkle the mousse cups with the toasted flaked almonds and dust heavily with icing sugar before serving.

COOK'S TIP

Melting Chocolate

Many of the recipes require melted chocolate and it is important to do this gently. Stand the bowl of chocolate over a saucepan of just simmering water and stir until the chocolate is smooth and creamy. Alternatively, melt chocolate in the microwave on LOW, stirring frequently.

CHOCOLATE AND LIME MOUSSE

SERVES 2

75 g (3 oz) plain chocolate	150 ml (¼ pint) double cream
2 eggs, separated	2.5 ml (½ level tsp) powdered gelatine
15 ml (1 tbsp) caster sugar	chocolate caraque or twists of lime, to decorate
finely grated rind and strained juice of 1 small lime	

1 Break the chocolate into small pieces. Place in a small heatproof bowl standing over a pan of simmering water and heat gently until the chocolate melts. (Alternatively, microwave on LOW for 4-5 minutes or until melted, stirring occasionally.) Cool slightly.

2 Whisk the egg yolks, sugar and lime rind in a bowl, using an electric whisk, until thick and mousse-like. Whisk in the chocolate, then 30 ml (2 tbsp) of the cream.

3 Sprinkle the gelatine over the lime juice in a small bowl and leave to soak for 2-3 minutes. Place the bowl over a saucepan of simmering water and stir until dissolved. (Or, microwave on HIGH for 30 seconds or until melted.) Whisk into the chocolate mixture.

4 Whisk the egg whites until stiff but not dry, then fold into the chocolate mixture.

5 Divide the mousse between two glasses and chill until set. Whip the remaining cream and use to decorate the desserts, with chocolate caraque or twists of lime. Leave at cool room temperature for 30 minutes before serving.

COOK'S TIP

Chocolate Caraque

Melt at least 100 g (4 oz) chocolate in a bowl over a pan of simmering water. Pour it in a thin layer on to a marble slab or cold baking sheet and leave to set until it no longer sticks to your hand when you touch it. Holding a large knife with both hands, push the blade across the surface of the chocolate to roll pieces off in long curls. Adjust the angle of the blade to get the best curls.

PETITS POTS
AU CHOCOLATE

SERVES 6

15 ml (1 tbsp) coffee beans	75 g (3 oz) plain chocolate
3 egg yolks	TO DECORATE
1 egg	150 ml (¼ pint) whipping cream
75 g (3 oz) caster sugar	chocolate shapes or coffee dragees
750 ml (1¼ pints) milk and single cream mixed	

1 Toast the coffee beans under a moderate grill for a few minutes, then set aside.

2 Beat the egg yolks, egg and sugar together in a bowl until very pale.

3 Place the milk, cream and coffee beans in a saucepan and bring to the boil. Strain the hot milk on to the egg mixture, stirring all the time. Discard the coffee beans. Return the mixture to the saucepan.

4 Break up the chocolate and add to the pan. Stir over gentle heat (do not boil) for about 5 minutes until the chocolate has almost melted and the mixture is slightly thickened. Whisk lightly until the mixture is evenly blended.

5 Stand six individual 150 ml (¼ pint) ramekin dishes or custard pots in a roasting tin, then pour in enough hot water to come halfway up the sides of the dishes. Pour the custard mixture slowly into the dishes, dividing it equally between them. Cover.

6 Bake in the oven at 150°C (300°F) mark 2 for 1-1¼ hours or until lightly set. Leave to cool completely.

7 To serve, whip the cream and spoon into a piping bag fitted with a large star nozzle. Pipe a whirl on top of each dessert. Decorate with chocolate shapes or coffee dragees.

COOK'S TIP

These little chocolate pots rely heavily on the flavour of the chocolate used. So it is essential to use a good quality variety.

MAGIC
CHOCOLATE PUDDING

SERVES 4-6

50 g (2 oz) butter or margarine	350 ml (12 fl oz) milk
75 g (3 oz) caster sugar	40 g (1½ oz) self-raising flour
2 eggs, separated	25 ml (5 level tsp) cocoa powder

1 Grease a 1 litre (1¾ pint) ovenproof dish.

2 Cream the butter and sugar together in a bowl until light and fluffy. Beat in the egg yolks and stir in the milk.

3 Sift the flour and cocoa powder together over the creamed mixture, then beat in until evenly mixed. Whisk the egg whites until stiff and fold into the mixture. Pour into the prepared dish.

4 Bake in the oven at 180°C (350°F) mark 4 for 35-45 minutes until the top is set and spongy to the touch. This pudding will separate into a custard layer with a sponge topping. Serve hot.

COOK'S TIP

This delicious chocolate pudding, which is a great hit with children, is called 'magic' because it separates magically during baking into a rich chocolate sauce at the bottom and a sponge cake on top.

BAKED CHOCOLATE MARBLE SPONGE

SERVES 8

	CHOCOLATE FUDGE SAUCE
75 g (3 oz) plain chocolate	75 ml (5 tbsp) single cream
175 g (6 oz) butter or margarine	25 g (1 oz) cocoa powder
175 g (6 oz) light soft brown sugar	100 g (4 oz) caster sugar
3 eggs, beaten	175 g (6 oz) golden syrup
200 g (7 oz) self-raising flour	25 g (1 oz) butter or margarine
45 ml (3 tbsp) milk	pinch of salt
50 g (2 oz) macaroons	2.5 ml (½ tsp) vanilla essence

1 Grease a 1.3 litre (2¼ pint) loaf dish.

2 Break the chocolate into small pieces. Place in a small heatproof bowl standing over a pan of simmering water and heat until the chocolate melts. (Alternatively, microwave on LOW for 3-4 minutes or until melted, stirring occasionally.) Leave to cool.

3 Cream the butter and sugar together in a bowl until pale and fluffy. Gradually beat in the eggs. Using a metal spoon, fold in the flour and milk.

4 Divide the mixture in two and flavour half with the cooled chocolate, folding it evenly through the mixture.

5 Place alternate spoonfuls of the mixtures in two layers in the prepared dish and zig-zag a knife through the mixture to make a marbled pattern. Roughly crush the macaroons and scatter over the top. Cover with foil.

6 Bake in the oven at 180°C (350°F) mark 4 for about 1¼ hours or until firm to the touch.

7 Meanwhile, combine all the ingredients for the fudge sauce, except the vanilla essence, in a saucepan over low heat and mix well. Slowly bring to the boil, stirring occasionally. Boil for 5 minutes, then add the vanilla essence.

8 Turn out the pudding and serve thickly sliced with the hot chocolate fudge sauce.

AMERICAN CHOCOLATE CUSTARD PIE

SERVES 8

1 quantity shortcrust pastry (see page 172)	3 egg yolks
FOR THE FILLING	40 g (1½ oz) butter or margarine
100 g (4 oz) sugar	5 ml (1 tsp) vanilla essence
50 g (2 oz) plain flour	225 ml (8 fl oz) double or whipping cream
pinch of salt	chocolate curls or grated chocolate, to decorate
450 ml (¾ pint) milk	
50 g (2 oz) plain chocolate	

1 Roll out the pastry on a lightly floured work surface and use to line a 23 cm (9 inch) loose-based fluted flan tin or ring placed on a baking sheet. Crimp the edges. Chill for 30 minutes. Prick the base of the pastry case.

2 Bake blind in the oven at 200°C (400°F) mark 6 for 10-15 minutes until set. Remove the paper and beans and bake for a further 5-10 minutes. Leave to cool.

3 To make the filling, mix the sugar, flour and salt in a large saucepan and stir in the milk.

4 Break the chocolate into small pieces and add to the pan. Heat gently until the chocolate has melted, stirring continuously.

5 Whisk until the chocolate and milk are blended, then increase the heat and cook for about 10 minutes, stirring constantly. Remove the pan from the heat.

6 Beat the egg yolks and whisk in a small amount of the hot chocolate sauce. Slowly pour the egg mixture into the saucepan, stirring rapidly. Cook over low heat stirring, for 10-15 minutes, until the mixture is very thick and creamy. Do not allow to boil.

7 Remove from the heat. Stir in the butter and vanilla essence, then pour into the cold pastry case. Cover to prevent a skin forming and chill for 3-4 hours until set.

8 Just before serving, whip the cream lightly and spread evenly over the chocolate filling. Decorate the top with chocolate curls or grated chocolate. Serve chilled.

MISSISSIPPI MUD PIE

SERVES 12-16

FOR THE BASE	FOR THE FILLING
100 g (4 oz) ginger biscuits, crushed	225 g (8 oz) butter or margarine
100 g (4 oz) digestive biscuits, crushed	175 g (6 oz) plain chocolate
75 g (3 oz) butter, melted	120 ml (8 tbsp) golden syrup
25 g (1 oz) soft light brown sugar	4 eggs, beaten
	50 g (2 oz) pecan nuts, chopped

1   Grease a 23 cm (9 inch) loose-based cake tin.
2   To make the base, mix the biscuits with the butter and sugar. Press into the bottom and 4 cm (1½ inches) up the sides of the prepared tin. Chill while making the filling.
3   To make the filling, put the butter, chocolate and syrup in a saucepan and heat very gently until melted, stirring all the time. (Alternatively, put the ingredients in a bowl and microwave on LOW for 4-6 minutes or until melted, stirring frequently.) Cool, then beat in the eggs and pecans. Pour the mixture into the biscuit crust.
4   Bake in the oven at 180°C (350°F) mark 4 for 1¼ hours or until just firm to the touch but still soft in the centre. Serve warm or cold.

COOK'S TIP

This rich and sticky pie originated in the United States, where it is served warm with hot fudge sauce or cold topped with whipped cream and grated chocolate. Either way, a small portion is all that is needed.

GOOEY CHOCOLATE BROWNIES

MAKES 24 SQUARES

550 g (1¼ lb) plain chocolate	225 g (8 oz) caster sugar
225 g (8 oz) butter, cut into pieces	75 g (3 oz) self-raising flour
3 eggs	2.5 ml (½ level tsp) salt
30 ml (2 tbsp) freshly made strong coffee	175 g (6 oz) walnut halves, chopped
	5 ml (1 tsp) vanilla essence

1   Grease and line a baking tin measuring 22 x 29 cm (8½ x 11½ inches) across the top and 19 x 26 cm (7½ x 10½ inches) across the base.
2   Using a very sharp knife, roughly chop 225 g (8 oz) of the chocolate. Break the remaining chocolate into small pieces and place in a heatproof bowl with the butter. Stand the bowl over a pan of simmering water and heat gently until the chocolate melts, stirring. (Alternatively, microwave on LOW for 10 minutes or until melted, stirring occasionally.) Leave to cool.
3   Mix the eggs, coffee and sugar together in a bowl, then gradually beat in the chocolate mixture. Fold in the flour, salt, walnuts, vanilla essence and chopped chocolate. Pour the mixture into the prepared tin.
4   Bake in the oven at 190°C (375°F) mark 5 for 45 minutes or until just firm to the touch in the centre. Leave to cool in the tin.
5   When the cake is completely cold, turn out on to a board and trim the edges. Cut into 24 squares. Serve on their own or with ice cream.

RK CHOCOLATE TRUFFLE CAKE

SERVES 24

	FOR THE FILLING
225 g (8 oz) plain chocolate	350 g (12 oz) plain chocolate, in pieces
100 g (4 oz) butter	
350 g (12 oz) caster sugar	175 g (6 oz) butter
2 eggs, separated	75 ml (5 tbsp) brandy
150 ml (¼ pint) soured cream	FOR THE ICING
350 g (12 oz) self-raising flour	200 g (7 oz) plain chocolate, in pieces
5 ml (1 tsp) bicarbonate of soda	200 ml (7 fl oz) double cream

1 Grease a 25 cm (10 inch) spring-release cake tin and line the base with greaseproof paper.
2 Break the chocolate into small pieces. Place in a large heatproof bowl with the butter and 150 ml (¼ pint) water, over a pan of simmering water and heat gently until the chocolate melts. Beat in the sugar, then leave to cool.
3 Beat in the egg yolks, then fold in the soured cream, flour and soda. Whisk the egg whites until stiff, then fold into the mixture. Pour into the prepared tin.
4 Bake in the oven at 180°C (350°F) mark 4 for 1 hour or until risen and firm. Turn out and cool on a wire rack.
5 To make the filling, place the chocolate in a large heatproof bowl with the butter, over a pan of simmering water and heat gently until melted, stirring. Stir in 45 ml (3 tbsp) of the brandy. Leave until slightly thickened.
6 Cut the cake into two layers and sprinkle with the remaining brandy. Place the top half in the base of the tin, cut side up. Pour in the truffle filling. Top with the second sponge. Chill until set. Unmould and stand on a wire rack.
7 To make the icing, put the chocolate in a large heatproof bowl with the cream, stand over a pan of simmering water and heat gently until the chocolate melts.
8 Cool until the icing coats the back of a spoon. Pour the icing over the cake, using a palette knife to cover the sides. Leave until set.

CHOCOLATE BOX GATEAU

SERVES 9

	300 ml (½ pint) double cream
3 eggs	700 g (1½ lb) mandarin oranges or tangerines, peeled and segmented
100 g (4 oz) caster sugar	
75 g (3 oz) plain flour	
30 ml (2 tbsp) cocoa powder	1 quantity apricot glaze (see page 173)
FOR THE FILLING AND DECORATION	
150 g (5 oz) plain chocolate	

1 Grease and flour an 18 cm (7 inch) square cake tin, then line the base with greaseproof paper.
2 To make the sponge, using an electric whisk, whisk the eggs and sugar together in a bowl until very thick and pale, and the mixture leaves a trail when the whisk is lifted. Sift the flour and cocoa over the mixture, then fold in using a large metal spoon. Transfer to the prepared tin.
3 Bake in the oven at 190°C (375°F) mark 5 for 30-35 minutes or until firm to the touch and shrunken from the sides of the tin. Turn out and cool on a wire rack.
4 Break the chocolate into small pieces. Place in a heatproof bowl standing over a pan of simmering water and heat gently until the chocolate melts.
5 Meanwhile, spread a sheet of foil on a baking sheet and mark a 22 cm (8½ inch) square. Spread the chocolate evenly over the square marked on the foil. Leave until set. When set, trim the edges and cut into 24 squares, measuring about 5 cm (2 inches).
6 Whip the cream until it just holds its shape. Cut the cake in half horizontally, then sandwich together with half of the cream and a few of the mandarins.
7 Arrange the rest of the fruit evenly all over the top of the cake and brush with warm apricot glaze.
8 Spread the remaining cream round the sides of the cake. Press on the chocolate squares, overlapping each one slightly. Decorate with flowers if desired.

CHOCOLATE ROULADE

SERVES 8-10

100 g (4 oz) plain chocolate	15 ml (1 tbsp) icing sugar
4 eggs, separated	150 ml (¼ pint) Greek yogurt
100 g (4 oz) caster sugar	few drops of rose water (optional)
FOR THE FILLING AND DECORATION	350 g (12 oz) raspberries
300 ml (½ pint) double cream	icing sugar, for dusting

1 Grease a 23 x 33 cm (9 x 13 inch) Swiss roll tin, line with greaseproof paper and grease the paper.
2 To make the roulade, break the chocolate into small pieces. Place in a heatproof bowl standing over a pan of simmering water and heat gently until the chocolate melts.
3 Whisk the egg yolks and sugar together in a bowl until very thick and pale in colour. Beat in the chocolate. Whisk the egg whites until stiff, then fold carefully into the chocolate mixture. Pour the mixture into the prepared tin and spread out evenly.
4 Bake in the oven at 180°C (350°F) mark 4 for 20-25 minutes until well risen and firm to the touch.
5 Lay a piece of greaseproof paper on a flat surface and sprinkle generously with caster sugar. When the roulade is cooked, turn it out on to the paper. Carefully peel off the lining paper. Cover the roulade with a warm, damp tea towel and leave to cool.
6 To make the filling, whip the cream with the icing sugar until it forms soft peaks. Set aside half for decoration. Fold the yogurt into the other half, with a few drops of rose water. Spread over the roulade and sprinkle with two thirds of the raspberries. Starting from one of the narrow ends, carefully roll it up, using the paper to help. Transfer the roulade to a serving plate and dust generously with icing sugar.
7 Decorate with the remaining cream and raspberries.

WHISKY MOCHA FLAN

SERVES 6-8

1 quantity shortcrust pastry (see page 172)	3 egg yolks
	15 ml (1 tbsp) caster sugar
FOR THE FILLING	150 ml (¼ pint) double cream
75 g (3 oz) plain chocolate, melted	FOR THE TOPPING
	200 ml (7 fl oz) double cream
10 ml (2 level tsp) powdered gelatine	15-30 ml (1-2 tbsp) whisky
150 ml (¼ pint) milk	15 ml (1 tbsp) caster sugar
15 ml (1 level tbsp) instant coffee granules	chocolate caraque, to decorate

1 Roll out the pastry on a lightly floured work surface and use to line a 23 cm (9 inch) fluted flan tin. Trim the edges, then prick with a fork. Chill for 30 minutes.
2 Bake blind in the oven at 220°C (425°F) mark 7 for 20-25 minutes. Leave to cool. Remove flan from tin.
3 Using a pastry brush, brush half of the melted chocolate evenly all over the inverted pastry case. Leave in a cool place until set. Turn the flan case over and brush the inside with the remaining chocolate; leave to set.
4 Sprinkle the gelatine over 30 ml (2 tbsp) water in a small bowl and leave to soak for 2-3 minutes. Place over a pan of simmering water and stir until dissolved.
5 Put the milk and coffee in a small saucepan. Heat gently until the coffee dissolves and the milk comes almost to the boil. Very lightly whisk the egg yolks and sugar in a bowl. Stir in the coffee-flavoured milk. Place bowl over a pan of hot water and cook, stirring, until thick enough to coat the back of the spoon. Strain into a clean bowl. Stir in the dissolved gelatine. Leave to cool.
6 Whip the cream until it will just hold soft peaks, then gently fold into the coffee custard. Spoon into the chocolate coated flan case. Chill until set.
7 To make topping, whip the cream with the whisky and sugar. Spread an even layer over the top of the flan. Decorate with the remaining cream and caraque. Chill.

CHOCOLATE PRALINE RING

SERVES 4-6

50g (2 oz) plain or milk chocolate	50 g (2 oz) caster sugar
200 ml (7 fl oz) milk	2.5 ml (½ level tsp) cornflour
15 ml (1 level tbsp) powdered gelatine	50 g (2 oz) praline, finely crushed (see page 53)
75 ml (5 tbsp) cold black coffee	75 ml (5 tbsp) double cream
3 eggs, separated	TO DECORATE
	whipped cream
	marrons glacés (optional)

1 Lightly oil a 1.1 litre (2 pint) ring mould.
2 Break the chocolate into small pieces. Place in a medium saucepan and add the milk. Heat gently until the chocolate melts. Bring to the boil, stirring all the time, until the chocolate mixture is smooth – about 2-3 minutes.
3 Sprinkle the gelatine over the coffee in a small bowl and leave to soak for 2-3 minutes. Place the bowl over a saucepan of simmering water and stir until dissolved.
4 Whisk the egg yolks, 25 g (1 oz) of the caster sugar and the cornflour together in a bowl until very thick and pale. Slowly whisk in the hot chocolate mixture.
5 Return the mixture to the rinsed-out pan and stir over a very gentle heat until it thickens enough to coat the back of a wooden spoon. Do not boil. Pour into a bowl.
6 Stir the dissolved gelatine into the chocolate mixture with 30 ml (2 tbsp) of the praline powder. Leave to cool.
7 When the custard is cool and just beginning to set, whip the cream until it just begins to hold its shape. Fold into the mixture. Whisk egg whites until stiff but not dry. Whisk in the remaining sugar, then fold into the custard.
8 Pour into the prepared ring mould and chill for about 3 hours to set.
9 To serve, dip the mould briefly into hot water and invert the ring on to a serving plate. Decorate with the remaining praline, whipped cream and marrons glacés.

CHOCOLATE CHESTNUT VACHERIN

SERVES 8

6 egg whites	500 g (1.1 lb) can sweetened chestnut purée
350 g (12 oz) caster sugar	300 ml (½ pint) double cream
75 g (3 oz) hazelnuts, skinned, toasted and finely chopped	a little icing sugar for dusting
175 g (6 oz) plain chocolate, in pieces	whipped cream and cocoa powder, to decorate

1 Line 3 baking sheets with non-stick baking parchment and draw a 20 cm (8 inch) circle on each. Invert the paper.
2 To make the meringue, whisk the egg whites in a bowl until very stiff, but not dry. Gradually whisk in the caster sugar a little at a time, whisking well between each addition until the meringue is smooth and shiny. Very lightly fold in the chopped hazelnuts.
3 Either spread the mixture over the marked circles, or transfer to a piping bag fitted with a plain 1 cm (½ inch) nozzle and pipe the meringue in a spiral over the marked circles, starting from the centre.
4 Bake at 140°C (275°F) mark 1 for 1-1½ hours or until dried out. Change the positions of the baking sheets during cooking so that the meringues dry out evenly. Remove from the oven and leave to cool, then carefully remove the lining papers.
5 Melt the chocolate in a heatproof bowl set over a pan of hot water. Soften the chestnut purée in a bowl and stir in the melted chocolate. Lightly whip the cream until soft peaks form and fold into the chestnut mixture.
6 To assemble the vacherin, sandwich the meringues together with a little of the chestnut cream. Cover the top and sides with the remainder and decorate with whipped cream and cocoa powder.

FROZEN DESSERTS

Nothing can compare with the superb flavour of homemade ices, whether you choose to make a simple refreshing sorbet, a rich velvety ice cream or an elaborate iced dessert. The choice of flavourings is endless – vanilla, coffee, chocolate, liqueurs, nuts and all kinds of fruits.

RASPBERRY REDCURRANT FREEZE

SERVES 4-6

350 g (12 oz) fresh or frozen raspberries	300 ml (½ pint) soured cream
225 g (8 oz) jar redcurrant jelly	

1 Put the raspberries and redcurrant jelly in a saucepan and heat gently, stirring frequently, until the fruit is soft. (Alternatively, microwave on HIGH for 4-5 minutes, stirring occasionally.)
2 Purée in a blender or food processor, then sieve to remove the seeds. Chill for about 1 hour until cold.
3 Whisk in the soured cream. Freeze by hand or in an ice cream machine (see page 159).
4 Leave at cool room temperature for 20-30 minutes to soften before serving.

COOK'S NOTE

The knack of successfully making smooth frozen desserts largely involves making sure that no large ice crystals form during freezing. This means that it is necessary to periodically whisk the freezing mixture by hand, if you do not own an ice cream machine which will do the job for you.

PEACH ICE CREAM

SERVES 6

350 g (12 oz) fresh ripe peaches	300 ml (10 fl oz) whipping cream
300 ml (½ pint) milk	peach slices and fan wafers, to decorate (optional)
grated rind and juice of 1 lemon	

1 Using a sharp knife, quarter the peaches and remove the skins, discarding the stones.
2 Roughly slice the peaches into a blender or food processor, add the milk, lemon rind and juice and the cream. Blend well until the mixture is quite smooth.
3 Pour the mixture into a shallow freezer container. Freeze for about 2 hours until mushy in texture.
4 Turn into a large, chilled basin and mash with a fork. Return to the freezer for 3-4 hours to become firm.
5 About 30 minutes before serving, remove from the freezer and leave the ice cream to soften at room temperature. Serve decorated with peach slices and a fan wafer, if wished.

COOK'S TIP

Refer to instructions on page 159 for freezing in an ice cream machine.

VANILLA
ICE CREAM

SERVES 4-6

1 vanilla pod	50-75 g (2-3 oz) caster sugar
300 ml (½ pint) milk	300 ml (10 fl oz) double cream
3 egg yolks	

1 Split the vanilla pod to reveal the seeds. Put the milk and vanilla pod into a heavy-based saucepan and bring almost to the boil. Remove from the heat, cover and leave to infuse for about 20 minutes.

2 Beat the egg yolks and sugar together in a bowl until well blended. Stir in the milk and strain back into the pan. Cook the custard over a gentle heat, stirring all the time, until it thickens very slightly. (Alternatively, cook the custard in a bowl standing over a pan of simmering water.) It is very important not to let the custard boil or it will curdle. Pour out into a bowl and leave to cool.

3 Whisk the cream into the cold custard mixture.

4 Freeze the ice cream mixture by hand or in an ice cream machine (see right). Leave at cool room temperature for 20-30 minutes to soften before serving.

VARIATIONS

Coffee Ice Cream

Add 150 ml (¼ pint) strong fresh cooled coffee to the cooled custard or 10 ml (2 level tsp) instant coffee granules to the milk. Omit the vanilla.

Chocolate Ice Cream

Put the milk in a saucepan with 125 g (4 oz) plain chocolate. Heat gently until the chocolate melts, then bring almost to the boil. Continue as left.

Fruit Ice Cream

Add 300 ml (½ pint) fruit purée, sweetened to taste, to the cooled custard.

MANGO
ICE CREAM

SERVES 4-6

450 ml (¾ pint) milk	2 ripe mangoes, skinned, sliced and stoned, or two 425 g (15 oz) cans mango slices, drained
1 vanilla pod	
4 egg yolks	juice of 1 lime
75 g (3 oz) sugar	300 ml (½ pint) double cream
	twists of fresh lime, to decorate (optional)

1 Pour the milk into a large, heavy-based saucepan. Add the vanilla pod and bring almost to the boil. Remove from the heat, cover and leave to infuse for at least 15 minutes. Remove the vanilla pod.

2 Put the egg yolks and sugar in a large bowl and beat together. Stir in the milk, then strain back into the pan.

3 Cook the custard gently, stirring until it coats the back of a wooden spoon. Do not boil. Cool completely for at least 1 hour.

4 Purée the mangoes in a blender or food processor until smooth. Stir the mango purée and lime juice into the cool custard. Whip the cream lightly, then fold into the mixture. Pour into a shallow freezer container.

5 Freeze the mixture for about 2 hours until mushy in texture. Turn into a large, chilled bowl and mash with a fork. Freeze for 3-4 hours until firm.

6 Soften in the refrigerator for about 1 hour before serving, decorated, if liked.

COOK'S TIP

Refer to instructions on page 159 for freezing in an ice cream machine.

BLACKBERRY ICE CREAM

SERVES 6-8

450 g (1 lb) blackberries, fresh or frozen	150 ml (¼ pint) whipping cream
30 ml (2 tbsp) thick honey	30 ml (2 tbsp) orange-flavoured liqueur
410 g (14 oz) can evaporated milk, chilled	45 ml (3 tbsp) lemon juice

1 Place the blackberries and honey in a small saucepan. Cover and cook gently until the fruit is soft and pulpy. Purée in a blender or food processor, then rub through a nylon sieve. Leave to cool.

2 Whip evaporated milk until thickened slightly. Whip cream to the same consistency, then fold gently together. Stir in the cold fruit purée, liqueur and lemon juice.

3 Freeze by hand or in an ice cream machine.

4 Leave at cool room temperature for 20-30 minutes to soften before serving. Scoop into individual glass dishes.

COOK'S TIP

To Freeze Ice Cream by Hand

Suggested freezing times are based on 900 ml (1½ pint) ice cream. If making a larger quantity, increase them.

1 Set the freezer to maximum or fast freeze about 1 hour before you intend to freeze the mixture.

2 Make the ice cream as directed in the recipe.

3 Pour the mixture into a shallow non-metal, freezer container. Cover and freeze for about 3 hours or until just frozen all over. It will have a mushy consistency.

4 Spoon into a bowl and mash with a fork or flat whisk to break down the ice crystals. Work quickly so that the ice cream does not melt completely.

5 Return the mixture to the shallow container and freeze again for about 2 hours or until mushy.

6 Mash again as step 4. If any other ingredients are to be added, such as nuts, then fold in at this stage.

7 Return to the freezer and freeze for about 3 hours or until firm.

PISTACHIO AND ALMOND ICE CREAM

SERVES 6

1.4 litres (2½ pints) milk	50 g (2 oz) ground almonds
15 ml (1 level tbsp) rice flour	few drops of rose water
175 g (6 oz) granulated sugar	150 ml (¼ pint) double cream
25 g (1 oz) pistachio nuts	shredded pistachio nuts, to decorate

1 Pour the milk into a large, heavy-based saucepan. Bring to the boil, then simmer gently for about 45 minutes or until the milk reduces by half. Cool slightly.

2 Mix the rice flour with a little of the cooled milk until smooth. Return to the pan and bring to the boil, stirring. Cook for 15 minutes, stirring frequently until the consistency of thin batter. Strain, add the sugar and stir until dissolved. Leave to cool.

3 Soak the pistachio nuts in boiling water for 1-2 minutes, then drain. Ease off the skins, then shred finely.

4 Stir the pistachios, ground almonds and rose water into the milk mixture. Whip the cream lightly, then fold in.

5 Freeze by hand or in an ice cream machine.

6 Leave at cool room temperature for 20-30 minutes to soften before serving. Serve, decorated with pistachios.

COOK'S TIP

Using an Ice Cream Machine

An ice cream machine will freeze an ice cream or sorbet mixture and churn it at the same time, thus eliminating the physical effort. The results will be smooth and even textured. There are several types of ice cream machine available, some use a salt solution and others a disc which needs to be frozen before use. Always follow manufacturer's instructions.

Generally speaking, the cooled mixture should be poured into the machine when the paddles are moving, otherwise it tends to freeze on to the base and sides of the bowl, stopping the paddles working. When making ice cream this way, if the recipe calls for whipped cream, it should be ignored. The cream can simply be added from the carton with the custard.

COFFEE AND
HAZELNUT ICE CREAM

SERVES 4-6

100 g (4 oz) shelled hazelnuts	300 ml (½ pint) double cream
50 ml (2 tbsp plus 4 tsp) coffee-flavoured liqueur	300 ml (½ pint) single cream
15 ml (1 tbsp) coffee and chicory essence	75 g (3 oz) icing sugar, sifted

1   Toast the hazelnuts under the grill for a few minutes, shaking the grill pan constantly so that the nuts brown evenly.
2   Tip the nuts into a clean tea-towel and rub to remove the skins. Chop finely.
3   Mix 30 ml (2 tbsp) coffee liqueur and the essence together in a bowl. Stir in the chopped nuts, reserving a few for decoration.
4   In a separate bowl, whip the creams and icing sugar together until thick. Fold in the nut mixture, then turn into a shallow freezerproof container. Freeze for 2 hours until ice crystals form around the edge of the ice cream.
5   Turn the ice cream into a bowl and beat thoroughly for a few minutes to break up the ice crystals. Return to the freezer container, cover and freeze for at least 4 hours, preferably overnight (to allow enough time for the flavours to develop).
6   To serve, transfer the ice cream to the refrigerator for 30 minutes to soften slightly, then scoop into individual glasses. Spoon 5 ml (1 tsp) coffee liqueur over each serving and sprinkle with the remaining nuts. Serve immediately.

COOK'S TIP

Refer to instructions on page 159 for freezing in an ice cream machine.

RASPBERRY
ROSE ICE CREAM

SERVES 6-8

300 ml (½ pint) milk	450 g (1 lb) raspberries
2 large handfuls of fragrant pink rose petals	15 ml (1 tbsp) rosewater
3 egg yolks	300 ml (½ pint) double cream
75 g (3 oz) caster sugar	raspberries and rose petals, to decorate

1   Put the milk and rose petals in a heavy-based saucepan and bring almost to the boil. Remove from the heat and leave to infuse for at least 30 minutes.
2   Beat the egg yolks and sugar together until well blended. Stir in the milk and rose petals, then strain back into the pan, discarding the rose petals. Cook over a gentle heat, stirring all the time until it thickens very slightly. Do not let the custard boil or it will curdle. Pour into a bowl and leave to cool.
3   While the custard is cooling, mash the raspberries then push through a nylon sieve to make a purée. Stir in the rosewater.
4   Whisk the cream into the cold custard mixture, then stir in the raspberry purée. Pour into a shallow non-metallic freezer container. Cover and freeze on fast freeze for about 3 hours or until just frozen.
5   Spoon into a bowl and mash with a fork to break down the ice crystals. Work quickly so that the ice cream does not melt completely.
6   Return the mixture to the container and freeze again for about 2 hours until mushy.
7   Mash again as step 4, then return to the freezer for a further 3 hours or until firm.
8   Remove from the freezer and leave at room temperature for about 20-30 minutes to soften. Serve sprinkled with a few raspberries and rose petals.

COCONUT ICE CREAM

SERVES 8

275 g (10 oz) granulated sugar	four 450 ml (¾ pint) cans coconut milk
600 ml (1 pint) water	mint sprigs, to decorate

1 To make the syrup, place the sugar and water in a medium saucepan. Heat gently until the sugar dissolves, then boil gently for 10 minutes without stirring. Leave to cool.

2 Mix the cold syrup with the coconut milk and pour into a shallow freezer container. Cover and freeze on fast freeze for about 3 hours or until just frozen all over. The mixture will have a mushy consistency.

3 Spoon into a bowl and mash with a fork to break down the ice crystals. Work quickly so that the ice cream does not melt completely.

4 Return the mixture to the container and freeze for about 2 hours, or until mushy. Mash as in step 3. Return to the freezer and freeze for about 3 hours or until firm.

5 Remove from the freezer and leave at room temperature for 20-30 minutes to soften before serving.

6 Serve scooped into balls and decorate with mint sprigs.

COOK'S TIP

The ice cream is best made with canned coconut milk, which is sold in Indian and oriental grocers. However it works almost as well if made with creamed coconut or dried coconut milk (sold in sachets). If using creamed coconut use four 225 g (8 oz) packets each made up with 450 ml (¾ pint) water. If using instant coconut milk powder you will also need four 100 g (3.5 oz) packets, each made up with 450 ml (¾ pint) water.

If using an ice cream machine, refer to the freezing instructions given on page 159.

PRALINE ICE CREAM WITH APRICOT COULIS

SERVES 2

FOR THE ICE CREAM	2.5 ml (½ tsp) vanilla essence
75 g (3 oz) unblanched almonds	FOR THE APRICOT COULIS
115 g (4½ oz) caster sugar	225 g (8 oz) fresh apricots, halved
3 eggs, separated	30 ml (2 tbsp) Southern Comfort
300 ml (½ pint) whipping cream	caster sugar, to taste

1 Lightly oil a baking sheet.

2 To make the praline, put the almonds and 75 g (3 oz) of the sugar in a heavy-based saucepan. Heat gently until the sugar melts and caramelises to a rich golden brown. Turn on to the prepared sheet and leave until cold and set. Break up with a rolling pin, then crush to a fine powder in a nut mill or food processor.

3 Put the egg yolks in a bowl over a pan of gently simmering water. Put the remaining sugar in a clean heavy-based pan with 120 ml (4 fl oz) cold water and heat gently until the sugar has dissolved. Increase the heat and boil for 3-5 minutes, without stirring, until a light syrup is formed. Remove from the heat and whisk into the egg yolks until thick, using an electric whisk.

4 Remove the bowl from the heat and whisk until cold. Stir in the cream, vanilla essence and praline. Stiffly whisk the egg whites, then fold into the mixture until evenly incorporated.

5 Freeze the mixture by hand or in an ice cream machine (see page 159).

6 To make the apricot coulis, poach the apricots in a heavy-based pan, with just enough water to cover the bottom, until soft. Press through a nylon sieve into a bowl. Stir in Southern Comfort and sugar. Cover and chill.

7 Leave the ice cream in the refrigerator for 30 minutes to soften before serving. Shape into six quenelles with dessertspoons and arrange on individual plates. Surround with the chilled apricot coulis.

LEMON GERANIUM ICE CREAM

SERVES 4-6

300 ml (½ pint) milk	100 g (4 oz) icing sugar
10-12 lemon-scented geranium leaves, crushed	300 ml (10 fl oz) whipping cream
3 egg yolks	lemon-scented geranium leaves, to decorate

1 Bring the milk and geranium leaves almost to the boil. Remove from the heat and leave to infuse for 30 minutes. Remove the geranium leaves.

2 Whisk the egg yolks and icing sugar together in a medium bowl until pale and frothy. Stir in the milk, then strain back into the pan.

3 Cook the custard gently over a low heat, stirring continuously, until it coats the back of a wooden spoon. Do not boil. This takes about 20 minutes.

4 Pour into a shallow freezer container, cool, then cover and freeze for 2 hours, until mushy.

5 Spoon into a bowl and beat to break down the ice crystals. Whip the cream until stiff, then fold into the mixture. Return to the freezer container and freeze for a further 2 hours.

6 Turn into a chilled bowl and beat well again. Return to the freezer and freeze until firm.

7 Transfer to the refrigerator to soften for 30 minutes before serving. Decorate with geranium leaves.

COOK'S TIP

Refer to instructions on page 159 for freezing in an ice cream machine.

TUTTI FRUTTI ICE CREAM

SERVES 8-10

90 ml (6 tbsp) dark rum	600 ml (1 pint) milk
50 g (2 oz) sultanas	1 vanilla pod or few drops of vanilla essence
50 g (2 oz) stoned dates	6 egg yolks
50 g (2 oz) glacé cherries	175 g (6 oz) caster sugar
50 g (2 oz) no-soak dried apricots	600 ml (1 pint) double cream, whipped

1 Pour the rum into a bowl. Add the sultanas, then roughly snip the dates, cherries and apricots into the bowl. Make sure all the fruit is coated with rum. Cover and leave to macerate for 2-3 hours, tossing occasionally.

2 Put the milk and vanilla pod or essence into a heavy-based saucepan and bring almost to the boil. Remove from the heat, cover and leave to infuse for 15 minutes.

3 Beat the egg yolks and sugar together in a bowl until pale and thick. Stir in the milk and strain back into the pan. Cook the custard over a gentle heat, stirring all the time, until it coats the back of a wooden spoon. Do not boil. Cover and leave to cool.

4 Pour into a chilled, shallow freezer container and freeze by hand to the end of step 5 (see page 159).

5 Whip the cream. Mash the ice cream, then fold in the cream and macerated fruit. Freeze until firm. (If using an ice cream machine, put the custard, cream and macerated fruit into the machine together.)

6 Leave at cool room temperature for 20-30 minutes to soften before serving.

VARIATION

For a short-cut version of this ice cream, use a 425 g (15 oz) can custard instead of making the egg custard. With vanilla flavouring added and the heady flavour of fruit macerated in rum, no-one will guess the custard came out of a can!

PRUNE AND BRANDY ICE CREAM

SERVES 8

225 g (8 oz) no-soak dried prunes	5 egg yolks
90 ml (6 tbsp) brandy	40 g (1½ oz) butter
30 ml (2 tbsp) lemon juice	50 g (2 oz) fresh brown breadcrumbs
100 g (4 oz) caster sugar	30 ml (2 tbsp) demerara sugar
450 ml (¾ pint) milk	450 ml (¾ pint) whipping cream, whipped
1 vanilla pod	

1 Cut all the prune flesh off the stones, then snip into small pieces. Place in a bowl with the brandy, lemon juice and 25 g (1 oz) of the caster sugar. Stir well to mix, then cover and leave to soak.

2 Put the milk and vanilla pod into a heavy-based pan and bring almost to the boil. Remove from the heat, cover and leave to infuse for 10 minutes.

3 Beat the egg yolks and remaining caster sugar together in a bowl until pale and frothy. Stir in the milk and strain back into the pan. Cook the custard over a gentle heat, stirring all the time, until thickened slightly. Do not boil. Leave to cool.

4 Melt the butter in a small frying pan, add the breadcrumbs and demerara sugar and cook over a moderate heat, stirring frequently until the crumbs turn golden brown and become crisp. Immediately, spoon the mixture out on to a plate. Leave to cool.

5 Freeze the ice cream mixture by hand to the end of step 5 (see page 159). Mash the ice cream, then fold in the whipped cream, the soaked prunes with any juices, and the crumb mixture. Freeze until firm.

6 Leave at cool room temperature for 20-30 minutes to soften before serving.

VARIATION

Use 225 g (8 oz) no-soak dried figs in place of the prunes and 90 ml (6 tbsp) port in place of the brandy.

CHRISTMAS PUDDING ICE CREAM

SERVES 4-6

100 g (4 oz) mixed no-soak dried fruit	450 ml (15 fl oz) single cream
60 ml (4 tbsp) light or dark rum	3 egg yolks
30 ml (2 tbsp) port	100 g (4 oz) caster sugar
grated rind and juice of 1 orange	150 ml (5 fl oz) whipping cream
	5 ml (1 level tsp) ground mixed spice

1 Mix the dried fruit, rum, port and orange rind and juice together, then set aside to macerate overnight.

2 Gently heat the single cream in a small saucepan to simmering point.

3 Whisk the egg yolks and sugar together in a medium bowl until pale and thick. Gradually pour on the hot cream, stirring continuously.

4 Strain the mixture into a medium heavy-based saucepan or double boiler and cook over a gentle heat, stirring continuously, until it coats the back of a wooden spoon; do not boil. This takes about 20 minutes. Set aside to cool.

5 Whip the cream until stiff, then fold into the cold custard with the dried fruit mixture and mixed spice.

6 Pour into a shallow freezer container, then cover and freeze for about 3 hours until mushy.

7 Turn into a chilled bowl and beat well. Return to the freezer container and freeze for a further 2 hours.

8 Beat the mixture again, then turn into a 1.1 litre (2 pint) bombe mould, cover and freeze for a further 2 hours until firm.

9 Transfer to the refrigerator to soften for 30 minutes before serving. Turn out on to a cold serving plate.

COOK'S TIP

Refer to instructions on page 159 for freezing in an ice cream machine.

FROZEN BRANDY CREAMS

SERVES 4

4 egg yolks	150 ml (¼ pint) double cream
150 g (5 oz) caster sugar	coffee dragees, to decorate
90 ml (6 tbsp) brandy	

1 Mix the egg yolks, sugar and brandy together in a medium bowl, stirring well.

2 Place the bowl over a pan of simmering water. Stir the mixture all the time for about 15 minutes until it thickens slightly and will just coat the back of the spoon. Do not overheat or the eggs may curdle. Remove from the heat and leave to cool for 30 minutes. (Alternatively, microwave on LOW for 4-6 minutes or until thickened. Cool.)

3 Lightly whip the cream and stir half into the cold brandy mixture. Pour into four small freezerproof soufflé or ramekin dishes. Cover and freeze for at least 5 hours until firm.

4 To serve, decorate each ramekin with a whirl of the remaining whipped cream, then top with a coffee dragee. Serve immediately.

COOK'S TIP

This works equally well with other liqueur flavours, such as almond or coffee.

FROZEN PASSION FRUIT SOUFFLE

SERVES 8

16 passion fruit	175 g (6 oz) caster sugar
6 egg yolks	600 ml (1 pint) double cream

1 Tie a double strip of greaseproof paper around a 900 ml (1½ pint) soufflé dish to make a 7.5 cm (3 inch) collar. Lightly brush the inside of the paper with oil.

2 Cut each passion fruit in half and scoop out the flesh and seeds into a nylon sieve, placed over a small bowl. Press with a spoon to extract all of the juice – about 150 ml (¼ pint).

3 Whisk the egg yolks in a large bowl with an electric mixer until very thick.

4 Put 60 ml (4 tbsp) of the passion fruit juice into a small saucepan with the caster sugar. Stir over a low heat until the sugar has dissolved. Bring to the boil and boil until the temperature reaches 110°C (230°F) on a sugar thermometer.

5 Whisk the syrup in a steady stream into the egg yolks, then continue whisking until the mixture cools and thickens. Gradually whisk in the remaining passion fruit juice, whisking until the mixture is thick and mousse-like.

6 Whip the cream until it just holds its shape. Fold the cream into the passion fruit mixture until no trace of white remains. Pour into the prepared dish, then freeze until firm. Once frozen, cover the top of the soufflé.

7 Remove the soufflé from the freezer 20-30 minutes before serving and carefully ease away the paper collar. Decorate with whipped cream and pistachios, if liked.

COOK'S TIP

This velvety smooth soufflé should be made the day before. The soufflé can be decorated with whipped cream and pistachio nuts, but as its impressive qualities are in the texture and fresh flavour, it doesn't necessarily need to be dressed-up.

FROZEN CHESTNUT BOMBE

SERVES 8-10

FOR THE BOMBE	TO DECORATE
1 quantity vanilla ice cream (see page 158)	300 ml (½ pint) whipping cream
285 g (10 oz) can whole chestnuts, drained	15 ml (1 tbsp) rum
30 ml (2 tbsp) icing sugar	marrons glacés or dragees and herb leaves
150 ml (¼ pint) soured cream	
100 g (4 oz) macaroons	
45 ml (3 tbsp) rum	

1 To make the bombe, remove the ice cream from the freezer and leave at cool room temperature for 45 minutes to soften.
2 Purée the chestnuts, icing sugar and soured cream in a blender or food processor until smooth. Add the ice cream and purée.
3 Roughly crush the macaroons and sprinkle with the rum. Fold into the ice cream mixture.
4 Pour into a 1.1 litre (2 pint) bombe mould or pudding basin. Cover and freeze for at least 5 hours or until firm.
5 To serve, dip the mould or bowl briefly in hot water, then unmould on to a serving plate. Return to the freezer for 10 minutes.
6 To make the decoration, whip the cream and rum until stiff. Spoon into a piping bag fitted with a large star nozzle. Pipe around the base of the bombe and up and over the sides. Decorate with marrons glacés or dragées and herb leaves. Leave in the refrigerator for 1 hour to soften before serving.

FROZEN CHOCOLATE AND MANGO CAKE

SERVES 8-10

1 chocolate Swiss roll sponge, made with 2 eggs (see page 171)	TO DECORATE
	chocolate caraque or curls and mango slices
½ quantity mango ice cream (see page 158)	
¼ quantity chocolate ice cream (see page 158)	

1 Trim the Swiss roll sponge and cut into three pieces the width and length of a 1.1 litre (2 pint) loaf tin.
2 Take the ice creams out of the freezer and leave at room temperature for 30 minutes or until soft enough to spread. Spread half the mango ice cream into the loaf tin and level the surface.
3 Place one piece of sponge on top of the mango ice cream in the loaf tin. Spread with the chocolate ice cream. Return to the freezer for 15 minutes to firm.
4 Place a second piece of sponge on top of the chocolate ice cream. Spread with the remaining mango ice cream. Top with the last piece of sponge. Cover and freeze for at least 3 hours or until firm.
5 One hour before serving, dip the tin briefly in hot water then unmould on to a serving plate. Leave in the refrigerator for 1 hour before serving. Decorate with chocolate caraque or curls and slices of mango.

COOK'S TIP

Use this as a basic recipe to make other ice cream cakes of your choice.

ORANGES EN SURPRISE

SERVES 6

6 large oranges	90 ml (6 tbsp) chunky orange marmalade
300 ml (½ pint) double cream	
50 g (2 oz) icing sugar	bay leaves or chocolate leaves, to decorate
90 ml (6 tbsp) orange-flavoured liqueur	

1 Cut a slice off the top of each orange and reserve. Scoop out all the flesh, pips and juice from the oranges and discard (the juice can be used for drinking or in other recipes). Wash, then dry thoroughly. Set aside.
2 Whip the cream and icing sugar together in a bowl until standing in stiff peaks. Mix the liqueur and marmalade together, then fold into the cream until evenly distributed.
3 Spoon the cream mixture into the orange shells, mounding it up over the top. Freeze for at least 4 hours, preferably overnight (to allow the flavours to develop).
4 Serve straight from the freezer, decorated with the reserved orange lids, bay leaves or chocolate leaves.

COOK'S TIP

Chocolate Leaves
To make these, using a small paintbrush, thinly spread melted chocolate on the undersides of clean, dry, undamaged rose leaves. Leave to set. Gently peel off chocolate.

ORANGE SHERBET

SERVES 8

178 ml (6¼ oz) carton frozen orange juice	600 ml (1 pint) milk
175 g (6 oz) caster sugar	300 ml (½ pint) single cream
45 ml (3 tbsp) golden syrup	shredded orange rind and mint sprigs, to decorate
45 ml (3 tbsp) lemon juice	

1 Tip the frozen undiluted orange juice into a deep bowl. Leave until beginning to soften, then add the sugar, golden syrup and lemon juice. Whisk until smooth.
2 Combine the orange mixture with the milk and cream and pour into a deep rigid container. Cover and freeze for 4-5 hours. There is no need to whisk the mixture during freezing.
3 Transfer to the refrigerator to soften 45 minutes or 1 hour before serving. Serve scooped into individual glasses or orange shells, decorated with orange shreds and sprigs of mint.

COOK'S TIP

There is always some confusion over the term 'sherbet' when used to describe a dessert. The word 'sherbet' is in fact the American term for a sorbet, although it is often mistakenly used to describe a water ice. Water ices are simple concoctions of sugar syrup and fruit purée or fruit juice, sometimes with liqueur or other alcohol added. Sorbets are a smoother version of water ices. They are made in the same way, with sugar syrup and fruit, but at the half-frozen stage they have whisked egg whites or other ingredients folded into them.

INDIVIDUAL COFFEE BOMBES

SERVES 6

1½ quantity coffee ice cream (see page 158)	50 g (2 oz) plain chocolate
FOR THE FILLING	45 ml (3 tbsp) double cream
25 g (1 oz) cake crumbs	30 ml (2 tbsp) rum or brandy
25 g (1 oz) ground almonds	chocolate leaves or curls, to decorate

1 Set the freezer to fast freeze. Put six 175 ml (6 fl oz) individual freezerproof pie or pudding moulds in the freezer to chill.

2 Leave the ice cream at room temperature for 20-30 minutes or until soft enough to spread.

3 Meanwhile, to make the truffle filling, mix the cake crumbs and almonds together in a bowl. Put the chocolate and cream in a small bowl standing over a pan of simmering water and stir until melted. Add the chocolate mixture to the crumb and almond mixture with the rum. Mix well.

4 Spread the softened ice cream around the base and sides of the pie moulds, leaving a cavity in the centre for the truffle mixture. Freeze for 1 hour or until firm.

5 Fill the centre of each mould with the truffle mixture and level the surface. Cover and freeze for 1 hour or until firm.

6 To serve, dip the moulds briefly in hot water, then unmould on to serving plates. Return to the freezer for 10 minutes to firm up. Decorate with chocolate leaves or curls to serve.

PERNOD PARFAIT

SERVES 8

125 g (4 oz) granulated sugar	450 ml (15 fl oz) whipping cream
4 egg yolks	
30 ml (2 tbsp) Pernod	150 ml (5 fl oz) whipping cream, to decorate

1 Place the sugar and 300 ml (½ pint) water in a heavy-based saucepan and heat gently until dissolved. Bring to the boil and boil steadily for 2 minutes.

2 Put the egg yolks in a bowl and beat, using an electric whisk, until pale and fluffy. Pour the hot syrup in a thin stream on to the egg yolks and continue beating until the mixture is cool. Beat in the Pernod.

3 Whip the cream until it just holds its shape, then fold into the egg mixture. Pour into eight freezerproof serving dishes or ramekins. Cover and freeze for 5 hours or overnight until firm.

4 To serve, whip the cream until it just holds its shape, then pipe a swirl on to each parfait. Serve immediately, with crisp dessert biscuits.

ORANGE WATER ICE

SERVES 6

175 g (6 oz) sugar	10 large oranges
450 ml (¾ pint) water	1½ lemons

1 To make the sugar syrup, place the sugar and water in a medium saucepan. Heat gently until the sugar dissolves, then boil gently for 10 minutes without stirring.
2 Meanwhile, using a potato peeler, thinly pare the rind from four oranges and the lemons. Add the orange and lemon rind to the sugar syrup and leave until cold.
3 Squeeze the juice from the four oranges and the lemons. Strain into a measuring jug – there should be 450 ml (¾ pint).
4 Strain the cold syrup into a shallow freezer container and stir in the fruit juices. Mix well. Cover and freeze for about 4 hours until mushy in texture.
5 Remove from the freezer and turn the frozen mixture into a bowl. Beat well with a fork to break down the ice crystals. Return to the freezer container and freeze for at least 4 hours or until firm.
6 Meanwhile, using a serrated knife, cut away the peel and pith from the remaining oranges.
7 Slice the oranges down into thin rings, ease out and discard any pips. Place the oranges in a serving bowl, cover tightly and refrigerate until serving time.
8 Place the water ice in the refrigerator for 45 minutes to soften before serving. Serve with the fresh orange slices.

VARIATIONS

Lemon Water Ice
With 6-8 lemons as a basis, follow the recipe using the pared rind of four lemons and enough juice to give 450 ml (¾ pint).

Coffee Granita
Put 30 ml (2 tbsp) sugar and 50 g (2 oz) finely ground Italian coffee in a jug. Pour over 600 ml (1 pint) boiling water and leave to stand for 1 hour. Strain the coffee through a filter paper or muslin, then freeze as in steps 4-5.

GERANIUM GRAPE SORBET

SERVES 6

100 g (4 oz) sugar	90 ml (6 tbsp) dry white vermouth
300 ml (½ pint) water	
15 ml (½ tbsp) chopped rose- or lemon-scented geranium leaves	2 egg whites
	rose- or lemon-scented geranium leaves, to decorate
700 g (1½ lb) seedless green grapes	

1 To make the sugar syrup, dissolve the sugar in the water over a low heat. Bring to the boil and boil gently for 10 minutes without stirring. Add the geranium leaves, cover and leave to cool.
2 Purée the grapes in a blender or food processor and then work through a sieve. There should be 600 ml (1 pint) purée. Add the vermouth and the strained sugar syrup, mix well and pour this mixture into a shallow freezer container. Freeze for about 1 hour until half frozen and mushy.
3 Turn the half frozen mixture into a large bowl and break up with a fork.
4 Whisk the egg whites until stiff and fold into the grape mixture. Return to the container and freeze for about 2-3 hours until firm. Serve straight from the freezer, decorated with geranium leaves.

COOK'S TIP

Using a Sorbetière
A sorbetière or ice cream machine will freeze a sorbet and churn it at the same time, to give a smooth, even textured result. When making sorbet, any egg white should be lightly whisked with a fork and added at the start of the churning process. Freezing time is usually about 20-30 minutes. The sorbet should then be transferred to the freezer and frozen for 1-2 hours to allow the flavours to develop. Soften slightly at room temperature before serving.

LEMON SORBET

SERVES 3-4

350 ml (12 fl oz) Stock syrup (see below)	pared rind and juice of 3 lemons
	1 egg white

1   Prepare the stock syrup as far as dissolving the sugar. Add the lemon rinds and simmer gently for about 10 minutes. Leave to cool completely.

2   Stir in the lemon juice and strain into a shallow freezer container. Cover and freeze for about 3 hours until mushy.

3   Whisk the egg white until stiff. Turn the sorbet into a bowl and beat gently to break down the ice crystals. Fold in the egg white.

4   Return to the freezer container, cover and freeze for 4 hours or until firm.

5   Leave in the refrigerator for about 40 minutes to soften slightly before serving. To freeze in an ice cream machine, see page 159.

VARIATION

Orange or Lime Sorbet

Make as above, using the pared rind and juice of 2 oranges or 5 limes instead of the lemons.

COOK'S NOTE

Stock Syrup

Put 100 g (4 oz) granulated sugar in a heavy-based saucepan. Add 300 ml (½ pint) water and heat gently until the sugar dissolves. Do not stir the ingredients but occasionally loosen the sugar from the base of the pan to help it dissolve. Bring to the boil and boil for 2 minutes. Cool and use as required in these sorbet recipes. Makes about 350 ml (12 fl oz).

KIWI FRUIT SORBET

SERVES 6

50 g (2 oz) sugar	kiwi fruit slices, to decorate
150 ml (¼ pint) water	orange-flavoured liqueur and wafers, to serve
6 kiwi fruit	
2 egg whites	

1   Place the sugar in a saucepan with the water. Heat gently until the sugar dissolves, then simmer for 2 minutes. Cool for 30 minutes.

2   Halve the kiwi fruit and peel thinly, using a potato peeler.

3   Place the fruit in a blender or food processor with the cool syrup. Work to a smooth purée, then pass through a nylon sieve to remove the pips. Pour into a chilled shallow freezer container. Freeze for 2 hours until mushy.

4   Beat the mixture with a fork to break down any ice crystals.

5   Whisk the egg whites until stiff, then fold through the fruit mixture until evenly blended. Return to the freezer for 4 hours.

6   Scoop into individual glass dishes, decorate with kiwi fruit and spoon over some liqueur. Serve with wafers.

APRICOT AND MINNEOLA SORBET

SERVES 8

two 420 g (15 oz) cans apricot halves in syrup	pared rind and juice of 1 minneola
	2 egg whites

1 Drain the apricots, reserving the syrup. Simmer the minneola rind in the apricot syrup for 2-3 minutes. Leave to cool, then strain.

2 Purée the apricots with 60 ml (4 tbsp) minneola juice in a blender or food processor. Press through a nylon sieve. Add the apricot syrup.

3 Freeze as for Lemon sorbet, adding the egg whites as directed (see page 169).

CHAMPAGNE SORBET

SERVES 4-6

350 ml (12 fl oz) Stock syrup (see page 169)	350 ml (12 fl oz) champagne
juice of 1 lemon	1 egg white

1 Mix the stock syrup, lemon juice and champagne together.

2 Freeze as for Lemon sorbet, adding the egg white as directed (see page 169).

MELON AND GINGER SORBET

SERVES 6

1 medium green or orange-fleshed melon, such as Ogen, Galia or Canteloupe	30 ml (2 tbsp) lemon juice
	350 ml (12 fl oz) Stock syrup (see page 169)
50 g (2 oz) stem ginger	2 egg whites

1 Purée the melon flesh, ginger and lemon juice in a blender or food processor. Press through a nylon sieve.

2 Add the stock syrup. Freeze as for Lemon sorbet, adding the egg whites as directed (see page 169).

RASPBERRY SORBET

SERVES 6

450 g (1 lb) raspberries	350 ml (12 fl oz) Stock syrup (see page 169)
30 ml (2 tbsp) lemon juice	
30 ml (2 tbsp) kirsch	2 egg whites

1 Purée the raspberries with the lemon juice and kirsch in a blender or food processor. Press through a nylon sieve.

2 Add to the stock syrup. Freeze as for Lemon sorbet, adding the egg whites as directed (see page 169).

BASIC RECIPES

You can't beat a light-as-a-feather sponge to create a mouth-watering dessert. Lots of gâteaux are based on a basic Genoese or whisked sponge. These are delicious enough simply to split and fill with fruit and cream, or can be transformed into decadent desserts with nuts, liqueurs and praline.

WHISKED SPONGE

MAKES TWO 18 CM (7 INCH) SPONGES

3 eggs

75 g (3 oz) caster sugar

75 g (3 oz) plain flour

1 Grease two 18 cm (7 inch) sandwich tins, line with greaseproof paper, then dust with a mixture of flour and caster sugar.
2 Put the eggs and sugar in a large heatproof bowl standing over a pan of hot water. Whisk until doubled in volume and thick enough to leave a thin trail on the surface when the whisk is lifted.
3 Remove from the heat and continue whisking for a further 5 minutes until the mixture is cool.
4 Sift half the flour over the mixture and fold in very lightly, using a large metal spoon. Sift and fold in the remaining flour in the same way.
5 Pour the mixture into the prepared tins, tilting the tins to spread the mixture evenly. Do not use a palette knife or spatula as this will crush out the air bubbles.
6 Bake in the oven at 190°C (375°F) mark 5 for 20-25 minutes until well risen, firm to the touch and beginning to shrink away from the sides of the tins. Turn out on to a wire rack and leave to cool.

COOK'S TIP

To make two 20 cm (8 inch) sponges, use 4 eggs, 100 g (4 oz) caster sugar and 100 g (4 oz) plain flour.

SWISS ROLL

1 Line a 33 x 23 cm (13 x 9 inch) Swiss roll tin with greaseproof paper.
2 Make the sponge as above but use 100 g (4 oz) plain flour and fold in with 15 ml (1 tbsp) hot water. Pour into the prepared tin. Tilt the tin backwards and forwards to spread the mixture in an even layer.
3 Bake in the oven at 200°C (400°F) mark 6 for 10-12 minutes until golden brown, well risen and firm.
4 Meanwhile, place a sheet of greaseproof paper over a damp tea towel. Dredge the paper with caster sugar.
5 Quickly turn out the cake on to the paper, trim off the crusty edges and spread with jam. Roll up the cake with the aid of the paper. Make the first turn firmly so that the whole cake will roll evenly and have a good shape when finished, but roll more lightly after this turn. Place seam-side down on a wire rack and dredge with caster sugar.

CHOCOLATE SWISS ROLL

Make the sponge as for Swiss roll (left) but replace 15 ml (1 tbsp) plain flour with 15 ml (1 tbsp) sifted cocoa powder. Turn out the cooked sponge, trim, then cover with a sheet of greaseproof paper and roll with the paper inside. When cold, unroll and remove the paper. Spread with whipped cream and re-roll. Dust with icing sugar.

GENOESE CAKE

MAKES ONE 23 CM (9 INCH) CAKE

75 g (3 oz) butter

6 eggs

75 g (3 oz) caster sugar

150 g (5 oz) plain flour

30 ml (2 tbsp) cornflour

1 Grease a 23 cm (9 inch) spring-release cake tin and line with greaseproof paper.
2 Put the butter into a saucepan and heat gently until melted, then remove from the heat and leave for a few minutes to cool slightly.
3 Put the eggs and sugar in a heatproof bowl standing over a pan of hot water. Whisk until pale and creamy and thick enough to leave a trail on the surface when the whisk is lifted. Remove from the heat and whisk until cool.
4 Sift the flours together into a bowl. Fold half the flour into the egg mixture with a metal spoon.
5 Pour half the cooled butter around the edge of the mixture. Gradually fold in the remaining butter and flour alternately. Fold in very lightly or the butter will sink and result in a heavy cake. Pour the mixture into the prepared tin.
6 Bake in the oven at 180°C (350°F) mark 4 for 35-40 minutes until well risen, firm to the touch and beginning to shrink away from the sides of the tin. Turn out on to a wire rack and leave to cool.

CHOCOLATE GENOESE CAKE

Substitute 25 g (1 oz) of the plain flour with cocoa powder. Sift the cocoa with the flours and proceed as above.

COOK'S TIP

Like the whisked sponge, a Genoese cake is made by the whisking method, but melted butter is added with the flour. This gives a delicate sponge with a moister texture than the plain whisked sponge and a richer buttery taste.

SHORTCRUST PASTRY

MAKES 225 G (8 OZ) PASTRY

This plain short pastry is probably the most widely used of all pastries. For shortcrust pastry, the proportion of flour to fat is 2:1, or twice the quantity. Therefore, for a recipe using quantities of shortcrust pastry other than 225 g (8 oz) simply use half the quantity of fat to the flour weight specified.

This quantity, is approximately equivalent to one 368 g (13 oz) packet ready-made shortcrust pastry.

225 g (8 oz) plain flour

pinch of salt

50 g (2 oz) butter or block margarine, chilled and diced

50 g (2 oz) lard, chilled and diced

chilled water, to mix

1 Place the flour and salt in a bowl and add the fat.
2 Using both hands, rub the fat lightly into the flour until the mixture resembles fine breadcrumbs.
3 Add 45-60 ml (3-4 tbsp) water, sprinkling it evenly over the surface. (Uneven addition may cause blistering when the pastry is cooked.)
4 Stir in with a round-bladed knife until the mixture begins to stick together in large lumps.
5 With one hand, collect the dough mixture together to form a ball. Knead lightly for a few seconds to give a firm, smooth dough. Do not overhandle the dough.
6 To roll out, sprinkle a very little flour on a working surface and the rolling pin (not on the pastry) and roll out the dough evenly in one direction only, turning it occasionally. The usual thickness is 3 mm (⅛ inch). Do not pull or stretch the pastry.
7 The pastry can be baked straight away, but it is better if allowed to 'rest' for about 30 minutes in the tin or dish, covered with foil or greaseproof paper, in the refrigerator.

PATE SUCREE

MAKES 100 G (4 OZ) PASTRY

100 g (4 oz) flour

pinch of salt

50 g (2 oz) caster sugar

50 g (2 oz) butter (at room temperature)

2 egg yolks

1 Sift the flour and salt on to a working surface. Make a well in the centre and add the sugar, butter and egg yolks.
2 Using the fingertips of one hand, pinch and work the sugar, butter and egg yolks together until well blended.
3 Gradually work in all the flour to bind the mixture together.
4 Knead lightly until smooth. Wrap the pastry in foil or greaseproof paper and leave to 'rest' in the refrigerator or a cool place for about 1 hour, or overnight if possible.

FLAN PASTRY

MAKES 100 G (4 OZ) PASTRY

100 g (4 oz) flour

pinch of salt

75 g (3 oz) butter or block margarine and lard, diced

5 ml (1 level tsp) caster sugar (optional)

1 egg, beaten

1 Place the flour and salt in a bowl. Rub the fat into the flour as for shortcrust pastry, until the mixture resembles fine breadcrumbs. Stir in the sugar if using.
2 Add the egg, stirring with a round-bladed knife until the ingredients begin to stick together in large lumps.
3 With one hand, collect the mixture together and knead lightly for a few seconds to give a firm, smooth dough. Wrap the pastry in greaseproof paper or foil and chill in the refrigerator for at least 30 minutes before use. Roll out as for shortcrust pastry.

CREME PATISSIERE

MAKES 600 ML (1 PINT)

600 ml (1 pint) milk

1 vanilla pod

4 eggs

75 g (3 oz) caster sugar

60 ml (4 level tbsp) plain flour

75 ml (5 level tbsp) cornflour

1 Put the milk and the vanilla pod in a heavy-based saucepan and heat gently until just boiling. Remove from the heat and leave to infuse for 30 minutes.
2 Cream the eggs and sugar together in a bowl until really pale and thick.
3 Sift the flour and cornflour into a bowl, then gradually add a little of the milk to make a smooth paste. Gradually beat the flour mixture into the egg mixture.
4 Remove the vanilla pod from the milk, then reheat until just boiling. Pour onto the egg mixture, in a steady stream, stirring all the time.
5 Strain the mixture back into the saucepan. Reheat gently, stirring all the time until the custard coats the back of a spoon. Pour into a clean bowl, cover the top with a piece of damp greaseproof paper and leave to cool.

BUTTER CREAM

MAKES 250 G (9 OZ)

75 g (3 oz) butter, softened

175 g (6 oz) icing sugar

few drops of vanilla flavouring

15-30 ml (1-2 tbsp) milk or warm water

1 Put the butter in a bowl and cream until soft. Sift and gradually beat in the icing sugar, then add the vanilla flavouring and milk or water. Beat until smooth.

VARIATIONS

Orange or Lemon
Replace the vanilla flavouring with a little finely grated orange or lemon rind. Add a little juice from the fruit instead of the milk, beating well to avoid curdling the mixture.

Coffee
Replace the vanilla flavouring with 10 ml (2 level tsp) instant coffee granules dissolved in some of the hot liquid; cool before adding to the mixture. Or replace 15 ml (1 tbsp) of the liquid with the same amount of coffee essence.

Chocolate
Dissolve 15 ml (1 level tbsp) cocoa powder in a little hot water and cool before adding to the mixture.

Mocha
Dissolve 5 ml (1 level tsp) cocoa powder and 10 ml (2 level tsp) instant coffee granules in a little hot water taken from the measured amount. Cool before adding to the mixture.

GLACE ICING

MAKES ABOUT 100 G (4 OZ)

100 g (4 oz) icing sugar

few drops of vanilla or almond flavouring (optional)

colouring (optional)

1 Sift the icing sugar into a bowl. Add a few drops of vanilla or almond flavouring if wished.

1 Gradually mix in 15 ml (1 tbsp) warm water. The icing should be thick enough to coat the back of a spoon. If necessary, add more water or sugar to adjust consistency. Add colouring, if liked, and use at once.

VARIATIONS

Orange or Lemon
Replace the water with 15 ml (1 tbsp) strained orange or lemon juice.

Chocolate
Dissolve 10 ml (2 level tsp) cocoa powder in the 15 ml (1 tbsp) hot water.

Coffee
Flavour the glacé icing with 5 ml (1 tsp) coffee essence or dissolve 10 ml (2 level tsp) instant coffee granules in the 15 ml (1 tbsp) hot water.

APRICOT GLAZE

MAKES 150 ML (¼ PINT)

100 g (4 oz) apricot jam

1 Put the jam and 30 ml (2 tbsp) water in a saucepan and heat gently, stirring, until the jam softens. Bring to the boil and simmer for 1 minute.
2 Sieve the glaze and use while still warm.

ROYAL ICING

MAKES ABOUT 900 G (2 LB)

4 egg whites

900 g (2 lb) icing sugar

15 ml (1 tbsp) lemon juice

10 ml (2 tsp) glycerine

1 Whisk the egg whites in a bowl until slightly frothy. Then sift and stir in about a quarter of the icing sugar with a wooden spoon. Continue adding more sugar gradually, beating well after each addition, until about three-quarters of the sugar has been added.
2 Beat in the lemon juice and continue beating for about 10 minutes, until the icing is smooth.
3 Beat in the remaining sugar until the required consistency is achieved.
4 Finally, stir in the glycerine to prevent the icing hardening. Cover and keep for 24 hours before using to allow air bubbles to rise to the surface.

FLAT ICING
1 Always apply royal icing over a layer of almond paste rather than directly on to the cake. Keep the bowl of icing covered with a damp cloth, to prevent it developing a crusty surface. Spoon almost half the icing on to the top of the cake and spread it evenly with a palette knife, using a padding action to remove any air bubbles.
2 Using an icing ruler or palette knife longer than the width of the cake, draw it steadily, without applying any pressure, across the top of the cake at an angle of 30°. Neaten the edges. Leave to dry for 24 hours before icing the sides.
3 To ice the sides, place the board on an icing turntable or on an upturned plate. Spread the remaining icing on the side of the cake and smooth it roughly with a small palette knife. Hold the palette knife or an icing comb upright and at an angle of 45° to the cake. Starting at the back, slowly rotate the turntable while moving the knife or comb slowly and evenly towards you to smooth the surface.
4 For a really smooth finish, let dry for 1-2 days, then apply a second thinner coat of icing. Use a piece of fine sandpaper to sand down any imperfections in the first coat. Allow to dry before piping on decorations.

INDEX